# Managing Credit Risk in
# Corporate Bond Portfolios

## *A Practitioner's Guide*

# THE FRANK J. FABOZZI SERIES

# Managing Credit Risk in Corporate Bond Portfolios

*A Practitioner's Guide*

## SRICHANDER RAMASWAMY

**WILEY**

John Wiley & Sons, Inc.

For general information on our other products and services, or technical support, please contact our Customer Care Department within the United States at 800-762-2974, outside the United States at 317-572-3993 or fax 317-572-4002.

Wiley also publishes its books in a variety of electronic formats. Some content that appears in print may not be available in electronic books.

For more information about Wiley products, visit our web site at www.wiley.com.

ISBN: 0-471-43037-4

Printed in the United States of America

10 9 8 7 6 5 4 3 2 1

# Contents

# Foreword

**S**ome of the greatest advances in finance over the past two to three decades have come in the field of risk management. Theoretical developments have enabled us to disaggregate risk elements and thus better identify and price risk factors. New instruments have been created to enable practitioners to more actively manage their risk profiles by shedding those exposures they are not well placed to hold while retaining (or leveraging) those that reflect their comparative advantage. The practical consequence is that the market for risk management instruments has grown exponentially. These instruments are now actively used by all categories of institution and portfolio managers.

Partly as a result of this, the business of portfolio management has become enormously more competitive. Falling interest rates have motivated clients to be more demanding in their search for yield. But it would probably have happened anyway. Institutional investors are continuously seeking a more efficient risk–return combination as well as deciding exactly where on the risk–return frontier they wish to position themselves. All this requires constant refinement of portfolio management techniques to keep up with evolving best practice.

The basic insights behind the new techniques of risk management depend on mathematical innovations. The sophistication of the emerging methodology has important strengths, but it also has limitations. The key strength is analytic rigor. This rigor, coupled with the computational power of modern information technology, allows portfolio managers to quickly assess the risk characteristics of an individual instrument as well as measure its impact on the overall risk structure of a portfolio.

The opposite side of the coin to analytic rigor is the complexity of the models used. This complexity opens a gap between the statistical measurement of risk and the economic intuition that lies behind it. This would not matter too much if models could always be relied on to produce the "right" results. After all, we do not need to understand internal combustion or hydraulic braking to drive a car. Most of the time, of course, models do produce more or less the right answers. However, in times of stress, we become aware of two key limitations. First, because statistical applications must be based on available data, they implicitly assume that the past is a good guide to the future. In extreme circumstances, that assumption may break down.

Second, portfolio modeling techniques implicitly assume low transaction costs (i.e., continuous market liquidity). Experience has taught (notably in the 1998 episode) that this assumption must also be used carefully.

Credit risk modeling presents added complications. The diversity of events (macro and micro) that can affect credit quality is substantial. Moreover, correlations among different credits are complex and can vary over time. Statistical techniques are powerful tools for capturing the lessons of past experience. In the case of credit experience, however, we must be particularly mindful of the possibility that the future will be different from the past.

Where do these reflections lead? First, to the conclusion that portfolio managers need to use all the tools at their disposal to improve their understanding of the forces shaping portfolio returns. The statistical techniques described in this book are indispensable in this connection. Second, that senior management of institutional investors and their clients must not treat risk management models as a black box whose output can be uncritically accepted. They must strive to understand the properties of the models used and the assumptions involved. In this way, they will better judge how much reliance to place on model output and how much judgmental modification is required.

Srichander Ramaswamy's book responds to both these points. A careful reading (which, admittedly, to the uninitiated may not be easy) should give the reader a better grasp of the practice of portfolio management and its reliance on statistical modeling techniques. Through a better understanding of the techniques involved, portfolio managers and their clients will become better informed and more efficient players in the financial system. This is good for efficiency and stability alike.

**Sir Andrew Crockett**
Former General Manager
Bank for International Settlements

# Preface

Currently, credit risk is a hot topic. This is partly due to the fact that there is much confusion and misunderstanding concerning how to measure and manage credit risk in a practical setting. This confusion stems mainly from the nature of credit risk: It is the risk of a rare event occurring, which may not have been observed in the past. Quantifying something that has not been previously observed requires using models and making several assumptions. The precise nature of the assumptions and the types of models used to quantify credit risk can vary substantially, leading to more confusion and misunderstanding and, in many cases, practitioners come to mistrust the models themselves.

The best I could have done to avoid adding further confusion to this subject is to not write a book whose central theme is credit risk. However, as a practitioner, I went through a frustrating experience while trying to adapt existing credit risk modeling techniques to solve a seemingly mundane practical problem: Measure and manage the relative credit risk of a corporate bond portfolio against its benchmark. To do this, one does not require the technical expertise of a rocket scientist to figure out how to price complex credit derivatives or compute risk-neutral default intensities from empirically observed default probabilities. Nevertheless, I found the task quite challenging. This book grew out of my conviction that the existing literature on credit risk does not address an important practical problem in the area of bond portfolio management.

But that is only part of the story. The real impetus to writing this book grew out of my professional correspondence with Frank Fabozzi. After one such correspondence, Frank came up with a suggestion: Why not write a book on this important topic? I found this suggestion difficult to turn down, especially because I owe much of my knowledge of bond portfolio management to his writings. Writing this book would not have been possible without his encouragement, support, and guidance. It has been both a pleasure and a privilege to work closely with Frank on this project.

While writing this book, I tried to follow the style that sells best on trading floors and in management meetings: Keep it simple. However, I may have failed miserably in this. As the project progressed, I realized that quantification of credit risk requires mathematical tools that are usually not taught at the undergraduate level of a nonscience discipline. On the positive side, however, I strove to find the right balance between theory and practice and to make assumptions that are relevant in a practical setting.

Despite its technical content, I hope this book will be of interest to a wide audience in the finance industry. Institutional investors will find the book useful for identifying potential risk guidelines they can impose on their corporate bond portfolio mandates. Risk managers will find the risk measurement framework offers an interesting alternative to existing methods for monitoring and reporting the risks in a corporate bond portfolio. Portfolio managers will find the portfolio optimization techniques provide helpful aids to portfolio selection and rebalancing processes. Financial engineers and quantitative analysts will benefit considerably from the technical coverage of the topics and the scope the book provides to develop trading tools to support the corporate bond portfolio management business.

This book can also serve as a one-semester graduate text for a course on corporate bond portfolio management in quantitative finance. I have used parts of this book to teach a one-quarter course on fixed income portfolio management at the University of Lausanne for master's-level students in banking and finance. To make the book student-friendly, I have included end-of-chapter questions and solutions.

Writing this book has taken substantial time away from my family. I thank my wife, Esther, for her support and patience during this project, my first son, Björn, for forgoing bedtime stories so that I could work on the book, and my second son, Ricardo, for sleeping through the night while I was busy writing the book. I am also very grateful for the support of the management of the Bank for International Settlements, who kindly gave me the permission to publish this book. In particular, I would like to thank Bob Sleeper for his encouragement and support, and for providing insightful comments on the original manuscript of this book. Finally, I wish to express my gratitude to Pamela van Giessen, Todd Tedesco, and Jennifer MacDonald at John Wiley for their assistance during this project.

The views expressed in this book are mine, and do not necessarily reflect the views of the Bank for International Settlements.

Srichander Ramaswamy

## CHAPTER 1

# Introduction

## MOTIVATION

Most recent books on credit risk management focus on managing credit risk from a middle office perspective. That is, measuring and controlling credit risk, implementing internal models for capital allocation for credit risk, computing risk-adjusted performance measures, and computing regulatory capital for credit risk are normally the topics dealt with in detail. However, seen from a front office perspective, the need to manage credit risk prudently is driven more by the desire to meet a return target than the requirement to ensure that the risk limits are within agreed guidelines. This is particularly the case for portfolio managers, whose task may be to either replicate or outperform a benchmark comprising corporate bonds. In performing this task, portfolio managers often have to strike the right balance between being a trader and being a risk manager at the same time.

In order to manage the risks of the corporate bond portfolio against a given benchmark, one requires tools for risk measurement. Unlike in the case of a government bond portfolio, where the dominant risk is market risk, the risk in a portfolio consisting of corporate bonds is primarily credit risk. In the portfolio management context, standard practice is to measure the risk relative to its benchmark. Although measures to quantify the market risk of a bond portfolio relative to its benchmark are well known, no standard measures exist to quantify the relative credit risk of a corporate bond portfolio versus its benchmark. As a consequence, there are no clear guidelines as to how the risk exposures in a corporate bond portfolio can be quantified and presented so that informed decisions can be made and limits for permissible risk exposures can be set. The lack of proper standards for risk reporting on corporate bond portfolio mandates makes the task of compliance monitoring difficult. Moreover, it is also difficult to verify whether the portfolio manager acted in the best interest of the client and in line with the spirit of the manager's fiduciary responsibilities.

The lack of proper risk measures for quantifying the dominant risks of the corporate bond portfolio against its benchmark also makes the task of choosing the right bonds to hold in the portfolio rather difficult. As the number of issuers in the benchmark increases, identifying a subset of bonds from the benchmark composition becomes cumbersome even with the help of several credit analysts. This is because corporate bond portfolio management concerns itself with efficient diversification of the credit risk through prudently selecting which bond obligors to include in the portfolio. In general, it has less to do with the identification of good credits seen in isolation. The diversification efficiency is measured relative to the level of credit diversification present in the benchmark portfolio. Selecting bonds such that the aggregate risks of the corporate portfolio are lower than those of the benchmark while simultaneously ensuring that the portfolio offers scope for improved returns over those of the benchmark invariably requires the use of quantitative techniques to drive the portfolio selection process.

This book was written to address these difficulties with respect to managing a corporate bond portfolio. In doing this, I have tried to strike a reasonable balance between the practical relevance of the topics presented and the level of mathematical sophistication required to follow the discussions. Working for several years closely with traders and portfolio managers has helped me understand the difficulties encountered when quantitative methods are used to solve practical problems. Invariably, many of the practical difficulties tend to be overlooked in a more academic setting, which in turn causes the proposed quantitative methods to lose practical relevance. I have made a strong attempt to not fall into this trap while writing this book. However, many of the ideas presented are still untested in managing real money.

## SUMMARY OF THE BOOK

Although this book's orientation is an applied one, some of the concepts presented here rely substantially on quantitative models. Despite this, most of the topics covered are easily accessible to readers with a basic knowledge of mathematics. In a nutshell, this book is primarily about combining risk management concepts with portfolio construction techniques and explores the role quantitative methods can play in this integration process with particular emphasis on corporate bond portfolio management. The topics covered are organized in a cohesive manner, so sequential reading is recommended. Briefly, the topics covered are as follows.

Chapter 2 covers basic concepts in probability theory and linear algebra that are required to follow certain sections in this book. The intention of this chapter is to fill in a limited number of possible gaps in the reader's knowledge in these areas. Readers familiar with probability theory and linear algebra could skip this chapter.

Chapter 3 provides a brief introduction to the corporate bond market. Bond collateralization and corporate bond investment risks are briefly discussed. This chapter also gives an overview of the practical difficulties encountered in trading corporate as opposed to government bonds, the important role corporate bonds play in buffering the impact of a financial crisis, the relative market size and historical performance of corporate bonds. The chapter concludes by arguing that the corporate bond market is an interesting asset class for the reserves portfolios of central banks and for pension funds.

Chapter 4 offers a brief review of market risk measures associated with changes to interest rates, implied volatility, and exchange rates. Interest rate risk exposure in this book is restricted to the price sensitivity resulting from changes to the swap curve of the currency in which the corporate bond is issued. Changes to the bond yield that cannot be explained by changes to the swap curve are attributed to credit risk. Taking this approach results in considerable simplification to market risk modeling because yield curves do not have to be computed for different credit-rating categories.

Chapter 5 introduces various factors that are important determinants of credit risk in a corporate bond and describes standard methods used to estimate them at the security level. It also highlights the differences in conceptual approaches used to model credit risk and the data limitations associated with parameter specification and estimation. Subsequently, quantification of credit risk at the security level is discussed in considerable detail.

Chapter 6 covers the topic of portfolio credit risk. In this chapter, the notion of correlated credit events is introduced; indirect methods that can be used to estimate credit correlations are discussed. An approach to determining the approximate asset return correlation between obligors is also outlined. Finally, analytical approaches for computing portfolio credit risk under the default mode and the migration mode are dealt with in detail assuming that the joint distribution of asset returns is multivariate normal.

Chapter 7 deals with the computation of portfolio credit risk using a simulation approach. In taking this approach, it is once again assumed that the joint distribution of asset returns is multivariate normal. Considering that the distribution of credit losses is highly skewed with a long, fat tail, two tail risk measures for credit risk, namely credit value at risk and expected shortfall risk, are introduced. The estimation of these tail risk measures from the simulated data is also indicated.

In Chapter 8, the assumption that the joint distribution of asset returns is multivariate normal is relaxed. Specifically, it is assumed that the joint distribution of asset returns is multivariate $t$-distributed. Under this assumption, changes to the schemes required to compute various credit risk measures of interest using analytical and simulation approaches are discussed.

Chapter 9 develops a framework for reporting the credit risk and market risk of a corporate bond portfolio that is managed against a benchmark. To highlight the impact of model errors on the aggregate risk measures computed, risk report generation under different modeling assumptions and input parameter values is presented. A simple performance attribution model for identifying the sources of excess return against the benchmark is also developed in this chapter.

Chapter 10 begins with a brief introduction to portfolio optimization techniques and the practical difficulties that arise in using such techniques for portfolio selection. This is followed by the formulation of an optimization problem for constructing a bond portfolio that offers improved risk-adjusted returns compared to the benchmark. Subsequently, an optimization problem for portfolio rebalancing is formulated incorporating turnover constraints so that the trade recommendations are implementable. Finally, a case study is performed using an actual market index to illustrate the impact of alternative parametrizations of the credit risk model on the optimal portfolio's composition.

Chapter 11 provides a brief overview of collateralized debt obligations and tradeable corporate bond baskets and discusses how the credit risks of such structured products can be analyzed using the techniques presented in this book. This chapter also provides a methodology for inferring the implied credit rating of such structured products.

A number of numerical examples are given in every chapter to illustrate the concepts presented and link theory with practice. All numerical results presented in this book were generated by coding the numerical algorithms in C language. In doing so, I made extensive use of Numerical Algorithms Group (NAG) C libraries to facilitate the numerical computations.

## CHAPTER 2

# Mathematical Preliminaries

The purpose of this chapter is to provide a concise treatment of the concepts from probability theory and linear algebra that are useful in connection with the material in this book. The coverage of these topics is not intended to be rigorous, but is given to fill in a limited number of possible gaps in the reader's knowledge. Readers familiar with probability theory and linear algebra may wish to skip this chapter.

## PROBABILITY THEORY

In its simplest interpretation, probability theory is the branch of mathematics that deals with calculating the likelihood of a given event's occurrence, which is expressed as a number between 0 and 1. For instance, what is the likelihood that the number 3 will show up when a die is rolled? In another experiment, one might be interested in the joint likelihood of the number 3 showing up when a die is rolled and the head showing up when a coin is tossed. Seeking answers to these types of questions leads to the study of distribution and joint distribution functions. (The answers to the questions posed here are 1/6 and 1/12, respectively). Applications in which repeated experiments are performed and properties of the sequence of random outcomes are analyzed lead to the study of stochastic processes. In this section, I discuss distribution functions and stochastic processes.

### Characterizing Probability Distributions

Probability distribution functions play an important role in characterizing uncertain quantities that one encounters in daily life. In finance, one can think of the uncertain quantities as representing the future price of a stock or a bond. One may also consider the price return from holding a stock over a specified period of time as being an uncertain quantity. In probability theory, this uncertain quantity is known as a *random variable*. Thus, the daily or monthly returns on a stock or a bond held can be thought of as random variables. Associated with each value a random variable can take is a probability, which can be interpreted as the relative frequency of occurrence of this value. The set of all such probabilities form the probability distribution of the random variable. The probability distribution for a random variable $X$ is usually represented by its cumulative distribution function. This function gives the probability that $X$ is less than or equal to $x$:

$$F(x) = P(X \leq x)$$

The probability distribution for $X$ may also be represented by its probability density function, which is the derivative of the cumulative distribution function:

$$f(x) = \frac{dF(x)}{dx}$$

A random variable and its distribution are called *discrete* if $X$ can take only a finite number of values and *continuous* if the random variable can take an infinite number of values. For discrete distributions, the density function is referred to as the probability mass function and is denoted $p(x)$. It refers to the probability of the event $X = x$ occurring. Examples of discrete distributions are the outcomes of rolling a die or tossing a coin. The random variable describing price returns on a stock or a bond, on the other hand, has a continuous distribution.

Knowledge of the distribution function of a random variable provides all information on the properties of the random variable in question. Common practice, however, is to characterize the distribution function using the moments of the distribution which captures the important properties of the distribution. The best known is the first moment of the distribution, better known by the term *mean* of the distribution. The first moments of a continuous and a discrete distribution are given, respectively, by

$$\mu = \int_{-\infty}^{\infty} x f(x) dx$$

and

$$\mu = \sum_{i=1}^{n} x_i p(x_i)$$

The mean of a distribution is also known by the term *expected value* and is denoted $E(X)$. It is common to refer to $E(X)$ as the expected value of the random variable $X$. If the moments are taken by subtracting the mean of the distribution from the random variable, then they are known as *central moments*. The second central moment represents the variance of the distribution and is given by

$$\sigma^2 = \int_{-\infty}^{\infty} (x - \mu)^2 f(x)dx \qquad \text{(continuous distribution)}$$

$$\sigma^2 = \sum_{i=1}^{n} (x_i - \mu)^2 p(x_i) \qquad \text{(discrete distribution)}$$

Following the definition of the expected value of a random variable, the variance of the distribution can be represented in the expected value notation as $E[(X - \mu)^2]$. The square root of the variance is referred to as the *standard deviation* of the distribution. The variance or standard deviation of a distribution gives an indication of the dispersion of the distribution about the mean.

More insight into the shape of the distribution function can be gained by specifying two other parameters of the distribution. These parameters are the *skewness* and the *kurtosis* of the distribution. For a continuous distribution, the skewness and the kurtosis are defined as follows:

$$\text{skewness} = \int_{-\infty}^{\infty} (x - \mu)^3 f(x)dx$$

$$\text{kurtosis} = \int_{-\infty}^{\infty} (x - \mu)^4 f(x)dx$$

If the distribution is symmetric around the mean, then the skewness is zero. Kurtosis describes the "peakedness" or "flatness" of a distribution. A leptokurtic distribution is one in which more observations are clustered around the mean of the distribution and in the tail region. This is the case, for instance, when one observes the returns on stock prices.

In connection with value at risk calculations, one requires the definition of the quantile of a distribution. The *p*th quantile of a distribution, denoted $X_p$, is defined as the value such that there is a probability $p$ that the actual value of the random variable is less than this value:

$$p = P(X \leq X_p) \equiv \int_{-\infty}^{X_p} f(x)dx$$

If the probability is expressed in percent, the quantile is referred to as a per-centile. For instance, to compute value at risk at the 90 percent level of con-fidence, one has to compute the 10th percentile of the return distribution.

## Useful Probability Distributions

In this section, I introduce different probability distributions that arise in connection with the quantification of credit risk in a corporate bond port-folio. Formulas are given for the probability density function and the cor-responding mean and variance of the distribution.

**Normal Distribution**   A normally distributed random variable takes values over the entire range of real numbers. The parameters of the distribution are directly related to the mean and the variance of the distribution, and the skewness is zero due to the symmetry of the distribution. Normal distribu-tions are used to characterize the distribution of returns on assets, such as stocks and bonds. The probability density function of a normally distrib-uted random variable is given by

$$f(x) = \frac{1}{\sqrt{2\pi}\sigma} \exp\left(-\frac{(x-\mu)^2}{2\sigma^2}\right)$$

If the mean $\mu$ is zero and the standard deviation $\sigma$ is one, the normally distrib-uted random variable is referred to as a standardized normal random variable.

**Bernoulli Distribution**   A fundamental issue in credit risk is the determination of the probability of a credit event. By the very nature of this event, histor-ical data on which to base such assessments are limited. Event probabilities are represented by a discrete zero–one random variable. Such a random variable $X$ is said to follow a Bernoulli distribution with probability mass function given by

$$p(x) = \begin{cases} 1 - p & \text{if } X = 0 \\ p & \text{if } X = 1 \end{cases}$$

where $p$ is the parameter of the distribution. The outcome $X = 1$ denotes the occurrence of an event and the outcome $X = 0$ denotes the nonoccurrence of the event. The event could represent the default of an obligor in the context of credit risk. The Bernoulli random variable is completely characterized by its parameter $p$ and has an expected value of $p$ and a variance of $p(1 - p)$.

**Gamma Distribution**   The gamma distribution is characterized by two param-eters, $\alpha > 0$ and $\beta > 0$, which are referred to as the shape parameter and the scale parameter, respectively. Although gamma distributions are not used directly for credit risk computations, special cases of the gamma distribution play a role when the normal distribution assumption for asset returns is relaxed. The probability density function of the gamma distribution is given by

$$f(x) = \begin{cases} \frac{1}{\Gamma(\alpha)\beta^{\alpha}} x^{\alpha-1} e^{-x/\beta}, & 0 < x < \infty \\ 0, & x \le 0 \end{cases}$$

where

$$\Gamma(\alpha) = \int_{0}^{\infty} x^{\alpha-1} e^{-x} \, dx$$

The mean and the variance of the gamma distribution are $\alpha\beta$ and $\alpha\beta^2$, respectively. The special case in which $\alpha = n/2$ (where $n$ is a positive integer) and $\beta = 2$ leads to a chi-square-distributed random variable with $n$ degrees of freedom.

**Beta Distribution** The beta distribution provides a very flexible means of representing variability over a fixed range. The two-parameter beta distribution takes nonzero values in the range between 0 and 1. The flexibility of the distribution encourages its empirical use in a wide range of applications. In credit risk applications, the beta distribution is used to model the recovery rate process on defaulted bonds. The probability density function of the beta distribution is given by

$$f(x, \alpha, \beta) = \begin{cases} \frac{\Gamma(\alpha + \beta)}{\Gamma(\alpha)\,\Gamma(\beta)} x^{\alpha-1}(1-x)^{\beta-1}, & 0 < x < 1 \\ 0, & \text{otherwise} \end{cases}$$

where $\alpha > 0$, $\beta > 0$, and $\Gamma(\cdot)$ is the gamma function. The mean and variance of the beta distribution are given, respectively, by

$$\mu = \frac{\alpha}{\alpha + \beta}$$

and

$$\sigma^2 = \frac{\alpha\beta}{(\alpha + \beta)^2 (\alpha + \beta + 1)}$$

**Uniform Distribution**   The uniform distribution provides one of the simplest means of representing uncertainty. Its use is appropriate in situations where one can identify the range of possible values, but is unable to decide which values within this range are more likely to occur than others. The probability density function of a uniformly distributed random variable defined in the range between $a$ and $b$ is given by

$$f(x) = \frac{1}{b - a}, \qquad a \leq x \leq b$$

The mean and the variance of the distribution are given, respectively, by

$$\mu = \frac{a + b}{2}$$

and

$$\sigma^2 = \frac{(b - a)^2}{12}$$

In the context of credit risk quantification, one can use the uniform distribution to describe the recovery rate process on defaulted bonds as opposed to describing this by a beta distribution. This is because when one simulates the credit loss for a portfolio, use of the beta distribution often generates recovery values that can be close to the par value of the bond. In practice, such recovery values are rarely realized. Simulating the recovery values from a uniform distribution can limit the range of possible recovery values.

For purpose of illustration, consider a recovery value of 47 percent and a volatility of recovery value of 25 percent (these values reflect the empirical estimates for unsecured bonds). The corresponding value of the parameters of the uniform distribution are $a = 0.037$ and $b = 0.903$. When using these parameter values to simulate recovery values, the maximum recovery value is limited to 90 percent of the par amount of the bond. If one chooses the recovery rate volatility to be 22 percent rather than 25 percent, then the recovery values in a simulation run are restricted to lie in the range 9 percent to 85 percent of the par amount of the bond.

## Joint Distributions

The study of joint probability distributions arises if there is more than one random variable to deal with. For instance, one may want to study how the default of one obligor influences the default of another obligor. In this case, one is interested in the joint probability that both obligors will default over a given time period. To examine this, one needs to define joint probability distribution functions. Specifically, the joint probability distribution of the random variables $X$ and $Y$ is characterized by the following quantity:

$$F(x, y) = P(X \leq x, Y \leq y)$$

The right-hand side of this equation represents the joint probability that $X$ is less than $x$ and $Y$ is less than $y$. The corresponding joint density function is given by

$$f(x, y) = \frac{\partial^2 F(x, y)}{\partial x\, \partial y}$$

The two random variables are said to be independent if the joint distribution function can be written as the product of the marginal distributions as given by

$$F(x, y) = F(x)\, F(y)$$

When dealing with more than one random variable, an important attribute of interest is the correlation between the random variables. Correlation determines the degree of dependence between the random variables in question. If the random variables are independent, then the correlation between the random variables is zero.

The definition of the coefficient of correlation between two random variables requires the introduction of another term, called the covariance. The covariance between two random variables $X$ and $Y$ is by definition the following quantity:

$$\sigma_{XY} = E[(X - \mu_X)(Y - \mu_Y)] = E(XY) - E(X)E(Y)$$

Here, $\mu_X$ and $\mu_Y$ are the expected values of the random variables $X$ and $Y$, respectively. If $\sigma_X$ and $\sigma_Y$ denote the standard deviations of the random variables $X$ and $Y$, respectively, then the coefficient of correlation between the two random variables is given by

$$\rho_{XY} = \frac{\sigma_{XY}}{\sigma_X \sigma_Y}$$

If the random variables are independent, then the expected value of their product is equal to the product of their expected values, that is,

$$E(XY) = E(X)E(Y)$$

As mentioned, in this case the correlation between the two random variables is zero, or equivalently, the random variables are uncorrelated. It is useful to note here that if two normally distributed random variables are uncorrelated, then the random variables are also independent. This is not true for random variables that have a different distribution.

## Stochastic Processes

The probability distribution functions discussed so far arise in the context of isolated experiments such as rolling a die or tossing a coin. In such experiments, a probability distribution function provides information on the possible values the random outcome of the experiment can take. However, if one is interested in studying the properties of the sequence of random outcomes when the experiment is performed repeatedly, one enters into the domain of stochastic processes. For instance, the evolution of the price of a stock over time can be thought of as a stochastic process. At any given point in time, the price of the stock can be regarded as a random variable.

This price process of a stock is usually referred to as a continuous-time stochastic process. In such a process, both time and the values the random variable can take are infinitely many. Consider rolling a die; the possible outcomes are limited to a set of six values. In this case, the stochastic process is referred to as a discrete-state stochastic process. If the time dimension is also allowed to take on only a discrete set of values, the process is referred to as a discrete-time, discrete-state stochastic process.

In connection with a stochastic process, one may be interested in making inferences based on the past values of the stochastic process that was observed. This leads to the topic of conditional distributions. In the case of rolling a die, observing the outcomes during a sequence of rolls provides no information on what the outcome of the next roll will be. In other words, the conditional and unconditional distributions are identical and the sequence of experiments can be termed independent. This is an extreme example where the past has no influence on the future outcomes of the experiment.

**Markov Chains**  An interesting variant to the foregoing case is when the experiment's next outcome depends only on its last outcome. A stochastic process that exhibits this property is known as a Markov process. Depending on whether the values the Markov process can take are restricted to a finite set or not, one can distinguish between discrete-state and continuous-state Markov processes. Furthermore, if the time instants at which we observe a discrete-state Markov process are also restricted to a finite set, then this Markov process is known as a Markov chain. Markov chains are used in the modeling of rating migrations of obligors.

To provide a formal definition of Markov chains, consider a discrete-time stochastic process, denoted $\{X_n, n \geq 0\}$, which takes values from a finite set $S$ called the state space of the process. The members of this set $i \in S$ satisfy the property $P(X_n = i) > 0$ for some $n > 0$, where $P(\cdot)$ denotes the probability of an event occurring. The process $\{X_n, n > 0\}$ is called a discrete-time Markov chain if it has the following property for any $n > 0$:

$$P(X_{n+1} = i_{n+1} | X_n = i_n, \cdots, X_0 = i_0) = P(X_{n+1} = i_{n+1} | X_n = i_n)$$

This conditional probability is referred to as the transition probability. If the transition probability is independent of $n$, then the process $\{X_n, n \geq 0\}$ is called a homogeneous Markov chain. For a homogenous Markov chain, the one-step transition probability from state $i \in S$ to state $j \in S$ is denoted by

$$P(X_{n+1} = j \in S | X_n = i \in S) = p_{ij}$$

If there are $m$ states in $S$, then the foregoing definition gives rise to $m \times m$ transition probabilities. These transition probabilities form the elements of an $m \times m$ matrix known as the probability transition matrix. I discuss the properties of this matrix in the section on linear algebra under the topic Markov matrix.

## LINEAR ALGEBRA

Linear algebra, as it concerns us in this book, is a study of the properties of matrices. A matrix is a rectangular array of numbers, and these numbers are known as the elements of the matrix. By an $m \times n$ matrix one means a matrix with $m$ rows and $n$ columns. In the special case where $n = 1$, the matrix collapses to a column vector. If $m = n$, then the matrix is referred to as a square matrix. In this book, we are only concerned with square matrices. For purpose of illustration, a $3 \times 3$ matrix $A$ is represented as

$$A = \begin{bmatrix} a_{11} & a_{12} & a_{13} \\ a_{21} & a_{22} & a_{23} \\ a_{31} & a_{32} & a_{33} \end{bmatrix}$$

It is also common to represent a matrix with elements $a_{ij}$ as $[a_{ij}]$. If the elements of the matrix $A$ are such that $a_{ij} = a_{ji}$ for every $i$ and $j$, then the matrix is referred to as a symmetric matrix. The addition of two $n \times n$ matrices $A$ and $B$ results in an $n \times n$ matrix $C$ whose elements are as follows:

$$c_{ij} = a_{ij} + b_{ij}, \qquad i, j = 1, 2, \ldots, n$$

The multiplication of an $n \times n$ matrix by an $n \times 1$ vector results in a vector of dimension $n \times 1$. For example, if $A$ is an $n \times n$ matrix and $\vec{x}$ is an $n \times 1$ vector, the product $A\vec{x}$ gives rise to an $n \times 1$ vector $\vec{b}$ whose elements are as follows:

$$b_i = \sum_{j=1}^{n} a_{ij} \times x_j, \qquad i = 1, 2, \ldots, n$$

Matrices and vectors are very useful because they make it possible to perform complex calculations using compact notation. I now introduce various concepts that are commonly used in connection with vectors and matrices.

## Properties of Vectors

If $\vec{x}$ is a vector, the product $\vec{x}^T\vec{x}$ is known as the inner product and is a scalar quantity. If $\vec{x}^T\vec{x} = 1$, then the vector $\vec{x}$ is referred to as a unit vector or normalized vector. The quantity $\|\vec{x}\| = \sqrt{\vec{x}^T\vec{x}}$ is called the 2-norm or simply the norm of the vector. Any vector can be normalized by dividing the elements of the vector by its norm.

Two vectors $\vec{x}_1$ and $\vec{x}_2$ are called linearly independent if the following relation holds only for the case when both $c_1$ and $c_2$ are equal to zero:

$$c_1\vec{x}_1 + c_2\vec{x}_2 = 0$$

If this relation holds for some nonzero values of $c_1$ and $c_2$, then the vectors are said to be linearly dependent.

## Transpose of a Matrix

The transpose of a matrix $A$, denoted $A^T$, is a matrix that has the first row of $A$ as its first column, the second row of $A$ as its second column, and so on. In other words, the $(i, j)$th element of the $A$ matrix is the $(j, i)$th element of the matrix $A^T$. It follows immediately from this definition that for symmetric matrices, $A = A^T$.

## Inverse of a Matrix

For any given $n \times n$ matrix $A$, if the $n \times n$ matrix $B$ is such that the product of the two matrices gives rise to a matrix that has all diagonal elements equal to one and the rest zero, then the matrix $B$ is said to be the inverse of the matrix $A$. The matrix with diagonal elements equal to one and all off-diagonal elements zero is referred to as the identity matrix and is denoted $I$. The inverse of the matrix $A$ is denoted $A^{-1}$. A necessary condition for a matrix to be invertible is that all its column vectors are linearly independent.

In the special case where the transpose of a matrix is equal to the inverse of a matrix, that is, $A^T = A^{-1}$, the matrix is referred to as an orthogonal matrix.

## Eigenvalues and Eigenvectors

The eigenvalues of a square matrix $A$ are real or complex numbers $\lambda$ such that the vector equation $A\vec{x} = \lambda\vec{x}$ has nontrivial solutions. The corresponding vectors $\vec{x} \neq 0$ are referred to as the eigenvectors of $A$. Any $n \times n$ matrix has $n$ eigenvalues, and associated with each eigenvalue is a corresponding eigenvector. It is possible that for some matrices not all eigenvalues and eigenvectors are distinct. The sum of the $n$ eigenvalues equals the sum of the entries on the diagonal of the matrix $A$, called the trace of $A$. Thus,

$$\text{trace } A = \sum_{i=1}^{n} a_{ii} = \sum_{i=1}^{n} \lambda_i$$

If $\lambda = 0$ is an eigenvalue of the matrix, the matrix is referred to as a singular matrix. Matrices that are singular do not have an inverse.

## Diagonalization of a Matrix

When $\vec{x}$ is an eigenvector of the matrix $A$, the product $A\vec{x}$ is equivalent to the multiplication of the vector $\vec{x}$ by a scalar quantity. This scalar quantity happens to be the eigenvalue of the matrix. One can conjecture from this that a matrix can be turned into a diagonal matrix by using eigenvectors appropriately. In particular, if the columns of matrix $M$ are formed using the eigenvectors of $A$, then the matrix operation $M^{-1}AM$ is a diagonal matrix with eigenvalues of $A$ as the diagonal elements. However, for this to be true, the matrix $M$ must be invertible. Stated differently, the eigenvectors of the matrix $A$ must form a set of linearly independent vectors.

It is useful to remark here that any matrix operation of the type $B^{-1}AB$ where $B$ is an invertible matrix is referred to as a similarity transformation. Under a similarity transformation, eigenvalues remain unchanged.

## Properties of Symmetric Matrices

Symmetric matrices have the property that all eigenvalues are real numbers. If, in addition, the eigenvalues are all positive, then the matrix is referred to as a positive-definite matrix. An interesting property of symmetric matrices is that they are always diagonalizable. Furthermore, the matrix $M$ constructed using the normalized eigenvectors of a symmetric matrix is orthogonal.

A well-known example of a symmetric matrix is the covariance matrix of security returns. For an $n$-asset portfolio, if the random vector of security returns is denoted by $\vec{r}$ and the mean of the random vector by $\vec{\mu}$, then the $n \times n$ matrix given by $E[(\vec{r} - \vec{\mu})(\vec{r} - \vec{\mu})^T]$ is termed the covariance matrix of security returns. Although covariance matrices are positive definite by definition (assuming the $n$ assets are distinct), covariance matrices estimated using historical data can sometimes turn out to be singular.

## Cholesky Decomposition

The Cholesky decomposition is concerned with the factorization of a symmetric and positive-definite matrix into the product of a lower and an upper triangular matrix. A matrix is said to be lower triangular if all its elements above the diagonal are zero. Similarly, an upper triangular matrix is one with all elements below the diagonal zero. If the matrix is symmetric and positive definite, the upper triangular matrix is equal to the transpose of the lower triangular matrix. Specifically, if the lower triangular matrix is denoted by $L$, then the positive-definite matrix $\Sigma$ can be written as $\Sigma = LL^T$. Such a factorization of the matrix is called the Cholesky decomposition.

The Cholesky factorization of a matrix finds application in simulating random vectors from a multivariate distribution. Specifically, if one has to generate a sequence of normally distributed random vectors having an $n \times n$ covariance matrix $\Sigma$, the Cholesky decomposition helps achieve this in two simple steps. In the first step, one generates a random vector $\vec{x}$ comprising $n$ uncorrelated standardized normal random variables. In the second step, one constructs the random vector $\vec{z} = L\vec{x}$, which has the desired covariance matrix. To see why this is true, first note that $\vec{z}$ is a zero-mean random vector because $\vec{x}$ is a zero-mean random vector. In this case, the covariance matrix of the random vector $\vec{z}$ can be written as

$$E(\vec{z}\,\vec{z}^T) = E(L\,\vec{x}\,\vec{x}^T L^T) = L E(\vec{x}\,\vec{x}^T) L^T$$

Because the random vector $\vec{x}$ comprises uncorrelated normal random variables, the covariance matrix given by $E(\vec{x}\,\vec{x}^T)$ is equal to the identity matrix. From this it follows that

$$E(\vec{z}\,\vec{z}^T) = L L^T = \Sigma$$

The elements of the matrix $L$ that represents the Cholesky decomposition of the matrix $\Sigma$ can be computed using the following rule:

$$l_{ii} = \sqrt{\left(\sigma_{ii} - \sum_{k=1}^{i-1} l_{ik}^2\right)}, \qquad i = 1, 2, \ldots, n$$

$$l_{ji} = \frac{1}{l_{ii}}\left(\sigma_{ji} - \sum_{k=1}^{i-1} l_{jk}\, l_{ik}\right), \qquad j = i + 1, \ldots, n$$

I mentioned that covariance matrices estimated from historical data could be singular. If this happens, we artificially add some variance to each of the random variables so that the covariance matrix is positive definite. For instance, if $E$ denotes a diagonal matrix with small positive elements, then the matrix $\Sigma + E$ has the property that it is positive definite and the Cholesky decomposition can be computed.

## Markov Matrix

A real $n \times n$ matrix $P = [p_{ij}]$ is called a Markov matrix if its elements have the following properties:

$$\sum_{j=1}^{n} p_{ij} = 1, \qquad i = 1, 2, \ldots, n$$

$$p_{ij} \geq 0, \qquad i, j = 1, 2, \ldots, n$$

This definition indicates that the elements in each row of a Markov matrix are non-negative and sum to one. As a result, any row vector having this property can be considered to represent a valid probability mass function. This leads to the interpretation of any vector having this property as a probability vector.

Markov matrices have some interesting properties. The matrix formed by taking the product of two Markov matrices is also a Markov matrix. If one multiplies a probability vector by a Markov matrix, the result is another probability vector. Markov matrices find applications in many different fields. In finance, Markov matrices are used to model the rating migrations of obligors. For instance, a 1-year rating transition matrix is simply a probabilistic representation of the possible credit ratings an obligor could have in 1 year. The probability of migrating to another rating grade is a function of the current credit rating of the obligor.

For purpose of illustration, consider the following Markov matrix:

$$P = \begin{bmatrix} 0.6 & 0.3 & 0.1 \\ 0.1 & 0.7 & 0.2 \\ 0 & 0 & 1 \end{bmatrix}$$

This Markov matrix has three states, which can be thought of as representing an investment-grade rating, a non-investment-grade rating, and a default state for the obligor, respectively. The first row represents the rating migration probabilities for an obligor rated investment grade. If these probabilities represent 1-year migration probabilities, one can interpret from the first row of the matrix that there is a 0.1 probability that the investment-grade obligor will default in 1 year from now. However, if one wants to know the probability that an investment-grade obligor will default in 2 years from now, one can compute this as follows:

$$[1 \quad 0 \quad 0]\begin{bmatrix} 0.6 & 0.3 & 0.1 \\ 0.1 & 0.7 & 0.2 \\ 0 & 0 & 1 \end{bmatrix}\begin{bmatrix} 0.6 & 0.3 & 0.1 \\ 0.1 & 0.7 & 0.2 \\ 0 & 0 & 1 \end{bmatrix} = [0.39 \quad 0.39 \quad 0.22]$$

In this computation, the probability vector $[1 \quad 0 \quad 0]$ denotes that the obligor has an investment-grade rating to start with. Multiplying this probability vector by $P$ gives the probability vector 1 year from now. If one multiplies this probability vector once more by $P$, one gets the probabilities of occupying different states 2 years from now. Actual computations carried out indicate that the probability that an investment-grade obligor will default in 2 years is 0.22.

In practice, rating agencies estimate multiyear rating transition matrices in addition to the standard 1-year rating transition matrix. A question of greater interest is whether one can derive a rating transition matrix for a 6-month or a 3-month horizon using the 1-year rating transition matrix. The short answer to this question is yes, and the way to do this is to perform an eigenvector decomposition of the 1-year rating transition matrix. If $M$ denotes the matrix of eigenvectors of the 1-year rating transition matrix $P$ and $\Lambda$ is a diagonal matrix whose diagonal elements are the eigenvalues of $P$, then one knows from the earlier result on the diagonalization of a matrix that the operation $M^{-1}PM$ gives the diagonal matrix $\Lambda$. From this it follows that

$$P = M\Lambda M^{-1}$$

The 3-month rating migration matrix, for instance, can now be computed as follows:

$$P^{1/4} = M\Lambda^{1/4}M^{-1}$$

The matrix $P^{1/4}$ computed by performing this operation is a valid Markov matrix provided $P$ represents a Markov matrix. Computing rating transition matrices for horizons less than 1 year using the foregoing matrix decomposition makes use of the result that the matrices $P$ and $P^{1/n}$ share the same eigenvectors. By performing the foregoing operations on the $3 \times 3$ matrix $P$, one can derive the following 3-month rating transition matrix:

$$P^{1/4} = \begin{bmatrix} 0.8736 & 0.1055 & 0.0209 \\ 0.0351 & 0.9088 & 0.0561 \\ 0 & 0 & 1 \end{bmatrix}$$

It is easy to verify that this matrix is a Markov matrix.

## Principal Component Analysis

Principal component analysis is concerned with explaining the variance–covariance structure of $n$ random variables through a few linear combinations of the original variables. Principal component analysis often reveals relationships that are sometimes not obvious, and the analysis is based on historical data. Our interest in principal component analysis lies in its application to the empirical modeling of the yield curve dynamics. For the purpose of illustrating the mathematical concepts behind principal component analysis, consider the $n$ random variables of interest to be the weekly yield changes for different maturities along the yield curve. Denote these random variables by $y_1, y_2, \dots, y_n$.

An algebraic interpretation of principal component analysis is that principal components are particular linear combinations of the $n$ random variables. The geometric interpretation is that these linear combinations represent the selection of a new coordinate system. Principal components depend solely on the covariance matrix $\Sigma$ of the $n$ random variables and do not require the multivariate normal distribution assumption for the random variables.

Denote the $n$ random variables by the vector $\vec{Y} = [y_1, y_2, \dots, y_n]^T$ and the eigenvalues of the $n \times n$ covariance matrix $\Sigma$ by $\lambda_1 \geq \lambda_2 \geq \cdots \geq \lambda_n \geq 0$. By definition, $\Sigma = E[(\vec{Y} - \vec{\mu})(\vec{Y} - \vec{\mu})^T]$, where $\vec{\mu}$ is the mean of vector $\vec{Y}$. Now consider the following linear combinations of $\vec{Y}$:

$$x_1 = \vec{\ell}_1^T \vec{Y} = \ell_{11}y_1 + \ell_{12}y_2 + \cdots + \ell_{1n}y_n$$

$$x_2 = \vec{\ell}_2^T \vec{Y} = \ell_{21}y_1 + \ell_{22}y_2 + \cdots + \ell_{2n}y_n$$

$$x_n = \vec{\ell}_n^T \vec{Y} = \ell_{n1}y_1 + \ell_{n2}y_2 + \cdots + \ell_{nn}y_n$$

In these equations, $\vec{\ell}_i$ are unit vectors and $x_1, x_2, \dots, x_n$ represent new random variables. The vector $\vec{\ell}_i$ is usually interpreted as a direction vector, which changes the coordinate axes of the original random variables. It is easy to verify that the variance of the random variable $x_i$ is given by

$$\text{var}(x_i) = \text{var}(\vec{\ell}_i^T \vec{Y}) = \vec{\ell}_i^T \Sigma \vec{\ell}_i$$

The covariance of the random variables $x_i$ and $x_k$ is given by

$$\text{cov}(x_i, x_k) = E\left[(\vec{\ell}_i^T \vec{Y} - \vec{\ell}_i^T \vec{\mu})(\vec{\ell}_k^T \vec{Y} - \vec{\ell}_k^T \vec{\mu})^T\right]$$
$$= \vec{\ell}_i^T E\left[(\vec{Y} - \vec{\mu})(\vec{Y} - \vec{\mu})^T\right]\vec{\ell}_k$$
$$= \vec{\ell}_i^T \Sigma \vec{\ell}_k$$

To compute the principal components, one first needs to define what principal components are. A simple definition of principal components is that they are uncorrelated linear combinations of the original random variables such that the variances explained by the newly constructed random variables are as large as possible.

So far, I have not mentioned how to choose the direction vectors to achieve this. In fact, it is quite simple. All one needs to do is to choose the direction vectors to be the normalized eigenvectors of the covariance matrix $\Sigma$. If one does this, the linear transformations give rise to random variables that represent the principal components of the covariance matrix. To see why this is the case, note that when the vector $\vec{\ell}_i$ is an eigenvector of the matrix $\Sigma$, then $\Sigma \vec{\ell}_i$ gives $\lambda_i \vec{\ell}_i$. From this it follows that

$$\text{var}(x_i) = \vec{\ell}_i^T \Sigma \vec{\ell}_i = \lambda_i \vec{\ell}_i^T \vec{\ell}_i = \lambda_i$$

In other words, the variances of the new random variables are equal to the eigenvalues of the covariance matrix. Furthermore, by construction, the random variables are uncorrelated because the covariance between any two random variables $x_i$ and $x_k$ is zero when $i \neq k$. The random variable $x_1$ is the first principal component and its variance, given by $\lambda_1$, is greater than the variance of any other random variables one can construct. The second principal component is $x_2$, whose variance is equal to $\lambda_2$.

The sum of the variances of the new random variables constructed is equal to the sum of the eigenvalues of the covariance matrix. The sum of the variances of the original random variables is equal to the sum of the diagonal entries of the covariance matrix $\Sigma$, which by definition is equal to the trace of the matrix. Because the trace of a matrix is equal to the sum of the eigenvalues of the matrix, one gets the following identity:

$$\sum_{i=1}^{n} \text{var}(y_i) = \sum_{i=1}^{n} \text{var}(x_i)$$

It immediately follows from this relation that the proportion of variance of the original random variables explained by the $i$th principal component is given by

$$\frac{\lambda_i}{\lambda_1 + \lambda_2 + \cdots + \lambda_n}$$

The principal components derived by performing an eigenvector decomposition of the covariance matrix are optimal in explaining the variance structure over some historical time period. Outside this sample period over which the covariance matrix is estimated, the eigenvectors may not be optimal direction vectors in the sense of maximizing the observed variance using a few principal components. Moreover, the principal component direction vectors keep changing as new data come in, and giving a risk interpretation to these vectors becomes difficult. Given these difficulties, one might like to know whether one could choose some other direction vectors that lend themselves to easy interpretation, but nonetheless explain a significant amount of variance in the original data using only a few components. The answer is yes, with the only requirement that the direction vectors be chosen to be linearly independent.

If, for instance, one chooses two direction vectors $\vec{\ell}_s$ and $\vec{\ell}_t$, denoted shift and twist vectors, respectively, then the variance of the new random variables is

$$\sigma_s^2 = \vec{\ell}_s^T \Sigma \vec{\ell}_s$$

$$\sigma_t^2 = \vec{\ell}_t^T \Sigma \vec{\ell}_t$$

The proportion of variance in the original data explained by the two depends on how much correlation there is between the two random variables constructed. The correlation between the random variables is given by

$$\rho = \frac{\text{cov}(\vec{\ell}_s, \vec{\ell}_t)}{\sigma_s \times \sigma_t} = \frac{\vec{\ell}_s^T \Sigma \vec{\ell}_t}{\sigma_s \times \sigma_t}$$

The proportion of total variance explained by the two random variables is

$$\frac{\sigma_s^2 + (1 - \rho)\sigma_t^2}{\lambda_1 + \lambda_2 + \cdots + \lambda_n}$$

## QUESTIONS

1. A die is rolled 10 times. Find the probability that the face 6 will show
   (a) at least two times and (b) exactly two times.

2. The number that shows up when a die is rolled is a random variable. Compute the mean and the variance of this random variable.
3. A normally distributed random variable has $\mu = 0.5$ and $\sigma = 1.2$. Compute the 10th percentile of the distribution.
4. A beta distribution with parameters $\alpha = 1.4$ and $\beta = 1.58$ is used to simulate the recovery values from defaulted bonds. Compute the probability that the recovery value during the simulations lies in the range 20 to 80 percent of the par value of the bond. What are the mean and the volatility of the recovery rate process simulated?
5. If a uniform distribution is used to restrict the simulated recovery rates to lie in the range 20 to 80 percent of the par value of the bond, what are the mean and the volatility of the recovery rate process?
6. Show that if $A$ and $B$ are any two $n \times n$ Markov matrices, then the product of the two matrices is also a Markov matrix.
7. For any Markov matrix $P$, show that $P^n$ and $P^{1/n}$ are also Markov matrices for any integer $n$.
8. I computed the 3-month rating transition matrix $P^{1/4}$ in the numerical example under Markov matrices. Compute the 1-month and 6-month rating transition matrices for this example.
9. Compute the eigenvalues, eigenvectors, and Cholesky decomposition of the following matrix:

$$A = \begin{bmatrix} 1 & -2 & 0 \\ -2 & 5 & 0 \\ 0 & 0 & 2 \end{bmatrix}$$

10. Compute the proportion of total variance explained by the first two principal components for the matrix $A$ in Question 9.
11. If the direction vectors are chosen to be $[1 \ \ 0 \ \ 1]^T$ and $[1 \ \ 0 \ \ 0]^T$ instead of the first two eigenvectors of the matrix $A$ in Question 9, compute the total variance explained by these two direction vectors.

## CHAPTER 3

# The Corporate Bond Market

In this chapter, I describe the features of corporate bonds and identify the risks associated with investment in corporate bonds. I then discuss the practical difficulties related to the trading of corporate bonds as opposed to government bonds arising from increased transaction costs and lack of transparent pricing sources. I highlight the important role played by corporate bonds in buffering the impact of financial crises and examine the relative market size and historical performance of corporate bonds. Finally, I provide some justification as to why the corporate bond market is an interesting asset class for the reserves portfolio of central banks and for pension funds.

## FEATURES OF CORPORATE BONDS

Corporate bonds are debt obligations issued by private and public corporations to raise capital to finance their business operations. The major corporate bond issuers can be classified under the following categories: (1) public utilities, (2) transportation companies, (3) industrial corporations, (4) financial services companies, and (5) conglomerates. Corporate bonds denominated in U.S. dollars are typically issued in multiples of $1,000 and are traded primarily in the over-the-counter (OTC) market.

Unlike owners of stocks, holders of corporate bonds do not have ownership rights in the corporation issuing the bonds. Bondholders, however, have priority on legal claims over common and preferred stockholders on both income and assets of the corporation for the principal and interest due to them. The promises of corporate bond issuers and the rights of investors who buy them are set forth in contracts termed *indentures*. The indenture, which is printed on the bond certificate, contains the following information: the duties and obligations of the trustee, all the rights of the bondholder, how and when the principal will be repaid, the rate of interest, the description of any property to be pledged as collateral, and the steps the bondholder can take in the event of default.

Corporate bonds are issued in the form of registered bonds or book-entry bonds. Registered bonds refer to those corporate bonds that are issued as certificates with the owner's name printed on them. There are no coupons attached for the owner to submit for payment of interest. The issuer's trustee sends the interest to the bondholder at the appropriate intervals and forwards the principal at maturity. Book-entry bonds are those that are issued without certificates. Book-entry bonds have largely replaced registered bonds as the prevailing form of issuance. With book-entry securities, a bond issue has only one master certificate, which is usually kept at a securities depository. The ownership of book-entry bonds is recorded in the investor's brokerage account and interest and principal payments are forwarded to this account.

Corporate bonds are broadly classified into investment-grade and non-investment-grade bonds. Investment-grade bonds are those that have a credit rating of BBB-minus or higher as rated by Standard & Poor's or, equivalently, a credit rating of Baa3 or higher as rated by Moody's. Companies that issue such bonds are assumed to have a reasonably good credit standing. Bonds that have a rating below this are referred to as non-investment-grade or high-yield bonds. Such bonds are issued by newer or start-up companies or companies that have had financial problems. The credit rating of the bond issuer provides bondholders with a simple system to measure the ability of the issuer to honor its financial obligations.

## Bond Collateralization

From the investor's perspective, corporate bonds offer an attractive yield pickup over comparable-maturity government bonds. However, whether the current yields will be realized over the investment horizon of interest depends on the ability of the issuer to honor the promised payments, which in turn is determined by the credit rating of the bond issuer. Generally, the lower the credit rating, the higher the yield pickup. An equally important factor that determines the yield differential versus the government bond is the collateral attached to the bond issue. Bonds that have collateral attached to them are called *secured* bonds and those with no collateral are called *unsecured* bonds. For identical bond maturities, secured bonds of any issuer have a lower yield relative to unsecured bonds of the same issuer. Depending on the nature of the collateral or its absence, corporate bonds can be further classified into debenture bonds, mortgage bonds, collateral trust bonds, or equipment trust certificates.

**Debenture Bonds**    Most corporate bonds are debentures, which means they are senior unsecured debt obligations backed only by the issuer's general credit and the capacity of its cash flow to repay interest and principal. Notwithstanding this, senior unsecured bonds generally have the protection of a negative pledge provision. This provision requires the issuer to provide security for the unsecured bonds in the event that it subsequently pledges its assets to secure other debt obligations. The intention is to prevent other creditors from obtaining a senior position at the expense of existing creditors. However, it is not intended to prevent other creditors from sharing in the position of debenture holders.

Another kind of debenture bond, which has lower priority on claims to senior unsecured bonds, is a subordinated bond. In exchange for this lower priority on claims in the event of bankruptcy, the yield on subordinated bonds is higher than on senior unsecured bonds.

**Mortgage Bonds** Bonds that have real estate or other physical assets pledged against them are referred to as mortgage bonds. The real assets pledged must have a market value greater than the bond issue size. Among corporates, the largest issuers of mortgage bonds are electric utility companies. Other utilities, such as telephone companies and gas pipeline and distribution firms, also use mortgage bonds to a limited extent as a source of financing. In the event of default on coupon or principal payment by the issuer, the pledged assets are sold off to repay the mortgage bondholders.

There are various kinds of mortgage bonds, such as first, prior, junior, second, and so on. This classification reflects the priority of the lien or legal claim the bondholder has against the specified pledged property. When investing in mortgage bonds, it is important to check how much of the other mortgage debt of the issuer is secured by the same collateral and whether the lien supporting the other mortgage debt has greater or lower priority than the issue that is being bought.

Another categorization of mortgage debt is in terms of open-ended and closed-end mortgage bonds. If the mortgage bonds are pledged with closed-end assets, these assets can only be sold to repay the interest and principal due for the particular issue in the event of default. On the other hand, if the mortgage bonds are pledged with open-ended assets, these assets may also be pledged against other open-ended issues.

**Collateral Trust Bonds** Collateral trust bonds are those that are secured by financial assets such as stocks, receivables, bonds, and securities other than real property. A trustee holds the eligible collateral and the collateral value must be at least equal to the value of the bonds. To ensure this is the case, the trustee periodically marks to market the collateral to ensure that the liquidation value is in excess of the amount needed to repay the entire outstanding bonds linked to it and the accrued interest. If this condition is not met, the issuer is required to bring in additional collateral, failing which, the trustee sells the collateral and redeems the bonds. Collateral trust bonds are typically issued by vehicle-leasing firms.

**Equipment Trust Certificates**   An equipment trust certificate is a bond that is collateralized by ownership of specific equipment, often capital in nature. Railroads and airlines issue this type of bond as a way to pay for new equipment at relatively low interest rates. Essentially this involves transferring the ownership of the asset, such as an aircraft or a locomotive, to a trustee, who then issues certificates indicating the beneficial ownership of the asset. Such equipment trust certificates are issued at 80 percent of the value of the equipment; the remaining 20 percent is paid by the railroad or airline seeking the finance. Due to the collateral value of the equipment trust certificates and superior standing in bankruptcy proceedings, ratings for equipment trust certificates are usually higher than on other debt securities issued by the same corporation.

**Remarks**   In general, bonds that are backed by some form of collateral are classified under securitized assets. If the collateral consists of receivables other than a mortgage loan, such as credit card receivables, auto loans, manufactured-housing contracts, and home-equity loans, then the collateralized bond is referred to as an asset-backed security (ABS). Bonds backed by first mortgages, although the most common securitized asset, are usually considered to be a separate investment category and are referred to as mortgage-backed securities (MBS). The analysis presented in this book is not applicable to mortgage-backed securities.

Although in principle the management of an ABS portfolio can be analyzed using the framework presented in this book, some features of ABSs such as internal and external forms of credit enhancement and whether the assets are amortizing require careful examination. Moreover, the loan originators of such securities, commonly referred to as the issuers of ABSs, are in fact the sponsors and not the issuers of these securities. This is achieved by the sponsor selling the assets to a special-purpose vehicle (SPV), the structural feature of which is to provide bankruptcy remoteness between the trust that issues the bonds and the loan sponsor who originates them. These factors tend to complicate the credit risk analysis of an ABS portfolio. Hence, the focus in this book is primarily on the portfolio management of unsecuritized corporate bonds.

## Investment Risks

An investor who buys corporate bonds is exposed to a variety of risks. The chief among them are market risk, credit risk, liquidity risk, and economic risk.

**Market Risk**   Prices of corporate bonds are sensitive to changes in the level of interest rates. Rising interest rates cause the prices of bonds to fall; the longer the maturity of the bond, the greater is the price depreciation. This risk, generally referred to as *interest rate* risk, is common to any fixed-income security. Another source of market risk can arise from early redemptions if the bond has a call provision. In this case, the issuer has the right to redeem the debt, fully or partially, before the scheduled maturity date of the bond. Call provisions limit the potential price appreciation when interest rates fall. Because the call provision puts the investor at a disadvantage, callable bonds carry higher yields than noncallable bonds. The relative percentage of unsecuritized corporate bonds with embedded options is, however, quite small. As of end of 2002, callable/puttable corporate bonds constituted 10.1 percent of the number of issues and 5.7 percent of market capitalization of the Lehman Brothers corporate bond index.

**Credit Risk** A major source of risk facing investors in the corporate bond market is whether the bond issuer has the financial capacity to meet the contractual coupon and principal payments. This risk is usually referred to as *default* risk, and it increases as the credit rating of the issuer declines. Apart from default risk, corporate bonds are also exposed to price changes that result from perceived changes in the ability of the issuer to meet the promised cash flows. This form of risk is usually referred to as *downgrade* risk. Default risk and downgrade risk are collectively called *credit* risk, and they constitute a major component of risk facing corporate bond investors.

**Liquidity Risk** The risk stemming from the lack of marketability of an instrument is referred to as *liquidity* risk. Bonds, such as U.S. Treasuries, that trade frequently and in large amounts have less liquidity risk than corporate bonds. An indicative measure of liquidity risk is the difference between the bid price and ask price of a security and the size that can be transacted at this bid price. The greater the bid–ask spread and/or the smaller the bid size, the greater the uncertainty is surrounding the true market value of the security. As the investor's holding period of the corporate bond increases, liquidity risk becomes only a small fraction of the overall risk facing a corporate bond investor. However, one has to bear in mind that when an investor tries to sell a corporate bond due to deteriorating credit conditions of the issuer, the liquidity risk facing the investor is greatest.

**Economic Risk** Economic risk refers to the vulnerability of the corporate bond's return to downturns in the economy. Unlike credit risk, which is specific to a particular issuer, economic risk affects the returns of all corporate bonds. This is because earnings capabilities of most companies are tied to the state of the economy. During periods of economic contraction, company earnings are reduced, which in turn reduces their capacity to meet payment obligations on outstanding debt. As a consequence, the general level of credit spreads relative to government debt increases across the entire spectrum of corporate bonds due to a decline in the ability of many corporations to service debt obligations. This results in a loss in market value of the corporate bond portfolio due to widening credit spreads for corporate borrowers across the entire spectrum.

## CORPORATE BOND TRADING

The over-the-counter nature of the corporate bond market leads to a privately negotiated secondary market where bonds tend to turn over infrequently. As a result, the corporate bond market suffers from the lack of transparency and availability of a central pricing mechanism. Indeed, price transparency is essential to building investor confidence, which in turn can result in an increase of trading volume. In fact, the trading volume in the corporate bond market is less than 1 percent of outstanding market capitalization, whereas in the case of the U.S. Treasury bond market, trading volume is close to 10 percent of the Treasury bond market capitalization. In this section, I discuss some practical issues connected with corporate bond trading namely, the trading costs involved, the impact on portfolio management styles, and pricing anomalies of corporate bonds.

### Trading Costs

I have already mentioned that the turnover in the corporate bond market is much lower than the turnover in the government bond market. The main reason for the lower turnover is the wider bid–ask spreads that are quoted for corporate bonds. Wider bid–ask spreads lead to high transaction costs if corporate bonds are frequently turned over. To minimize the transaction costs, most investors try to follow a buy-and-hold strategy when investing in corporate bonds. Such a strategy has the detrimental effect of further increasing bid–ask spreads on bonds that are not recent issues. Corporate bonds denominated in U.S. dollars are usually quoted in terms of yield spread over comparable-maturity U.S. Treasuries.[1] Typical bid–ask spreads on such quotes can vary from 5 to as much as 10 basis points, which is roughly 10 times greater than the bid–ask yield spreads observed on U.S. Treasuries.

The wider bid–ask spreads and smaller bid sizes for corporate bonds tend to make this asset class lack the traditional liquidity enjoyed by government bonds. In broad terms, a liquid financial asset is one for which large numbers of buyers and sellers are present so that incoming orders can be matched without affecting the market price of the asset. Although corporate bonds are less liquid than government bonds, it is important to note that illiquidity is not a static attribute of corporate bonds. On the contrary, significant fluctuations in the liquidity of corporate bonds can often occur in response to changes in macroeconomic trends or perceived risks of particular corporate sectors. The corporate bond market has a history of alternating between periods of confidence and transparency marked by multiple dealer quotes and tight bid–ask spreads and periods of gloom and uncertainty characterized by low trading volumes and wide bid–ask spreads.

To understand why trading costs are high for corporate bonds, it is important to examine the mechanics of corporate bond trading. As previously stated, corporate bonds are primarily traded in the secondary market. The secondary market trading is done through bond dealers in investment banks rather than through exchanges or on electronic platforms. Bond dealers serve as intermediaries between investors wanting to buy and sell corporate bonds. Because investors turn over corporate bonds less frequently, matching the buy and sell orders for dealers can take sometimes several days, and in the worst case, even several weeks. During this period, the dealer is forced to hold an inventory of the bond, which needs to be financed until a seller can be found. While the corporate bond is held in inventory, the dealer faces the risk that the price of the bond can fall due to either a negative earning surprise announcement or an actual downgrade of the corporation that issued the bond. Moreover, the inventory cost increases over time because risk managers penalize stale inventories with higher capital charges. To compensate for these risks, corporate bond dealers usually charge wider bid–ask spreads to cushion their potential losses.

Having examined why trading costs for corporate bonds are high, I turn to the following practical questions: How much does it cost to trade a corporate bond, and do the trading costs differ for different bond maturities? The trading cost of any bond is a function of the quoted bid–ask yield spread and the duration of the bond. Specifically, if $D$ denotes the modified duration of the bond and $\Delta s$ the bid–ask yield spread, then the trading cost for the bond is given by[2]

$$\text{Trading cost} = D \times \Delta s$$

This formula suggests that trading costs for a corporate bond with longer maturity are greater. If, for instance, the bid–ask yield spread is 5 basis points and the modified duration of the bond is 4 years, then the trading cost is 20 cents for a $100 face value of the bond. In a portfolio context, the trading cost is measured in terms of the annual turnover of the portfolio.[3] Assuming that the average duration of the portfolio is 4 years and the portfolio turnover is 100 percent during the year, the annual trading costs for the portfolio is roughly 20 basis points if the bid–ask yield spread is 5 basis points. This trading cost is quite high relative to the trading costs involved in managing a government bond portfolio. As a numerical comparison, trading costs for a government bond portfolio having the same duration and turnover ratio are about 3 to 4 basis points.

## Portfolio Management Style

The higher trading costs for corporate bond portfolios influence portfolio management styles that are pursued to add value against a given benchmark. Considering that average portfolio trading costs are fairly deterministic, corporate portfolio managers try to minimize this consciously by limiting the portfolio turnover. Typical annual turnover ratios for actively managed corporate bond portfolios are about 75 percent, whereas for government bond portfolios ratios can be in the region of 150 percent. As a result, the increase in trading costs to manage a corporate bond portfolio is roughly in the region of 10 basis points per annum more than that incurred to manage a government bond portfolio. When later I explore alternative asset allocation strategies to improve the investment returns on assets under management, I will take into account this additional trading cost for a corporate bond portfolio.

As a consequence of the higher transaction costs incurred for managing corporate bonds, portfolio management styles of corporate and government bond portfolio managers differ. In particular, investment strategies of corporate bond portfolio managers tend to focus on analyzing the long-term fundamentals of bond issuers so that a buy-and-hold strategy can be pursued while seeking to outperform a given benchmark. Portfolio managers in charge of managing government bond portfolios, on the other hand, tend to pursue yield-curve strategies to add value against their benchmarks. In addition, government bond portfolio managers may be able to repo out bonds that go on specials, and this could generate some additional income.

With respect to managing a corporate bond portfolio, I identified transaction costs as an important factor that influences the trading styles of portfolio managers. I now highlight some practical difficulties involved in managing a corporate bond portfolio as opposed to a government bond portfolio. Much of the practical difficulties stem from the smaller issue size of corporate bonds, and as a consequence, the smaller bid sizes for dealer quotes. To provide a concrete example, the issue sizes of investment-grade corporate bonds are typically in the range of $150 to $500 million and the bid sizes of dealer quotes are usually valid for $5 million. Transacting larger trade sizes on such bonds can drive the bid prices lower. In the U.S. Treasury market, executing a trade worth $100 million nominal amount has a negligible market impact even for off-the-run securities. Clearly, the lack of market depth when trading corporate bonds makes the task of managing large corporate bond portfolios difficult. Other practical difficulties with regard to managing a corporate bond portfolio relate to the difficulty of finding offers on bonds that a portfolio manager may be willing to buy or finding bids on bonds he or she may wish to sell. In particular, during periods of market turmoil, unwinding "bad credits" may incur considerable loss and, in worst-case situations, there may be no bids for them.

## Pricing Anomalies

Other facts concerning corporate bond trading relate to the dispersion of price quotes on bonds with very similar attributes. For instance, corporate bond yields can vary significantly among issuers belonging to the same corporate sector that have identical credit rating and comparable bond maturities. This makes the task of building generic-yield curves based on credit rating and the corporate sector difficult, if not impossible. However, the practical value of such curves from a pricing perspective is questionable. To provide a concrete example, the bid yields on dollar-denominated debt as of 2 January 2003 for three BBB-rated issuers were as follows:

General Motors (6.75 percent, 15JAN2006)       Bid yield = 5.752 percent
Daimler Chrysler (7.25 percent, 18JAN2006)     Bid yield = 4.023 percent
Ford Motor Credit (6.875 percent, 01FEB2006) Bid yield = 6.972 percent

There are several factors that influence large yield differences observed among issuers belonging to the same rating class. Finer ratings within a rating category and the placement of issuers on credit watch tend to explain some differences. The age of the bond, namely whether it was recently issued, also influences the yield differentials to a certain extent due to the liquidity effect. Another factor that influences the yield of a corporate bond apart from the credit rating is the market perception regarding the expected recovery amount on the bond in the event of issuer default. Even after accounting for these factors, the yield differentials among issuers with identical ratings can still be significant.

These issues indicate that the pricing of corporate bonds can be rather tricky. Price quotes for corporate bonds obtained from different brokers or dealers tend to vary considerably. The lack of reliable pricing sources for corporate bonds makes the task of marking to market corporate bond portfolios difficult. In many cases, the bond prices supplied by the index provider are commonly used. However, one has to bear in mind that when existing bonds in the portfolio are sold, the realized market price can be quite different from the valuation price. Explaining these differences, especially to clients, can be quite problematic.

In order to improve the transparency of traded prices for corporate bonds, since July 2002 the National Association of Securities Dealers

(NASD) has made it compulsory for all NASD member firms to report OTC trades on corporate bonds that fall into the category of TRACE-eligible security. TRACE stands for Trade Reporting and Compliance Engine; TRACE-eligible security covers most corporate bonds denominated in U.S. dollars and registered with the Security and Exchange Commissions (SEC). Initial price dissemination to the public is currently limited to investment-grade bonds having an issue size of $1 billion or more and some selected non-investment-grade bonds.

## ROLE OF CORPORATE BONDS

Corporate bonds are usually seen as offering economic enterprises an alternative funding source besides equity financing and bank loans. Considering that taking a bank loan or issuing a corporate bond to raise money can be regarded as a firm's debt financing options, either form of financing will result in the same debt-to-equity ratio for the firm. As a consequence, a microeconomic view might suggest that the firm's prospects will not depend on which form of debt financing is used. However, from a macroeconomic perspective, striking the right balance between the two debt financing options can have broader implications, especially for systemic risks faced by countries. In this section, I examine these issues and highlight the important role corporate bonds play in a nation's broader economic goals.

Financial episodes in the recent past have shown that economies with well-developed capital markets experience milder economic crises than those lacking this alternative funding source. In the case of Sweden, for example, a significant fall in real estate prices triggered a banking crisis in the early 1990s primarily because of the large exposures banks had to the real estate sector. The corporate sector, however, which had access to a variety of non-bank funding sources, rebounded relatively quickly to trigger a speedy recovery of the economy. Although the commitment of Swedish authorities to address the banking sector's problem was a contributing factor, the diversity of funding sources for corporates also played an important role. The United States had a similar experience during the banking-related problems arising from a fall in real estate value in the early 1990s. Again, access to alternative funding sources for corporates played a key role in the recovery process. The experience of Australia during the Asian crisis also provides an interesting case study. Despite its close trade and financial ties to Asia, the Australian economy experienced few signs of contagion arguably because of well-developed capital markets and a strong banking sector.

Notwithstanding these examples, one may be tempted to argue that alternative funding sources may not be necessary to soften the impact of financial crises. For instance, one could argue in favor of exercising the policy options available to central banks, such as injecting liquidity into the banking system and reducing interest rates, as a means of reducing the severity of the financial crisis. Experience has shown that the recovery from financial shocks using these monetary tools may well depend on access to alternative funding sources. Specifically, in the case of the United States, funding from the capital markets for corporates almost dried up in the aftermath of the Russian default in August 1998. However, easing of interest rates and injection of liquidity into the banking system by the Federal Reserve ensured that corporates could gain access to bank lending temporarily until the capital markets recovered from the financial shock. On the other hand, the experience of Japan has been quite the opposite. Despite the fact that the Bank of Japan has eased interest rates progressively and injected liquidity into the banking sector, bank lending has responded little and economic recovery has been slow. An interesting observation to make here is that in contrast to the United States, Japanese corporates depend heavily on banks for funding and the nonbank lending has not been sufficient to avoid a credit crunch.

Alan Greenspan summed up his observations on the availability of alternative funding sources for an economy as follows: "Multiple alternatives to transform an economy's savings into capital investment offer a set of backup facilities should the primary form of intermediation fail."[4] He further argued that if anecdotal evidence suggests that diversity of funding sources provides insurance against a financial problem turning into economy-wide distress, then steps to foster the development of capital markets in those economies should be given priority. Moreover, diverse capital markets compete with bank lending, and, as a consequence, the borrowing costs for corporates are lower during normal times.

Fostering the development of capital markets, however, is a difficult task especially if the necessary infrastructure required to support it is lacking. This includes improved accounting standards, bankruptcy procedures, legal frameworks, and disclosure. Establishing these becomes a precondition for the smooth functioning of capital markets.

Although I highlighted the weaknesses and economic risks posed by reliance on bank lending as the primary source of funding, I did not question why this practice tends to worsen economic crises. A recent paper by Nils Hakansson identified two principal effects that contribute to this problem.[5] First, the effects of misdirected government credit allocation preferences will tend to be magnified. Second, the absence of a sizable corporate bond market will aggravate the imperfections present in any financial regulatory system. In the end, the inferior risk assessment by the oversized banking system together with other inherent weaknesses that may be present in the system will tend to overwhelm. This will then lead to production overcapacity and nonperforming loans, and finally to economic crisis.

Hakansson argued further that government-induced credit allocation preferences and the lack of a developed corporate bond market sometimes forces unfavored industries to borrow abroad. When faith in the local currency begins to fade, the scramble for foreign currency funds by these debtors may spark an economic crisis. Another problem that can arise due to the lack of a well-developed corporate bond market is that some of the nation's basic investment needs, such as infrastructure projects, may be delayed or inadequately funded. Worse still, in the absence of suitable investment alternatives, local investors might prefer to invest abroad, thus depriving the nation of scarce capital resources.

When one understands the shortcomings of an overbearing banking system, it becomes rather easy to see the role corporate bonds play in an economy. Besides serving as a backup funding source during periods of credit crunches, corporate bonds help in lowering the funding costs for corporates by competing with bank lending and offer investors alternative investment opportunities. More important, however, is that a well-developed corporate bond market brings market discipline. The term *market discipline* broadly refers to the infrastructure and best market practices required to support the smooth functioning of capital markets. This includes financial reporting practices for companies that are relevant and reliable, a strong community of credit analysts, respected rating agencies that provide an impartial assessment of the corporates, bankruptcy laws and courts to process the claims of bond holders, and absence of interference from governments.

To put it in a nutshell, the existence of well-developed corporate bond markets reduces systemic risks and the severity of financial crises. This is because such an environment is associated with greater accounting transparency, a larger community of credit analysts, the presence of respected credit rating agencies, and the existence of efficient procedures for corporate reorganization and liquidation. Because of the potential benefits strong local bond markets can bring, policy makers and international organizations have embraced this principle, and efforts are under way to develop the local bond markets in many emerging economies. Notwithstanding these efforts, the development of a local corporate bond market in many emerging markets is still constrained by several factors. Among these, the following are important:

- A lack of liquidity in secondary markets and of a meaningful investor base with developed credit assessment skills.
- High costs of local issuance and crowding out by government bond issuance.
- The lack of a stable and large institutional investor base and/or restrictions on their asset holdings.
- Restriction of access to local bond issuance to top-tier corporates in many countries.

Despite these difficulties, considerable progress has been made in many emerging markets in developing the corporate bond market as an alternative funding source for corporations.

## RELATIVE MARKET SIZE

The corporate bond market is large and diverse with daily trading volume estimated to be close to $20 billion. The total market capitalization of global corporate bonds as of February 2003 was roughly USD 3,330 billion, an amount that is rather significant. In percentage terms, this amounts to roughly 19 percent of the market capitalization of Lehman's global multiverse index.[6] To provide an indication of the relative market size of corporate bonds versus other fixed-income asset classes, Exhibit 3.1 gives a breakdown of the market capitalization of various asset classes in Lehman Brothers multiverse bond index.

From Exhibit 3.1, one can see that the market capitalization of global corporate bonds is roughly the same as the market capitalization of mortgages. It is also useful to note here that asset-backed securities constitute only 3 percent of the market capitalization of corporate bonds. This is quite interesting because it indicates that the relative proportion of secured bonds

**EXHIBIT 3.1**  Market Capitalization of Asset Classes (February 2003)

| Description | Number of Issues | Market Capitalization (USD million) |
|---|---|---|
| Multiverse | 11,360 | 17,907,223 |
| Government | 2,212 | 9,868,696 |
| Treasuries | 804 | 8,087,998 |
| Agencies | 1,408 | 1,780,698 |
| Corporate | 5,645 | 3,409,902 |
| Industrial | 3,704 | 1,645,205 |
| Utility | 755 | 385,255 |
| Financial institutions | 1,816 | 1,379,442 |
| Noncorporate | 937 | 996,294 |
| Sovereign | 423 | 419,159 |
| Supranational | 234 | 301,312 |
| Others | 280 | 275,624 |
| Securitized | 2,567 | 3,632,338 |
| Mortgages | 2,401 | 3,531,021 |
| Asset Backed | 166 | 101,317 |

*Source:* The Lehman Brothers Global Family of Indices. Copyright 2002, Lehman Brothers. Reproduced with permission from Lehman Brothers Inc. All rights reserved.

issued by corporates is only around 3 percent. In terms of currency composition, roughly 60 percent of the corporate bonds are denominated in U.S. dollars, 23 percent in euros, 9 percent in yen, 6 percent in pounds sterling, and the rest in other currencies. It is evident from this breakdown that U.S. dollar-denominated bonds constitute the bulk of the outstanding corporate bonds.

The foregoing observations suggest that corporate bonds as an asset class offer investors a large pool of debt securities with significant market capitalization. Equally important from an investor's perspective is to know how this market capitalization has evolved over time. Such an examination reveals that the outstanding issue size of corporate bonds has increased significantly over recent years. This may suggest that corporates are increasingly seeking debt financing through corporate bond issuance. For purpose of illustration, the increase in outstanding issue size of euro-denominated corporate bonds over the period January 1999 to February 2003 was 48 percent, and for U.S. dollar-denominated corporate bonds it was 42 percent over the same period.

An interesting observation to make here is that the increase in market capitalization of corporate bonds happened during a time when the supply of U.S. Treasury debt was shrinking. To provide some comparisons, the market capitalization of investment-grade corporate bonds denominated in U.S. dollars rose from \$690 billion as of end of 1992 to \$1,730 billion as of end of 2002. Over the same period, the market capitalization of U.S. Treasuries (excluding T–bills) dropped from \$1,790 billion to \$1,700 billion. Exhibit 3.2 shows the evolution of the market capitalization of various

**EXHIBIT 3.2**   Market Capitalization of US Dollar-Denominated Asset Classes

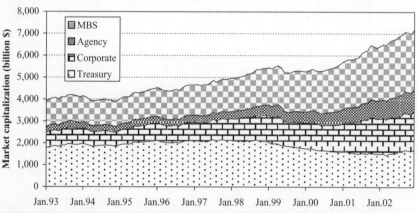

U.S. dollar-denominated fixed-income assets over the period January 1993 to December 2002.

## HISTORICAL PERFORMANCE

When investors evaluate the potential benefits of investing in an asset class, an analysis of the historical performance of the asset class in relation to others is carried out as a routine exercise. Despite the fact that historical performance is not an indicator of future performance, analyzing historical data has several advantages. For instance, such an analysis can reveal relationships between different asset classes that are otherwise not obvious. Furthermore, an analysis of the historical returns data is required if one wishes to evaluate the potential risks associated with investment decisions. The advantages of examining historical data when making investment decisions was best summarized by William Sharpe: "Although it is always perilous to assume that the future will be like the past, it is at least instructive to find out what the past was like. Experience suggests that for predicting future values, historic data appear to be quite useful with respect to standard deviations, reasonably useful for correlations, and virtually useless for expected returns. For the latter, at least, other approaches are a must."[7] In this section, I examine the historical performance of investment-grade corporate bonds as an asset class and compare this with the performance of U.S. Treasuries and Standard & Poor's 500 stock index.

To compute different statistical measures of performance, the historical data used cover the 30-year period between January 1973 and January 2003. Monthly returns over this period for U.S. dollar-denominated investment-grade corporate bonds (COR), U.S. Treasuries (UST), and Standard and Poor's 500 index (S&P) were used to compute the relevant statistical measures. Exhibit 3.3 shows the statistical performance measures for different

**EXHIBIT 3.3** Statistical Performance Measure for Asset Classes (January 1973 to January 2003)[a]

| Description | UST | COR | S&P |
|---|---|---|---|
| Annualized return (%) | 8.91 | 9.01 | 6.83 |
| Annualized volatility (%) | 5.51 | 7.58 | 15.98 |
| Sharpe ratio | 0.214 | 0.169 | −0.056 |
| Probability that annual return is positive (%) | 94.50 | 85.90 | 72.40 |
| Conditional expected return if positive (%) | 9.83 | 11.75 | 17.48 |
| Probability that annual return is negative (%) | 5.50 | 14.10 | 27.60 |
| Conditional expected return if negative (%) | −2.24 | −4.56 | −12.44 |

[a]UST, U.S. Treasuries; COR, corporate bonds; S&P, Stand & Poor's 500 index.

**EXHIBIT 3.4**  Correlation Matrix of Monthly
Returns (January 1973 to January 2003)[a]

|       | UST  | COR  | S&P  |
| ----- | ---- | ---- | ---- |
| UST   | 1.00 | 0.90 | 0.20 |
| COR   | 0.90 | 1.00 | 0.35 |
| S&P   | 0.20 | 0.35 | 1.00 |

[a]UST, U.S. Treasuries; COR, corporate bonds;
S&P, Standard & Poor's 500 index.

asset classes and Exhibit 3.4 shows the correlation between the monthly
returns of different asset classes.

The first three measures in Exhibit 3.3 are the standard risk–return
measures computed for different asset classes. In terms of annual returns
generated, the stock index was the worst performer. Although corporates
did marginally better than U.S. Treasuries, if one accounts for the additional transaction costs involved in replicating a corporate bond index, the
annualized returns may be marginally below the Treasuries. The risk-free
rate of return over the 30-year period is 7.73 percent (using 1-month libid
rates). In terms of risk, the equity returns are more than two times riskier
than corporate bond returns and almost three times as risky as Treasury
returns. Seen from the Sharpe ratio perspective, U.S. Treasuries were the
best performer over this period.

The method used to estimate the other statistical measures given in
Exhibit 3.3 is as follows. Probability that the annual return is positive or
negative is estimated by computing every month the total return over the
preceding 12 months. These returns are then grouped into negative and
positive returns, and the relative frequency of occurrence of a positive or a
negative annual return is used to determine the probability of a positive or
a negative return. The average return of each group is then determined to
compute the conditional expected returns for a 1-year horizon. The historical returns over a 30-year period suggest that there is a 27.6 percent chance
that the return over any 1-year period on the S&P 500 index will be negative. Given that the return is negative during a particular year, the expected
value of this negative return is −12.44 percent. For a portfolio that replicates the U.S. dollar-denominated investment-grade corporate index, the
probability of a negative return during any year is only 14.1 percent and the
conditional expected value of this return is −4.56 percent.

Examining Exhibit 3.4, we see that there is a very high correlation
between investment-grade corporate bond returns and U.S. Treasury
returns. This implies that there is little to gain in terms of diversification
from holding a portfolio consisting of U.S. Treasuries and corporate
bonds. On the other hand, a portfolio consisting of Treasury securities and
equities offers the best diversification, with a correlation coefficient of .20.

**EXHIBIT 3.5**  Statistical Performance Measure for Asset Classes (January 1975 to January 2000)[a]

| Description | UST | COR | S&P |
|---|---|---|---|
| Annualized return (%) | 9.02 | 9.83 | 12.81 |
| Annualized volatility (%) | 5.69 | 7.77 | 14.90 |
| Sharpe ratio | 0.098 | 0.176 | 0.292 |
| Probability that annual return is positive (%) | 93.75 | 87.50 | 81.60 |
| Conditional expected return if positive (%) | 10.27 | 12.41 | 17.77 |
| Probability that annual return is negative (%) | 6.25 | 12.50 | 18.40 |
| Conditional expected return if negative (%) | −2.21 | −4.31 | −8.13 |

[a]UST, U.S. Treasuries; COR, Corporate bonds; S&P, Standard & Poor's 500 index.

The S&P 500 index returns and investment-grade corporate bond returns have a correlation coefficient of .35, which is higher than the correlation between equity returns and Treasury returns. This is not surprising considering that corporate bonds tend to perform badly whenever equity returns are negative, and this explains why these two assets classes are more correlated.

Analyzing historical data, though useful, can sometimes be misleading. To demonstrate this, the various performance statistics using monthly data over the period January 1975 to January 2000 are presented in Exhibits 3.5 and 3.6. The risk-free return over this period is 8.46 percent.

The inferences one would draw on future expected returns using the two data sets are quite different even though there is a significant time overlap between the two. The figures in Exhibit 3.5 suggest that equities outperform U.S. Treasuries by roughly 3.8 percent per annum over the long term. Exhibit 3.3, on the other hand, suggests that equities underperform Treasuries by 2.1 percent over the long term. These observations confirm the remarks of William Sharpe that past returns are virtually useless for predicting future returns. However, the volatility of returns is broadly similar across the two time periods. For instance, annual volatility of investment-grade corporate bonds is roughly in the range 7.5 to 7.7 percent. The correlation

**EXHIBIT 3.6**  Correlation Matrix of Monthly Returns (January 1975 to January 2000)[a]

| | UST | COR | S&P |
|---|---|---|---|
| UST | 1.00 | 0.93 | 0.30 |
| COR | 0.93 | 1.00 | 0.38 |
| S&P | 0.30 | 0.38 | 1.00 |

[a]UST, U.S. Treasuries; COR, corporate bonds; S&P, Standard & Poor's 500 index.

between corporate bond returns and S&P 500 index returns is in the range .35 to .40, whereas the correlation between corporate bond returns and Treasury returns is around .90.

An analysis of historical data also reveals that if the return of the investment-grade corporate bond index during a year is negative, then the expected value of this negative return is roughly −4.5 percent. The probability of a negative return during any year for the corporate bond index is about 14 percent. A final point of interest is that among the three asset classes considered here, the investment-grade corporate bond index has the most robust Sharpe ratio over both time periods. The implication is that excess returns over the risk-free rate have been more stable for corporate bonds than for Treasuries or equities during the time periods considered here.

## THE CASE FOR CORPORATE BONDS

The corporate bond market represents a mature asset class with significant market capitalization and broad diversification across different sectors and credit ratings. Looking back over history, there is evidence that returns from investment-grade corporate bonds exhibit more stable Sharpe ratios than returns from U.S. Treasuries or equities. In addition, corporate bond returns are more correlated than Treasury returns with equity index returns. The implication is that when the equity market rallies, corporate bonds perform better than Treasuries, because credit spreads narrow. On the other hand, a continued fall in equity prices has an adverse impact on corporate bond returns. However, the downside risks of corporate bonds are considerably lower than for equities. As a result, including corporate bonds in the asset composition mix of long-term investors offers increased diversification benefits and reduces the fluctuations in annual returns. In this section, I discuss the advantages of investing in corporate bonds from the perspective of two investor groups: central bank reserve managers and pension fund plan sponsors.

### Central Bank Reserves

Currency reserves, in general, are held by central banks for a variety of reasons, which include among others transaction needs, intervention needs, and wealth diversification needs. Transaction needs are of minor importance to developed economies that have good access to international capital markets. On the other hand, for countries that have strict exchange rate controls, transaction needs may play a more important role. Intervention needs arise when countries desire to have convertible currencies and at the same time wish to reserve the power to influence exchange rates. This type of demand for reserves is considered by far the most important for those countries that have well-developed capital markets. Lastly, wealth effects may play some role in the final choice of the asset mix and currency composition of the reserves. During recent years, the wealth effect has become more important as the need for central banks to be more transparent on the role and use of currency reserves, which are considered to be part of the national savings, has grown. Moreover, the size and growth of currency reserves may provide signals to global financial markets on the credibility of the country's monetary policy and creditworthiness. In such a case, the return on the reserves held may not be inconsequential. In fact, the desire to improve the return on reserves has been on the agenda of reserve managers across the globe in recent years. In the discussion to follow, I highlight the important factors leading to a change in focus from liquidity management to returns management among reserve managers and indicate why corporate bonds as an asset class are an interesting investment alternative to government bonds when higher return on reserves becomes an explicit objective.

**Changing Objectives**    Foreign currency reserves play a crucial role in the liquidity management by countries that do not always have ready and inexpensive access to international capital markets. Considering its importance, central banks have held a significant proportion of their foreign exchange reserves in a portfolio of short-dated financial instruments to facilitate liquidity management. This portfolio, usually referred to as the liquidity portfolio, serves the purposes of foreign currency debt servicing, offsetting balance of payments, and ensuring the smooth functioning of the foreign exchange markets. Among these, the need for liquidity in a central bank reserves portfolio is usually dominated by the role intervention plays in the central bank's management of reserves. However, this view is changing as a consequence of the liberalization of capital markets and the growth of international financial flows, which render foreign currency intervention having at best only a transitory impact on the exchange rate of a given country. Moreover, central banks realize that they have a greater number of options available to meet funding requirements. For instance, in the 1980s, currency intervention was usually done in spot markets, leading to a need for cash liquidity that was funded by the sale of securities. The existence of an active repo market, at least for government securities, has called into question the need to invest a significant proportion of foreign currency reserves in short-dated instruments.

In the past, central banks were less concerned about the relative proportion of reserves held in the liquidity portfolio because liquidity management was regarded as being the motive for holding reserves. In recent years, this notion has been challenged as a result of experiences of countries faced with economic crises. Specifically, the series of crises in the emerging markets during the 1990s found several countries short of foreign currency reserves, a shortage that often constrained subsequent policy choices and in several cases made even worse the recessions that followed. On the other hand, countries with significant levels of reserves (China and Hong Kong) were able to hold their exchange rates steady despite a regional crisis. This experience led to the general impression that increased capital flows require central banks to hold more reserves than when capital flows were smaller or subject to controls. In fact, many reserve managers now share the opinion that emerging market countries need to hold much larger levels of reserves than previously felt necessary.

How large the reserves need to be depends on factors such as volatility of the real or the financial economy, the level of current account deficits, and whether the country is operating under a fixed or a floating exchange rate regime. Furthermore, the globalization of capital markets has made the task of predicting volatility of capital flows difficult, and, as a consequence, the level of reserves required to absorb these fluctuations is higher. Another reason for holding large reserves is the observation that the size of reserves is a key element determining sovereign credit ratings. Foreign investors, lacking any firm basis on which to assess the adequacy of a country's reserves, may simply look at the level of reserves relative to that in comparable countries. Although higher levels of reserves are considered desirable, current opinion among central bankers is that there is no objective way of calibrating the desired level of currency reserves for a country.

As a consequence of the desire to hold larger reserves, foreign currency reserves have grown significantly in many countries despite the fact that global growth has weakened over this period. In some countries, reserves have gone to 200 percent of short-term foreign debt and are still rising. The accumulation of foreign currency reserves has been high on the agenda of many central banks, and as this gathers momentum, the debate on the investment objectives of the reserves is also gaining importance. One consequence of reserve buildup in hard currencies is that it incurs costs in real resources. For instance, the budget cost of paying higher interest rates for domestic borrowings employed to purchase lower yielding hard currency assets is a transfer of real resources. For this reason, the decision to build up currency reserves involves a difficult cost–benefit analysis.

This brings up the following question: What is the cost of holding reserves? This is a difficult question and there is no clear answer. If the benefits of holding reserves are hard to quantify, the costs are even harder to measure. If foreign borrowing is used to build up reserves, countries in effect pay the foreign credit spread over U.S. Treasuries or comparable paper. This spread, which is negligible for borrowers at the upper end of the investment grade, is quite significant as the sovereign rating becomes more speculative. However, this calculation might overstate the cost of reserves by failing to take into account the possible effect of reserve levels on the assessment of sovereign credit rating. On the assumption that higher reserve levels lead to an improved credit rating, both domestic and foreign borrowing costs will be reduced. Furthermore, one can conjecture that the corporate sector in a country with high reserve levels may also benefit by being able to borrow at lower interest rates in the international markets.

An alternative way to measure the cost of holding reserves is to stress the opportunity costs and attempt to analyze the macroeconomic consequences of reserve accumulation. For instance, the opportunity costs of reserves accumulated from a succession of current account surpluses are the returns on forgone domestic investment. However, the marginal productivity of capital is hard to measure.

Although additional costs incurred in maintaining higher reserve levels are difficult to measure, reserve managers are becoming conscious of the need to increase return on reserves as a means to reduce the costs when reserves held are well in excess of the liquidity requirements of a central bank. This has prompted many central banks to regard the reserve management operation to a limited extent as a profit center and the reserves themselves as a store of wealth that generates revenue. With this change in perception, the reserve management function has taken over the additional task of an asset management function where the assets under management are the currency reserves of the central bank.

**Composition of Currency Reserves**    Official foreign currency reserves held by central banks as of end of 2001 amounted to $2,021 billion, and roughly 75 percent of this was held in dollar-denominated assets.[8] The high dollar component in the reserves indicates that the U.S. dollar continued to be the main reserve currency for central banks; the euro was still well behind with roughly 14 percent share. Having made the case why reserve managers target higher returns on reserves, it will be of interest to examine the instruments in which the official reserves are invested to achieve the higher return target. This gives an indication of the extent to which the desire to generate higher returns on reserves is implemented in practice. Unfortunately, finding good data on the composition of currency reserves at the instrument level is extremely difficult. Considering that the dollar-denominated assets make up 75 percent of the reserves, I focus on identifying the composition of the dollar-denominated reserve holdings at the instrument-level. Exhibit 3.7 shows the instrument-level composition of the U.S. dollar reserves as of March 2000.

Data on identified official holdings of dollar-denominated assets given in Exhibit 3.7 suggest that U.S. Treasury securities represented more than half (58 percent) of the dollar holdings of central banks. Identified dollar holdings, however, aggregate to a sum well short of the estimated dollar reserves

**EXHIBIT 3.7**   Instrument Composition of U.S. Dollar Reserves at End of March 2000 (In Billions of U.S. Dollars)

| | Short term | Long term | Total |
|---|---|---|---|
| Treasury securities | 165 | 492 | 657 (58%) |
| Other assets | 262 | 211 | 565 (42%) |
|   Deposits in the United States | 32 | — | |
|   Money market paper in the | | | |
|     United States | 104 | — | |
|   Offshore deposits | 126 | — | |
|   Agency securities | — | 91 | |
|   Corporate bonds | — | 12 | |
|   Equity | — | 96 | |
| Total | 427 | 703 | 1130 (100%) |
| Memorandum items: Share of Treasury | | | |
|   securities in assets of the given maturity | 39% | 70% | |
| Total estimated U.S. dollar reserves at | | | |
|   end of 1999 | | | 1359 |

*Source:* Robert McCauley and Ben Fung, "Choosing Instruments in Managing Dollar Foreign Exchange Reserves," *BIS Quarterly Review*, March 2003, p. 41, Table 1. Copyright 2003, Bank for International Settlements. Reprinted with permission.

($1,130 billion versus $1,359 billion). Under the assumption that the official estimates of U.S. Treasury holdings by central banks are accurate, U.S. Treasury securities constitute only 48 percent of the dollar-denominated assets. Still, the relative proportion of Treasury securities in dollar-denominated reserve holdings is quite high. Also of interest to note here is that the next asset class in which significant investments are made is in equities. However, March 2000 was the period when equities reached their highs, and since then they have declined significantly. Although no official data are yet available, one might guess that the relative proportion of equities in dollar-denominated reserve assets must have declined considerably as of the end of 2002.

The investment in corporate bonds, an asset class of interest in the context of this book, is very small, amounting to less than 1 percent of the estimated dollar reserves. Apart from equities, the non-Treasury component of long-term dollar-denominated reserves has been primarily invested in U.S. agency securities or bonds issued by supranationals. This is an indication that reserve managers continue to be wary of taking on credit risk as a means of improving the return on reserves. This is because loss resulting from credit risk is still considered a taboo among central banks. Based on anecdotal evidence, targeting higher return on reserves has been achieved mainly by increasing the duration of the reserves portfolio in recent years. In a falling interest rate environment, this strategy so far has been quite rewarding.

The composition of dollar-denominated assets at the instrument level indicates that there is not much diversification in terms of asset classes in the reserves portfolio. To a limited extent, the overreliance on Treasuries is a reflection of the lack of adequate skills among reserve managers to manage risks other than duration. For instance, inclusion of mortgage-backed securities requires the ability to model, measure, and manage prepayment risks. Including investment-grade corporate bonds requires the ability to measure and manage credit risk. Although lack of skills is a constraining factor, it is not the only constraint faced by central banks. Other reasons commonly cited by central bankers include inadequate risk management systems, lack of an incentive structure, and high job rotation among reserve managers, which hampers developing expertise.

If increasing return on reserves is regarded as an explicit objective, duration extension as a means to achieve higher returns in a low-interest-rate environment will expose central banks to substantial downside risks. In this situation, pursuing higher returns would necessitate reviewing the asset composition of the reserves and finding an appropriate trade-off between the level of market risk and credit risk that is being taken.

**Why Corporate Bonds?**    In pursuit of the objective of improving return on reserves, most central banks face the following investment constraint: little or no risk of a negative return over a 1-year investment period. This constraint is mainly a consequence of the greater public scrutiny of the investment practices of a central bank and the negative publicity investment-related losses on reserves are subject to. To reduce the risk of a negative return, most central banks rule out the inclusion of equities in the reserves portfolio because the volatility of equity returns is quite high. This leaves central banks with primarily two alternatives for improving the return on reserves: Either take more interest rate risk or take more credit risk. I will argue that including corporate bonds in the reserves portfolio, which amounts to taking more credit risk, is a better alternative to targeting higher returns without increasing the downside risk potential.

In examining the historical performance of different asset classes, I compared the performance of investment-grade corporate bonds against U.S. Treasuries. The corporate bond investment universe I considered included bonds rated BBB-minus and above and maturities up to 30 years. Even if one assumes that central banks will diversify into corporate bonds to target higher returns, most central banks would be unwilling to invest in bonds rated below single-A. Furthermore, the investment maturities are usually restricted to be below 10 years even for Treasury securities.[9] To make the investment performance comparisons between corporates and Treasuries meaningful in a central bank context, I restrict the corporate bond universe to be A-minus or better and the investment maturity to be

**EXHIBIT 3.8**   Performance of One- to Five-Year Sector Duration-Neutral Portfolios (January 1999 to January 2003)

| | | Annualized Market | |
| Description | Annual return (%) | volatility (%) | capitalization[a] ($ billion) |
| --- | --- | --- | --- |
| Corporates A-minus or better | 7.77 | 2.45 | 410 |
| U.S. Treasuries | 6.86 | 2.83 | 840 |

[a]Market capitalization as of January 2003.

between 1 and 5 years. Exhibit 3.8 shows the performance of duration-neutral portfolios, one replicating the 1- to 5-year sector of dollar-denominated corporate bonds rated A-minus or better and the other replicating the 1- to 5-year sector of U.S. Treasuries over the period January 1999 to January 2003. The correlation between the monthly returns of these two portfolios over this period is .92.

The figures in Exhibit 3.8 are quite interesting because they show that corporate bonds outperformed Treasuries during a period when equity markets fell significantly and credit spreads widened. Moreover, this outperformance was accompanied by lower volatility of returns of the corporate bond portfolio compared to the volatility of returns of a Treasury portfolio with identical duration. The implication is that long-term investors are adequately compensated for the additional risks involved when investing in corporate bonds. The additional risks include credit risk and liquidity risk, and these appear to demand a significant risk premium in recent years following the Asian and Russian financial crises.

Although it is tempting to argue that investing in corporate bonds will bring diversification benefits to the reserves portfolio, note that the correlation between corporate bond portfolio returns and Treasury portfolio returns is greater than .9. Such a high level of correlation implies that it is difficult to motivate investment in corporate bonds from the diversification perspective. A better justification for investing in corporate bonds by central banks is that it lowers the volatility of returns of the reserves portfolio while at the same time providing long-term yield enhancement over Treasuries.[10]

To compute the downside risk of investing in corporate bonds as opposed to Treasuries on a duration-neutral basis, one can examine the worst-case underperformance of the corporate bond portfolio relative to the Treasury portfolio over any 1-year period. Based on the historical data covering the period January 1999 to January 2003, the worst-case underperformance was 80 basis points. This occurred during the 1-year period between 1 August 2001 and 31 July 2002, a period of widening credit spreads after the tragic events of the September 11 attack.

The historical data used to compare relative performances of corporate and Treasury portfolios are representative of a recessionary time period. I showed by examining data over this period that the corporate bond portfolio outperformed a duration-neutral Treasury portfolio. In a period of economic expansion when interest rates are bound to increase, corporates may still offer scope for outperforming Treasuries. This is because economic expansions are associated with increasing equity prices, and this has the effect of narrowing the credit spreads for corporate bonds. Under this scenario, the potential downside risk for a corporate bond portfolio is lower than for a Treasury portfolio of similar duration. These effects are more pronounced for investment maturities in the short end of the yield curve, a sector that happens to be the natural choice for central banks.

## Pension Funds

Pension funds can be broadly classified into defined contribution schemes and defined benefit schemes. A defined contribution scheme involves a contractual commitment to contribute a certain amount of money to a pension plan, with no guarantee as to how much money will be in the plan at retirement and no guarantee as to the annual retirement benefit the employee will receive. A defined benefit scheme, on the other hand, makes no guarantee as to the amount of the contribution the corporation will make, but it does guarantee a defined annual retirement benefit to the employee. It is evident from this definition that in a defined contribution scheme the employee bears all market risk and captures all the rewards in the event of strong market performance. In a defined benefit scheme, however, the corporation bears the market risk and suffers the penalty of increased pension contributions if pension assets do not meet the liabilities. In this section, I focus mainly on the defined benefit scheme.

The objective of a defined benefit pension fund's asset allocation policy is to fully fund accrued pension liabilities at the lowest cost to the plan sponsor subject to an acceptable level of risk. The major risk plan sponsors face is the higher contributions that will be required if the pension assets fail to generate returns that cover the actuarial liabilities. This risk is referred to as surplus risk, which is the risk that the assets will fall short of liabilities. To reduce this risk, pension fund asset allocation decisions require an asset-liability modeling framework. A pension scheme is said to be fully funded if the market value of the financial assets in the pension fund is equal to the present value of the pension liabilities. Clearly, the method used to compute the present value of assets and liabilities has an influence on the deficit or surplus that is being reported.

In the past, accounting practices dealt with the problem of fluctuating market value of assets by smoothing them out. The actuarial liabilities of a pension fund are usually measured on the basis of the projected unit credit method. Computing actuarial liabilities using this method requires making assumptions regarding mortality and disability rates, progression of salaries and future inflation rates, long-term return on assets and applicable discount rates, and projections for withdrawing participants and retirements. The applicable discount rate in the past was chosen to be the effective yield on long-term bonds and equities, and the discount rate used displayed very little variations from one year to another. Such an approach to valuing assets and liabilities of pension funds has the effect of reducing the volatility of the surplus, and consequently the surplus risk (or equivalently, deficit risk) was kept to a minimum.

More recently, the accounting practices for reporting and dealing with a pension fund deficit or surplus have undergone dramatic changes.[11] The recommendations under International Accounting Standard 19 for defined benefits scheme are the following:

- Current service cost should be recognized as an expense.
- All companies should use the projected unit credit method to measure their pension expense and pension obligation.
- The rate used to discount postemployment benefit obligation should be determined by reference to market yields at balance sheet date on high-quality corporate bonds of maturity comparable to plan obligations.
- Postemployment benefit obligations should be measured on a basis that reflects (a) estimated future salary increases, (b) the benefits set out in the terms of the plan at the balance sheet date, and (c) estimated future pension increases.
- If the net cumulative unrecognized actuarial gains and losses exceed the greater of 10 percent of the present value of the plan obligation or 10 percent of the fair value of plan assets, that excess must be amortized over a period not longer than the estimated average remaining working lives of employees participating in the plan. Faster amortization is permitted.
- Plan assets should be measured at fair value.

These changes in accounting practices are intended to serve the following objectives:

- The employer's financial statements reflect the assets and liabilities arising from the retirement benefit obligations and any related funding measured at current market prices.
- The operating costs of providing retirement benefits are recognized in the periods in which the benefits are earned by employees.
- Financing costs and any other changes in the value of the assets and liabilities are recognized in the periods in which they arise.

**Implications for Pension Funds**   The valuation of pension liabilities using a discount rate based on current yield of a high-quality corporate bond (AA-rated is the one used) of comparable maturity as the plan obligation has important implications for surplus risk. In particular, use of the market value of pension assets and the discount rate based on the current yield of an AA-rated corporate bond for computing actuarial liabilities can lead to greater volatility of the pension fund surplus. To see why this may be the case, consider the case where the pension assets are primarily invested in equities. During period of recession, equity markets perform badly and the market value of pension assets declines. Bond yields, on the other hand, decline during this period when central banks ease monetary policy. As a consequence, the appropriate discount rates to be used for computing the present value of actuarial liabilities are lower, and this in turn leads to higher pension liabilities. The combination of a lower market value for assets and a higher value for liabilities leads to a large deficit in the pension scheme if one assumes that it was fully funded to begin with.

During economic expansions, the opposite is true. Large surpluses can be built up if the pension assets are primarily made up of equities. These surpluses can quickly turn into deficits in a matter of a few years of falling equity markets. In fact, many pension funds have suffered from overexposure to equity markets in recent years and are currently underfunded. In the United Kingdom, for instance, a typical pension fund has more than 60 percent exposure to equities, although in the United States this percentage is somewhat lower.

Reducing the exposure to equities and simultaneously increasing the exposure to corporate bonds in pension funds is a natural hedge to reduce the surplus risk. Although increasing the proportion of corporate bonds (or other fixed-income securities) results in a reduction in surplus risk, pension plan sponsors also have to ensure that the expected return on assets is in line with the growth rate in real earnings. This is because investment returns determine the rate at which contributions into the pension fund accumulate over time, and the growth rate in real earnings determines the size of contributions into the scheme and the pension liability at the retirement date. Investments in equities or property provide better hedge for the growth rate in real earnings, whereas investing in bonds reduces the surplus risk. Hence, the optimal asset allocation for a pension fund depends on the trade-off between surplus risk and the expected return on assets.

In general, the asset allocation decision critically depends on the assumed risk premiums for different assets. If one believes that the inflation rates and equity risk premium will be lower for this decade than for the previous two decades, pension sponsors are better off investing a greater proportion of the pension assets in fixed-income securities. Within the fixed-income asset class, corporate bonds offer greater opportunity to increase expected returns on the pension assets and, consequently, lower the contribution rate for pension plan sponsors. This is because of the higher yields investors demand for holding this asset class as opposed to government bonds. Furthermore, the higher correlation between corporate bond returns and equity returns observed in the historical data suggests that in the event of a strong equity market performance, corporate bonds provide a greater upside than government bonds.

## QUESTIONS

1. What are the different forms of bond collateralization used for securitization?
2. What are the major investment risks facing a corporate bond investor?
3. What factors contribute to higher trading costs for corporate bonds?
4. A corporate bond portfolio has an average duration of 2.5 years and average bid–ask yield spread of 5 basis points. If the annual portfolio turnover is 125 percent, compute the costs arising from trading.
5. What role does corporate bonds play in an economy?
6. What purpose does historical performance analysis serve?
7. What are the major challenges faced by reserve managers in central banks?
8. How would you justify an increased exposure to corporate bonds for the reserves portfolio?
9. How do the new accounting rules for pension fund reporting influence the asset allocation decision for pension funds?
10. What is surplus risk and how can it be reduced?

## CHAPTER 4

# Modeling Market Risk

In broad terms, portfolio management refers to the process of managing a portfolio's risk relative to a benchmark with the purpose of either tracking or adding value against the benchmark. In the context of managing a corporate bond portfolio, the major sources of risk are a change in the interest rates or a change in the credit rating of the bond issuer. In addition, bond holdings in currencies other than the portfolio's base currency are exposed to exchange rate risk as well. The price risk resulting from a change in the credit rating of the bond issuer is usually attributed to credit risk, whereas price risks resulting from a change in the interest rate and exchange rate are classified under market risk. In the event that the portfolio and the benchmark have different exposures to the various risk factors that influence the price dynamics of corporate bonds, the portfolio's returns and the benchmark's returns can deviate from one other. Clearly, the job of a portfolio manager is to exploit the upside potential when deviating from the benchmark neutral position while controlling the downside risk. Considering that a prerequisite for controlling the downside risk is the ability to measure risk exposures relative to the benchmark, the implementation of an appropriate risk model is a logical first step in this process.

In this chapter, I first discuss different measures that can be used to quantify interest rate risk. Subsequently, I develop a risk model that can be used to quantify the market risk of the corporate bond portfolio against the benchmark.

## INTEREST RATE RISK

In this section, I discuss the impact of interest rate changes on the price of securities that provide future cash flows. Because the present value of such securities is the discounted value of the future cash flows, changes to the interest rates change the appropriate discounts to be used for the cash flows. As a consequence, the price of the security changes. In some cases, changes to the interest rate can change the cash flows themselves. This is the case for bonds with embedded options. In this section, I discuss various risk measures that are commonly used to quantify the price sensitivity of debt instruments to changes in the interest rate curve.

## Modified Duration

The price of any security that offers future cash flows depends on the current term structure of interest rates. Changes to the interest rate term structure result in a change in the price of the interest rate-dependent security. The price of a corporate bond, which provides future cash flows, is therefore sensitive to changes in the interest rate term structure. It is common practice to refer to the term structure of interest rates simply as the *yield curve*. The price sensitivity of the bond is usually a function of how the yield curve's shape changes.

To measure the price sensitivity to parallel shifts of the yield curve, the most commonly used risk measure is *modified duration*. In simple terms, modified duration is the percentage change in a bond's price for a 100-basis point parallel shift in the yield curve, assuming that the bond's cash flows do not change when the yield curve shifts. Mathematically, modified duration is defined as the negative of the percentage change in price given a 100-basis points change in yield to maturity:

$$D = -\frac{1}{P_{\text{dirty}}} \frac{dP_{\text{dirty}}}{dy} \tag{4.1}$$

In this equation, $P_{\text{dirty}}$ is the dirty price (quoted or clean price plus accrued interest) of the bond for \$1 face value, which I will simply refer to as the price of the bond. Considering that yield to maturity is the interest rate that makes the present value of a bond's cash flows equal to its price, the price–yield relationship for a bond is given by

$$P_{\text{dirty}} = \sum_{i=1}^{N} \frac{Cf_i}{(1 + y/n)^{nt_i}} \tag{4.2}$$

In equation (4.2), $Cf_i$ is the $i$th cash flow at time $t_i$ and $n$ is the number of coupons per annum. From equations (4.1) and (4.2), the modified duration of the bond is given by

$$D = \frac{1}{(1 + y/n)} \frac{1}{P_{\text{dirty}}} \sum_{i=1}^{N} \frac{t_i \times Cf_i}{(1 + y/n)^{nt_i}} \tag{4.3}$$

## Convexity

For estimating price changes resulting from a small parallel shift of the yield curve, modified duration provides a reasonable approximation. When the yield curve shifts are larger, however, modified duration fails to provide a good approximation of price changes. This is because the price–yield relationship is nonlinear as modeled by equation (4.2). Also, modified duration captures only the effects of the first-order term in a Taylor series expansion of this nonlinear function. Including higher order terms of the Taylor series expansion can provide an improved estimate of the price change resulting from yield curve shifts. Common practice is to include the second-order term, which is referred to as *convexity*. Convexity captures the curvature of the price–yield relationship; in mathematical terms, it is defined as

$$C = \frac{1}{P_{\text{dirty}}} \frac{d^2 P_{\text{dirty}}}{dy^2} \tag{4.4}$$

Using the price–yield relationship (4.2) and the convexity definition given by equation (4.4), one can show that the convexity of the bond satisfies the following equation:

$$C = \frac{1}{(1 + y/n)^2} \frac{1}{P_{\text{dirty}}} \sum_{i=1}^{N} \frac{t_i \times (1 + nt_i) \times Cf_i}{n \times (1 + y/n)^{nt_i}} \tag{4.5}$$

### Approximating Price Changes

These two risk measures—modified duration and convexity—provide a good approximation of a bond's price change resulting from a change in the yield to maturity of that bond. Both measures are widely used in the context of bond portfolio management to control interest rate risk. For instance, using modified duration and convexity measures, one obtains the approximate price change of a bond due to a change in the yield to maturity by an amount $\Delta y$:

$$\Delta P_{\text{dirty}} = -P_{\text{dirty}} \cdot D \cdot \Delta y + 0.5 P_{\text{dirty}} \cdot C \cdot \Delta y^2 \tag{4.6}$$

It is important to note that both modified duration and convexity provide local approximations to the price–yield relationship of a bond. Hence, when the yield changes are large, the estimated price change using equation (4.6) may not be very accurate. However, for the purposes of modeling interest rate risk, these local approximations are usually good, as market-driven yield changes are usually not very large (typically less than 50 basis points).

## Bonds with Embedded Options

When computing modified duration and convexity measures, one assumes that future cash flows are not altered if the yield to maturity of the bond changes. This is not true for bonds with embedded options, especially as the bond price gets close to the strike price. For example, the price of a callable bond is capped at the strike price as the yield levels decline and the embedded call option is in-the-money. For this reason, a corporate bond with an embedded call option can be viewed as a portfolio comprising a noncallable bond and a short-call option on the bond. Because the bondholder is short a call option, the bondholder must receive a premium up front for the call option sold to the bond issuer. This up-front premium is usually reflected through a lower traded price of the callable bond as opposed to a noncallable bond with similar maturity and cash flows. Hence, callable bonds trade at higher yields than noncallable bonds of the same issuer with similar maturity. The corresponding yield pickup of the callable bond is referred to as the *option-adjusted spread*.

Bonds with embedded options exhibit a price–yield relationship that is different from an option-free or conventional bond. In particular, the differences are more pronounced as the embedded option gets closer to being in-the-money. The distortion in the price–yield relationship of bonds with embedded options in relation to option-free bonds arises from a phenomenon called *price compression*. Price compression occurs in the region around the strike price of the option where yield changes have very little influence on the price of the bond. This suggests that modified duration and convexity may not capture the true risk from yield changes of bonds with embedded options. In order to model the price compression process into the risk measures, one has to take into account the risk characteristics of the bond's embedded option. The relevant risk measures for an option are the so-called delta and gamma of the option, which model first- and second-order changes, respectively, to the option price due to a change in the price of the bond without the embedded option. Specifically, for a callable bond, if $P_{NC}$ denotes the dirty price of the noncallable part of the bond and $P_O$ the price of the embedded call option, then delta and gamma are given, respectively, by

$$\text{delta} = \frac{dP_O}{dP_{NC}} \tag{4.7}$$

and

$$\text{gamma} = \frac{d^2 P_O}{dP_{NC}^2} \tag{4.8}$$

Risk measures that take into account the price risk of the embedded options are referred to as *option-adjusted* risk measures. Thus, the appropriate risk measures that capture the price risk from yield changes of bonds with embedded options are *option-adjusted duration* and *option-adjusted convexity*. It is also common to refer to these measures as *effective duration* and *effective convexity*, respectively. One can show that effective duration and effective convexity for a callable bond are given, respectively, by

$$D_{\text{eff}} = D \times \frac{P_{NC}}{P_{CB}} \times (1 - \text{delta}) \tag{4.9}$$

$$C_{\text{eff}} = \frac{P_{NC}}{P_{CB}} \left[ C \times (1 - \text{delta}) - P_{NC} \times \text{gamma} \times D^2 \right] \tag{4.10}$$

In these equations, $P_{CB}$ is the dirty price of the callable bond and $D$ and $C$ are the modified duration and convexity of the bond, respectively, without the embedded call option.

For putable bonds, where the bondholder is long a put option, the corresponding equations for effective duration and effective convexity are given, respectively, by

$$D_{\text{eff}} = D \times \frac{P_{NP}}{P_{PB}} \times (1 + \text{delta}) \tag{4.11}$$

and

$$C_{\text{eff}} = \frac{P_{NP}}{P_{PB}} \left[ C \times (1 + \text{delta}) + P_{NP} \times \text{gamma} \times D^2 \right] \tag{4.12}$$

In equations (4.11) and (4.12), $P_{PB}$ is the dirty price of the putable bond and $P_{NP}$ is the dirty price of the bond without the put option. Note that delta for a callable bond is positive, whereas for a putable bond delta is negative. One can easily deduce from equations (4.9) to (4.12) that as the embedded option becomes worthless, delta and gamma tend to zero and the callable or putable bond trades as a conventional bond. In this case, effective duration and effective convexity are equal to modified duration and convexity of a conventional bond. On the other hand, if the embedded option is in-the-money, delta is 1 for a callable bond and $-1$ for a putable bond and gamma is 0 for both. This has the implication that effective duration and effective convexity are both equal to 0 under this scenario.

I mentioned earlier that callable bonds have a yield pickup over comparable-maturity noncallable bonds. In case the bondholder is long a put option, which is the case for putable bonds, then the bondholder must pay a premium up front to acquire this put option. As a result, putable bonds trade at lower yields than conventional bonds of identical maturity. To compare the relative attractiveness of a callable or a putable bond with conventional bonds, the term *effective yield* is usually used. Effective yield is the implied yield of the noncallable or nonputable part of the bond.

In the rest of this book, I use only the measures effective yield, effective duration, and effective convexity to quantify the corporate bond's yield and price risk to yield changes. Unless explicitly stated otherwise, I refer to these measures simply as yield, duration, and convexity, respectively, and use the abbreviations $y$, $D$, and $C$, respectively, to denote them.

## PORTFOLIO AGGREGATES

The discussion so far has focused on quantifying the price risk of a single corporate bond in response to changes in yield. From a portfolio management perspective, it is more important to estimate the price risk from yield changes for an entire corporate bond portfolio. This is done by defining the aggregate risk measures *effective portfolio duration* and *effective portfolio convexity*, which are simply the weighted averages of effective duration and effective convexity of the individual bonds in the portfolio.

For purposes of illustration, consider the portfolio to comprise cash holdings and $N$ corporate bonds. If $A_c$ denotes the amount in cash and $NE_i$ the nominal exposure to the $i$th corporate bond having a dirty price $P_{\text{dirty},i}$ for \$1 face value, then the market value of the portfolio is given by

$$M_P = A_c + \sum_{i=1}^{N} NE_i \times P_{\text{dirty},i} \qquad (4.13)$$

If $w_i$ denotes the weight of the $i$th bond in the portfolio, it is easy to verify that

$$w_i = \frac{NE_i \times P_{\text{dirty},i}}{M_P} \qquad (4.14)$$

Similarly, the weight of cash in the portfolio is given by

$$w_c = \frac{A_c}{M_P} \qquad (4.15)$$

Following standard market convention that a cash position is not subject to market risk, the duration and convexity of the cash holdings can be set to zero. Hence, the effective portfolio duration and effective portfolio convexity are given, respectively, by

$$D_P = \sum_{i=1}^{N} w_i D_i \qquad (4.16)$$

and

$$C_P = \sum_{i=1}^{N} w_i C_i \qquad (4.17)$$

Another portfolio aggregate that is often computed is the average effective yield of the portfolio. Specifically, if $R_c$ denotes the interest rate earned on cash and $y_i$ the effective yield of the $i$th bond in the portfolio, then the effective yield of the portfolio is given by

$$y_P = w_c R_c + \sum_{i=1}^{N} w_i y_i$$

Effective portfolio duration defined in equation (4.16) has the risk interpretation of representing the percentage change in a portfolio's market value for a 100-basis point change in effective yield of every bond in the portfolio. Including the portfolio's effective convexity improves this price risk estimate. For instance, the approximate change in market value of a portfolio resulting from a change $\Delta y_P$ to the effective yield of the portfolio is given by

$$\Delta M_P = -M_P \cdot D_P \cdot \Delta y_P + 0.5 M_P \cdot C_P \cdot \Delta y_P^2 \qquad (4.19)$$

## DYNAMICS OF THE YIELD CURVE

The portfolio aggregate risk measures defined in the preceding section provide an approximate measure of price risk due to yield changes. However, it is important to realize that these risk measures are derived under the implicit assumption that the yield of every bond in the portfolio will change by an identical amount. Under this assumption, the par yield curve shape change is restricted to a parallel shift. Note that a *par* yield curve is the yield curve obtained by interpolating the effective yield of bonds with different maturities. The extent to which portfolio duration and portfolio convexity capture market risk arising from yield changes depends on the extent to which parallel shifts of the yield curve are representative of yield curve shape changes.

To investigate whether parallel shifts explain a significant proportion of the change in shape of the yield curve, one can examine the proportion of yield curve variability explained by parallel shifts using historical data. If changes to the yield curve are primarily parallel shifts, then yield changes across different maturities should be perfectly correlated. However, empirical evidence suggests that yield changes for different maturities are only strongly but not perfectly correlated, leading to the conclusion that parallel shifts do not fully model the dynamics of the yield curve. Of course, the evidence that yield changes across different maturities are strongly correlated implies that yield curve shape changes could be explained using relatively few factors. One way to identify these factors is to carry out a principal component decomposition of the sample covariance matrix of yield changes. This makes it possible to identify those factors that explain a significant proportion of the total variance in the sample data. In simple terms, *principal component decomposition* refers to the process of constructing new random variables through linear combinations of original random variables with the primary objective of achieving data reduction. In the present case, these random variables correspond to yield changes across different maturities of the par yield curve.

To illustrate the mathematical concept behind principal component decomposition, consider a random vector $\vec{x} = [x_1, x_2, \ldots, x_m]^T$ having a covariance matrix $\Omega$ with eigenvalues $\lambda_1 \geq \lambda_2 \geq \cdots \geq \lambda_m \geq 0$. Now construct new random variables $z_1, z_2, \ldots, z_m$ that are some linear combinations of the random variables $x_1, x_2, \ldots, x_m$. This linear transformation generates the new random variable $z_i = \vec{\ell}_i^T \vec{x}$, which has a variance given by

$$\text{Var}(z_i) = \vec{\ell}_i^T \Omega \, \vec{\ell}_i \qquad (4.20)$$

If one chooses $\vec{\ell}_i$ to be the normalized eigenvector corresponding to the $i$th eigenvalue, then the variance of the random variable $z_i$ (usually referred to as the $i$th principal component) is equal to the eigenvalue $\lambda_i$. The proportion of the total variance of the original random variables explained by the $i$th principal component is given by $\lambda_i / (\lambda_1 + \cdots + \lambda_m)$. To achieve data reduction, one usually chooses the first $p$ principal components that explain a significant proportion of the total variance in the original data set.

The advantage of carrying out a principal component analysis is that it often reveals relationships that are not otherwise evident from an examination of the original data. For instance, a principal decomposition carried out on the historical yield changes for different maturities reveals that three factors, namely shift, twist, and curvature, are sufficient to explain the dynamics of the yield curve. For purposes of illustration, Exhibit 4.1 shows the proportion of total variance explained by the first three principal components for swap curves in the U.S. dollar and euro markets. The covariance matrix used in the calculation was computed using times series comprising weekly changes of quoted swap rates for different maturities over the period July 1999 to June 2002.

**EXHIBIT 4.1**   Proportion of Variance Explained by Principal Components

| Factor Type | USD Swap Curve (%) | EUR Swap Curve (%) |
| --- | --- | --- |
| Shift (S) | 90.8 | 94.0 |
| S + twist (T) | 98.4 | 96.6 |
| S + T + curvature | 99.2 | 98.7 |

Examining Exhibit 4.1, one can conclude that two principal components, namely level shift and twist (flattening or steepening of the yield curve), sufficiently explain a significant proportion of the historical changes to the yield curve. Based on this evidence, I use only two factors for modeling the yield curve risk.

In general, it is not necessary for the two risk factors to be the fundamental direction vectors obtained through principal component decomposition. In practice, it is only important to choose two fundamental direction vectors that are easy to interpret and explain a significant proportion of the total variance of the original variables. The choice of the principal component vectors is primarily motivated by the fact that these are optimal direction vectors for the sample period over which they are computed. Outside this sample period, however, these direction vectors may not be optimal in the sense of being able to model the maximum variance for the number of risk factors chosen. For these reasons, I choose risk factors that are identical across different markets but nonetheless model a significant proportion of the variance. In particular, the market risk model presented in the next section uses a $-10$-basis point parallel shift and a 10-basis point flattening of the par yield curve as the two risk factors to model yield curve risk. Exhibit 4.2 shows the two risk factors used to model the yield curve risk.

**EXHIBIT 4.2**   Shift and Twist Risk Factors

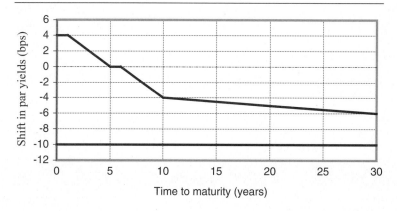

Note that the twist risk factor is modeled to be flat over the maturity ranges 0 to 1 year and 5 to 6 years.

To investigate whether the chosen shift and twist risk factors explain a significant proportion of the total variance, I again use the same (weekly) data set (of swap rate changes over the period July 1999 to June 2002) and compare this with the figures in Exhibit 4.1. In computing the proportion of total variance modeled by these two risk factors, one needs to account for the fact that the twist risk factor may not be orthogonal to the shift risk factor (indicating that these two risk factors may be correlated). If the variance of the shift and twist risk factors is denoted $\sigma_s^2$ and $\sigma_t^2$, respectively, then the variance explained by these factors (under the assumption that the correlation between them is $\rho$) is given by

$$\sigma_{\text{explained}}^2 = \frac{\sigma_s^2 + (1 - \rho)\sigma_t^2}{\lambda_1 + \lambda_2 + \cdots + \lambda_m} \tag{4.21}$$

Note that the individual factor variances can be computed using equation (4.20) where the normalized vector $\vec{\ell}_i$ is chosen to correspond to the risk factor being modeled. The correlation $\rho$ between the risk factors is given by

$$\rho = \frac{\vec{\ell}_s^T \Omega \vec{\ell}_t}{\sigma_s \times \sigma_t} \tag{4.22}$$

where $\vec{\ell}_s$ and $\vec{\ell}_t$ denote the normalized shift risk vector and twist risk vector, respectively. The results obtained by carrying out this analysis are shown in Exhibit 4.3.

Comparing Exhibits 4.1 and 4.3, one can infer that the chosen shift and twist risk factors jointly explain more than 95 percent of the variance for the U.S. dollar swap curve. The proportion of variance explained for the euro swap curve is slightly less than this value. The empirical evidence reported here provides a strong motivation for using these two risk factors to model the yield curve dynamics. Additionally, the direction vectors they represent are generic for any yield curve and are therefore easier to interpret than principal components.

**EXHIBIT 4.3**   Proportion of Variance Explained by Chosen Risk Factors

| Factor Type | USD Swap Curve (%) | EUR Swap Curve (%) |
|---|---|---|
| Shift | 90.0 | 82.7 |
| Shift + twist | 95.6 | 92.3 |

## OTHER SOURCES OF MARKET RISK

Managing credit risk is usually the primary focus of corporate bond portfolio managers. For this reason, identifying corporate borrowers with either a stable credit rating or the potential to improve their credit rating is the major preoccupation of portfolio managers. However, some corporate borrowers who meet these criteria may issue bonds in a currency that is different from the corporate bond portfolio's base currency. As a result, it is quite possible that a particular corporate bond the portfolio manager wishes to buy is issued in a currency different from the portfolio's base currency. In this case, the portfolio manager has to hedge the exchange rate risk arising from the purchase of a bond denominated in a foreign currency. The exchange rate risk is usually hedged through the purchase of currency forwards.

In general, the guidelines for managing the corporate bond portfolio specify whether exchange rate risk is permitted. In most cases, only a small percentage of foreign currency risk is permitted to ensure that, from an operational point of view, frequent currency rebalancing is not necessary. In order to identify both intentional and unintentional market risk exposures arising from exchange rate risk, one has to include exchange rate risk in the market risk calculation.

Another source of market risk arises from changes in implied yield volatility, which in turn has an impact on the prices of callable and putable bonds. In the next section, I develop a market risk model that takes into account yield curve risk, exchange rate risk, and implied yield volatility risk for managing a corporate bond portfolio.

## MARKET RISK MODEL

In this section, I focus on developing a market risk model to measure the portfolio's market risk exposure relative to the benchmark. Considering that a risk model's key function is to identify sources of mismatch between portfolio and benchmark returns, the first step is to select a set of risk factors that drive security returns. For a corporate bond portfolio, an obvious choice for the market risk factors would be yield curve shape changes in all markets relevant to the portfolio and the benchmark. I indicated earlier that two risk factors are generally sufficient to explain a significant proportion of the yield curve shape changes. The component of risk modeled by these two factors is usually referred to as the *systematic* risk. In developing the market risk model, I restrict attention to modeling only systematic risk and work with weekly time series data. Issuer-specific risk arising from holding specific corporate names in the portfolio is modeled under credit risk.

Common to any market risk model is the underlying assumption that historical risk factor realizations serve as good approximations for characterizing the distribution of risk factors in the future. Under this assumption, the covariance matrix computed using historical volatilities and correlations of relevant market risk factors serves as a suitable risk model. I indicate in this section how to construct such a market risk model. Having argued that two risk factors are sufficient to model the changes to the swap curve, I first illustrate how the shift and twist risk factors for any given yield curve can be estimated.

Denote the par yields by $y_i^k(t)$ at time $t$, where $i$ refers to the maturity and $k$ refers to the specific yield curve under consideration. For the sake of consistency, assume that for every yield curve the index $i$ runs from 1 to $n$. The time series of weekly yield changes for the $i$th maturity point on the yield curve for the $k$th yield curve is given by

$$\Delta y_i^k(t) = y_i^k(t) - y_i^k(t-1), \qquad i = 1,\ldots,n \qquad (4.23)$$

The earlier analysis indicated that these yield changes can be modeled using a shift component and a twist component. For instance, if one denotes $\Delta s = -10$ basis points as the shift component across all maturities and $\Delta t_i$ as the twist component for the $i$th maturity for a 10-basis point flattening of the yield curve shown in Exhibit 4.2, then the yield changes (assumed to be in basis points) can be represented as

$$\Delta y_i^k(t) = a_t^k \Delta s + b_t^k \Delta t_i + e_i^k, \qquad i = 1,\ldots,n \qquad (4.24)$$

In equation (4.24), $a_t^k$ and $b_t^k$ are coefficients associated with shift and twist risk factors, respectively, that model weekly yield changes. To determine these coefficients, one needs to minimize the sum of the squared residuals $e_i^k$ for $i = 1, \ldots, n$. One can show in this case that $a_t^k$ and $b_t^k$ are given, respectively, by

$$a_t^k = \frac{\left( \sum_{i=1}^{n} \Delta t_i^2 \sum_{i=1}^{n} \Delta y_i^k - \sum_{i=1}^{n} \Delta t_i \sum_{i=1}^{n} \Delta t_i \Delta y_i^k \right)}{\left( n \sum_{i=1}^{n} \Delta t_i^2 - \left( \sum_{i=1}^{n} \Delta t_i \right)^2 \right) \Delta s} \qquad (4.25)$$

and

$$b_t^k = \frac{\left( n \sum_{i=1}^{n} \Delta t_i \Delta y_i^k - \sum_{i=1}^{n} \Delta t_i \sum_{i=1}^{n} \Delta y_i^k \right)}{\left( n \sum_{i=1}^{n} \Delta t_i^2 - \left( \sum_{i=1}^{n} \Delta t_i \right)^2 \right)} \qquad (4.26)$$

The next task is to identify the relevant yield curves to be used to model market risk for a corporate bond portfolio. Considering that the intention is to model only market risk arising from systematic risk factors, the appropriate yield curves are the swap curves in different currency markets. One can justify such a choice on the basis of the strong correlation corporate bond yield changes have with changes in swap rates. Assuming the corporate bond portfolio is restricted to comprise only bonds issued in either U.S. dollars or euros, the yield curves to be considered for modeling market risk are the swap curves in U.S. dollar and euro markets.

When the portfolio or benchmark returns are also dependent on exchange rate movements, the market risk model has to include factors that capture this risk component. Again, if one restricts the permissible exchange rate risk to U.S. dollars against euros, one additional risk factor is required to capture this component of market risk. In order to model the risk exposure to changes in the exchange rate, assume that this risk factor models a 1 percent appreciation of the foreign currency against the base currency of the portfolio. In this case, the coefficient $c_t$ associated with the chosen risk factor using weekly exchange rate data is given by

$$c_t = 100 \times \frac{x_t - x_{t-1}}{x_{t-1}} \qquad (4.27)$$

In equation (4.27), $x_t$ denotes the exchange rate of the foreign currency at time $t$ expressed in units of foreign currency required to buy one unit of the portfolio's base currency.

Finally, to model the market risk resulting from changes in implied yield volatility, one includes the implied yield volatility risk factor. This risk factor is intended to capture the price risk arising from changes in the implied yield volatility when callable or putable bonds are held in the portfolio or benchmark. If one assumes the implied yield volatility risk factor models a 1 percent increase in implied yield volatility, then the coefficient $v_t$ associated with implied yield volatility risk factor is given by

$$v_t = 100 \times \frac{\sigma_t - \sigma_{t-1}}{\sigma_t} \qquad (4.28)$$

In equation (4.28), $\sigma_t$ refers to the implied yield volatility for some suitable option contract at time $t$ (a 1-month swaption on the 5-year swap rate is used in this risk model). Again assume that the implied yield volatility time series is constructed using weekly data.

One can now construct the risk model for computing the exposure of the portfolio relative to the benchmark to various market risk factors. The relevant risk factors comprise the shift and twist risk factors for the U.S.

**EXHIBIT 4.4**   Market Risk Model

|           | USD Shift | USD Twist | EUR Shift | EUR Twist | FX Factor | Yield Vol |
|-----------|-----------|-----------|-----------|-----------|-----------|-----------|
| USD shift | 1.110     | 0.251     | 0.518     | −0.051    | −0.158    | −0.128    |
| USD twist | 0.251     | 1.051     | 0.044     | 0.318     | −0.004    | −0.107    |
| EUR shift | 0.518     | 0.044     | 0.467     | −0.019    | −0.062    | −0.096    |
| EUR twist | −0.051    | 0.318     | −0.019    | 0.727     | 0.032     | −0.191    |
| FX factor | −0.158    | −0.004    | −0.062    | 0.032     | 0.918     | −0.319    |
| Yield vol.| −0.128    | −0.107    | −0.096    | −0.191    | −0.319    | 11.528    |

dollar and euro swap curves, the exchange rate risk factor and the implied yield volatility factor. In this case, one can construct the vector time series of the risk factor coefficients using weekly data, denoted $\{\dot{\phi}(t)\} = \{[a_t^{usd}\ b_t^{usd}\ a_t^{eur}\ b_t^{eur}\ c_t\ v_t]\}$. The risk model for measuring exposures to systematic risk factors turns out to be simply the covariance matrix $\Sigma = [\sigma_{ij}]$, where $\sigma_{ij}$ denotes the covariance between the $i$th and $j$th time series components in $\dot{\phi}(t)$. Exhibit 4.4 shows the six-factor market risk model estimated using weekly data over the period 31 March 1999 to 3 April 2001.

Given the risk model (or equivalently the risk factor covariance matrix), one can compute the tracking error of the portfolio versus the benchmark arising from mismatches in the exposures to market risk factors. As a prerequisite for this, one has to compute the sensitivities to various market risk factors that have been modeled.

To indicate the computation of the sensitivities to market risk factors, first assume that the market value of the portfolio is given by $M_P$. Now consider a shift of $\Delta s = -10$ basis points to the U.S. dollar swap curve. Under the assumption that the U.S. dollar swap curve dynamics capture the systematic risk of corporate bonds denominated in U.S. dollars, the yields of all U.S. dollar-denominated bonds change by $-10$ basis points. Under this scenario, the market value of the portfolio is different if corporate bonds denominated in U.S. dollars are held in the portfolio. Generically denoting this risk factor as $k$, the sensitivity to the $k$th risk factor in basis points is given by

$$S_P^k = 10,000 \times \frac{M_P^k - M_P}{M_P} \qquad (4.29)$$

In equation (4.29), $M_P^k$ is the new market value of the portfolio under the risk scenario. One can similarly compute the sensitivity in basis points to the $k$th risk factor for the benchmark, which is given as

$$S_B^k = 10,000 \times \frac{M_B^k - M_B}{M_B} \qquad (4.30)$$

Note that for estimating sensitivity to exchange rate risk, one has to shock the relevant foreign currency to appreciate by 1 percent against the base currency of the portfolio. Similarly, to estimate the sensitivity to changes in implied yield volatility, one has to shock the implied yield volatilites of all callable and putable bonds to increase by 1 percent and then revalue the portfolio and benchmark under this scenario.

For the chosen risk model, let $\vec{S}_P$ and $\vec{S}_B$ denote the vectors of factor loadings (or sensitivity) in basis points for the portfolio and benchmark, respectively. The annualized ex ante tracking error of the portfolio denoted in basis points arising from exposures to market risk factors is given by

$$T_e = \sqrt{52(\vec{S}_P - \vec{S}_B)^T \Sigma (\vec{S}_P - \vec{S}_B)} \qquad (4.31)$$

The scaling factor of 52 in equation (4.31) is required to annualize the tracking error computed using weekly time series data.

The annualized volatility of the portfolio in basis points can be determined from the following equation:

$$\sigma_P = \sqrt{52\, \vec{S}_P^T \Sigma \vec{S}_P} \qquad (4.32)$$

The risk factor sensitivities introduced here are useful in the context of formulating an optimization problem to find portfolios that replicate the risk factors of a given corporate bond benchmark. This is discussed in Chapter 10.

## QUESTIONS

1. The dirty price of a bond maturing in 4.25 years with a 5 percent coupon rate paid on a semiannual basis is $102.50. Compute the yield to maturity, modified duration, and convexity of the bond. Using modified duration and convexity, find the approximate price change for a 25-basis points increase in yield.

2. A portfolio manager holds two bonds in his portfolio, both paying semiannual coupons. The nominal amount invested in bond A is $1 million and this bond is trading at a dirty price of $101.50. Bond A matures in 2.25 years and has a coupon rate of 4.5 percent. The nominal amount invested in bond B is $2.5 million and bond B is trading at a dirty price of $105.25. Bond B matures in 8.75 years and has a coupon rate of 5 percent. Compute the yield to maturity, modified duration, and convexity of the bond portfolio. If the portfolio manager's performance is measured

against a 1- to 5-year sector benchmark having a modified duration of 2.25 years, what is the view of the portfolio manager?

3. Explain the motivation for doing a principal component decomposition of the yield curve.

4. A portfolio manager prefers to use two risk factors to model the yield curve dynamics but would like one factor to be the duration (implying a parallel shift of yield curve as one factor). Explain what criterion you would use to identify the second risk factor to ensure that the two factors explain a large proportion of the variance in the yield curve.

5. What is the tracking error of a portfolio? A portfolio has a monthly tracking error of 25 basis points. What is its annualized tracking error?

6. For the two-bond portfolio given in Question 2, find the shift risk and twist risk sensitivities in basis points for the portfolio using the risk factors given in Exhibit 4.2.

## CHAPTER 5

# Modeling Credit Risk

Credit risk constitutes the dominant part of the risk in a corporate bond portfolio. As a consequence, the ability to model credit risk accurately plays an important role in deciding whether the risk in a corporate bond portfolio can be managed effectively. However, modeling credit risk is a much more difficult task than modeling market risk. Most of the difficulties relate to the differences in the conceptual approaches used for modeling credit risk and data limitations associated with parameter specification and estimation. Hence, there is invariably a subjective element to the modeling of credit risk and, as such, credit risk modeling is a mixture of art and science. This subjective element is much more evident when one aggregates credit risk at the portfolio level, which is discussed in the next chapter. In this chapter, I discuss various factors that are important determinants of credit risk in a corporate bond and indicate the methods used to estimate these at the security level. Subsequently, I introduce standard risk measures that are used to quantify credit risk.

## ELEMENTS OF CREDIT RISK

Credit risk, in broad terms, refers to the risk of a loss arising from the obligor or issuer not being in a position to service the debt obligations. Also attributed to credit risk is the mark-to-market loss of a bond resulting from a change in the market perception of the issuer's ability to service the debt in the future. In most cases, this change in the market perception will be either preceded or succeeded by a change in the credit quality of the issuer. In computing credit risk at the security level, the following factors play important roles:

- *Probability of default.* This is the probability that the issuer will default on its contractual obligations to repay its debt. Because probability of default (PD) is a function of the time horizon over which one measures the debt-servicing ability, it is standard practice to assume a 1-year horizon to quantify this.

- *Recovery rate.* This is the extent to which the face value of an obligation can be recovered once the counterparty has defaulted. The recovery rate (RR) is usually taken to be the price at which the security trades in the secondary market immediately after the issuer has defaulted on contractual payments. Among other variables, seniority of the bond and the prevailing economic environment are important determinants of recovery rates.
- *Rating migration.* Short of default, this is the extent to which the credit quality of the issuer improves or deteriorates as expressed by a change in the probability of default. This affects the relative spread versus the risk-free yield curve at which the corporate bond trades.

In the following sections, I discuss each of these factors in greater detail, and, wherever relevant, indicate methods commonly employed to estimate the quantities of interest.

## Probability of Default

The key determinant of the credit risk of an issuer is the uncertainty regarding the issuer's ability to service debt obligations as expressed through the default probability. In general, the approaches used to determine default probabilities at the issuer level fall into two broad categories. The first is empirical in nature and requires the existence of a public credit-quality rating scheme. The second is based on Merton's options theory framework and is therefore a structural approach. The empirical approach to estimating the default probability makes use of a *historical* database of corporate defaults to form a static pool of companies having a particular credit rating for a given year. Annual default rates are then calculated for each static pool, which are then aggregated to provide an estimate of the average historical default probability for a given credit rating. If one uses this approach, then the default probabilities for any two issuers having the same credit rating will be identical. On the other hand, the option pricing approach to estimating default probability uses *current* estimates of the firm's assets, liabilities, and asset volatility and hence is related to the dynamics of the underlying structure of the firm. I discuss each of these approaches in greater detail in what follows.

**Empirical Approach** Many major rating agencies, including Moody's Investors Service, Standard & Poor's Corporation, and Fitch Ratings determine the probability of default using the empirical approach. Rating agencies assign credit ratings to different issuers based on extensive analysis of both the quantitative and the qualitative performance of a firm. This analysis is intended to capture the level of credit risk (how credit ratings are assigned is beyond the scope of this book). For the purpose of illustrating the empirical approach used to determine default probabilities for different credit ratings, I discuss Moody's methodology.

Moody's rating symbols for issuer ratings reflect opinions on the issuer's ability to honor senior unsecured financial obligations and contracts denominated in foreign and/or domestic currency. The rating gradations provide bondholders with a simple system to measure an issuer's ability to meet its senior financial obligations. Exhibit 5.1 shows the various rating symbols assigned by Moody's with a short description of the rating implication.

**EXHIBIT 5.1** Credit Quality Implication for Moody's Rating Symbols

| Rating Symbol | Rating Implication |
|---|---|
| Aaa | Issuers rated Aaa offer exceptional financial security, although the credit-worthiness of these entities is likely to change, such changes most unlikely may not impair their fundamentally strong position |
| Aa | Issuers rated Aa offer excellent financial security; compared to Aaa issuers, long-term risks of Aa issuers are somewhat greater |
| A | Issuers rated A offer good financial security; however, elements may be present that suggest a susceptibility to impairment in the future |
| Baa | Issuers rated Baa offer adequate financial security; however, certain protective elements may be lacking or may be unreliable over any great period of time |
| Ba | Issuers rated Ba offer questionable financial security; often the ability of these issuers to meet obligations may be moderate and not well safeguarded in the future |
| B | Issuers rated B offer poor financial security; assurance of payment of obligations over any long period of time is small |
| Caa | Issuers rated Caa offer very poor financial security; they may be in default on their obligations or there may be present elements of danger with respect to payment of obligations on schedule |
| Ca | Issuers rated Ca offer extremely poor financial security; such issuers are often in default on their obligations or have other marked shortcomings |
| C | Issuers rated C are the lowest rated class of entity and are usually in default on their obligations, and potential recovery values are low |

*Source:* "Rating Definitions," Moody's Investors Service. © Moody's Investors Service, Inc., and/or its affiliates. Reprinted with permission. All rights reserved.

In addition to the these generic rating categories, Moody's applies numerical modifiers 1, 2, and 3 to the rating categories from Aa to Caa. The modifier 1 indicates that the issuer is in the higher end of its letter-rating category, the modifier 2 indicates a mid-range ranking, and the modifier 3 indicates that the issuer is in the lower end of the letter-rating category. It is customary to refer to a rating change from grade Aa1 to Aa2 as a *one-notch rating downgrade*. Bonds issued by firms rated between Aaa to Baa are referred to as *investment-grade* bonds; the rest are referred to as *non-investment-grade* bonds.

It is important to emphasize here that Moody's ratings incorporate assessments of both the likelihood and the severity of default. Considering that a particular issuer could have debt issues with different collateral and seniority, Moody's approach leads to different ratings for a particular issuer's different debt issues. However, when an issuer is deemed to have defaulted on a particular debt issue, cross-default clauses require all out-standing debt of the issuer to be considered as having defaulted. This in turn leads to the following question: What events signal the default of an issuer? Moody's definition of default considers three types of default events:

1. There is a missed or delayed disbursement of interest and/or principal including delayed payments made within a grace period.
2. An issuer files for bankruptcy or legal receivership occurs.
3. A distressed exchange occurs where: (1) the issuer offers bondholders a new security or package of securities that amounts to a diminished financial obligation or (2) the exchange has the apparent purpose of helping the borrower default.

These definitions of default are meant to capture events that change the relationship between the bondholder and the bond issuer in such a way as to subject the bondholder to an economic loss.

The empirical approach relies on historical defaults of various rated issuers. This requires forming a static pool of issuers with a given rating every year and computing the ratio of defaulted issuers after a 1-year peri-od to the number of issuers that could have potentially defaulted for the given rating. If, during the year, ratings for certain issuers are withdrawn, then these issuers are subtracted from the potential number of issuers who could have defaulted in the static pool. Specifically, the 1-year default rates for A-rated issuers during a given year represent the number of A-rated issuers that defaulted over the year divided by the number of A-rated issuers that could have defaulted over that year. Annual default rates cal-culated in this manner for each rating grade are then aggregated to provide an estimate of the average historical default probability for a given rating grade.

I mentioned that although different debt issues of a particular issuer could have different ratings assigned depending on the seniority of the issue, cross-default clauses require all outstanding debt of a particular issuer to default at the same time. This raises an important question when managing corporate bond portfolios, namely, whether the issuer rating or the rating of the bond issue is to be considered when inferring the probability of default. The short answer to this question is that it depends on how credit risk will be quantified for the given bond. The approach taken here to quantify bond-level credit risk requires that the credit rating of the bond issuer is the one to be used. This will be evident when I discuss the quantification of credit risk at the bond level.

**Merton's Approach** Merton's approach to estimating the probability of default of a firm builds on the limited liability rule, which allows shareholders to default on their obligations while surrendering the firm's assets to its creditors. In this framework, the firm's liabilities are viewed as contingent claims on the assets of the firm and default occurs at debt maturity when the firm's asset value falls below the debt value. Assuming that the firm is financed by means of equity $S_t$ and a single zero-coupon debt maturing at time $T$ with face value $F$ and current market value $B_t$, one can represent the firm's assets at time $t$ as

$$A_t = S_t + B_t \qquad (5.1)$$

The probability of default in Merton's framework for the firm is the probability that the firm's assets are less than the face value of the debt, which is given by

$$PD = \text{prob}[A_T < F] \qquad (5.2)$$

To determine the probability of default in Merton's framework, one needs to select a suitable model for the process followed by $A_t$. A standard assumption is to postulate that $A_t$ follows a log-normal process with growth rate $\mu$ and asset return volatility $\sigma_A$, as follows:

$$A_t = A_0 \exp\left[(\mu - 0.5\sigma_A^2)t + \sigma_A\sqrt{t}\,z_t\right] \qquad (5.3)$$

In equation (5.3), $z_t$ is a normally distributed random variable with zero mean and unit variance. Using equation (5.3) in conjunction with equation (5.2), one can denote the probability of default as

$$PD = \text{prob}\left[\ln A_0 + (\mu - 0.5\sigma_A^2)T + \sigma_A\sqrt{T}\,z_T < \ln F\right] \qquad (5.4)$$

In equation (5.4), one takes the logarithm on both sides of the inequality because doing so does not change the probabilities. Rearranging the terms in equation (5.4), one can represent the probability of default for the firm as

$$\text{PD} = \text{prob}\left[z_T < -\frac{\ln(A_0/F) + \left(\mu - 0.5\sigma_A^2\right)T}{\sigma_A\sqrt{T}}\right] \tag{5.5}$$

Because $z_T$ is a normally distributed random variable, the probability of default can be represented as

$$\text{PD} = N(-D) \tag{5.6}$$

where

$$D = \frac{\ln(A_0/F) + \left(\mu - 0.5\sigma_A^2\right)T}{\sigma_A\sqrt{T}} \tag{5.7}$$

$$N(-D) = \frac{1}{\sqrt{2\pi}}\int_{-\infty}^{-D}\exp(-0.5x^2)dx \tag{5.8}$$

In equation (5.7), $D$ represents the distance to default, which is the distance between the logarithm of the expected asset value at maturity and the logarithm of the default point normalized by the asset volatility.

Although Merton's framework for determining the probability of default for issuers is rather simple, applying this directly in practice runs into difficulties. This is because firms seldom issue zero-coupon bonds and usually have multiple liabilities. Furthermore, firms in distress may be able to draw on lines of credit to honor coupon and principal payments, resulting in a maturity transformation of their liabilities.

To resolve these difficulties, the KMV Corporation suggested some modifications to Merton's framework to make the default probability estimate meaningful in a practical setting[1] (KMV refers to the probability of default as the expected default frequency, or EDF). For instance, rather than using the face value of the debt to denote the default point, KMV suggests using the sum of the short-term liabilities (coupon and principal payments due in less than 1 year) and one half of the long-term liabilities. This choice is based on the empirical evidence that firms default when their asset value reaches a level between the value of total liabilities and the value of short-term liabilities. Furthermore, because the asset returns of the firms may in practice deviate from a normal distribution, KMV maps the distance to default variable D to a historical default statistics database to estimate the probability of default. In the KMV framework, default probabilities for issuers can take values in the range between 0.02 and 20 percent.

To illustrate the KMV approach, let DPT denote the default point and $E(A_T)$ the expected value of the firm's assets 1 year from now. Then the distance to default is given by

$$D = \frac{\ln[E(A_T)/\text{DPT}]}{\sigma_A\sqrt{T}} = \frac{\ln(A_0/\text{DPT}) + (\mu - 0.5\sigma_A^2)T}{\sigma_A\sqrt{T}} \qquad (5.9)$$

In equation (5.9), the market value of the firm's assets is not observed because the liabilities of the firm are not traded. What can be observed in the market is the equity value of the firm because equity is traded. Because the value of the firm's equity at time $T$ can be seen as the value of a call option on the assets of the firm with a strike price equal to the book value of the liabilities, one has the following equation:

$$S_T = A_T \times N(d_1) - e^{-rT} \times \text{DPT} \times N(d_2) \qquad (5.10)$$

In equation (5.10), $N(\cdot)$ is the cumulative standard unit normal distribution, $r$ is the risk-free interest rate, and the variables $d_1$ and $d_2$ are given, respectively, by

$$d_1 = \frac{\ln(A_T/\text{DPT}) + (r + 0.5\sigma_A^2)T}{\sigma_A\sqrt{T}} \qquad (5.11)$$

and

$$d_2 = d_1 - \sigma_A\sqrt{T} \qquad (5.12)$$

It is possible to show that equity return and asset return volatility are related through the following relation:

$$\sigma_S = \frac{A_T}{S_T} \times N(d_1) \times \sigma_A \qquad (5.13)$$

From this relation, it is possible, using an iterative procedure, to solve for the asset value and asset return volatility given the equity value and equity return volatility. Knowing the asset return volatility and asset value, one can compute the distance to default using equation (5.9), from which probability of default can be inferred.

**Relative Merits** The empirical and structural approaches to determining issuers' probability of default can produce significant differences. Both approaches have their relative advantages and disadvantages. For instance, the empirical approach has the implicit assumption that all issuers having the same credit rating will have an identical PD. Furthermore, this default probability is equal to the historical average rate of default. Use of the structural approach, on the other hand, results in PD being more responsive to changes in economic conditions and business cycles because it incorporates current estimates of the asset value and asset return volatility of the firm in deriving this information. One drawback, however, is that the historical database of defaulted firms comprises mostly industrial corporates. As a consequence, use of an industrial corporate default database to infer the PD of regulated financial firms could potentially result in biased PD estimates. Seen from a trading perspective, credit spreads for corporates tend to be influenced much more by agency ratings and credit rating downgrades than by EDF values. This has the consequence that bond market participants tend to attach greater significance to rating agency decisions for pricing. For the purpose of modeling portfolio credit risk and selecting an optimal corporate bond portfolio to replicate the benchmark risk characteristics, I demonstrate the usefulness of both approaches in the chapters to follow.

**On Rating Outlooks** Rating agencies provide forward-looking assessments of the issuers' creditworthiness over the medium term. Such forward-looking credit assessments are referred to as *rating outlooks*. Outlooks assess the potential direction of an issuer's rating change over the next 6 months to 2 years. A positive outlook suggests an improvement in credit rating, a negative outlook indicates deterioration in credit rating, and a stable outlook suggests a rating change is less likely to occur. Bond prices tend to react to changes in rating outlook although no actual change in credit rating has occurred. In particular, the impact on prices is much more significant if the issuer is Baa because a rating downgrade can result in the issuer being rated non-investment grade. Furthermore, if a particular sector (such as telecom) has a negative rating outlook, a change in rating outlook from stable to negative for an issuer in this sector can also have a significant effect on bond prices.

These observations raise the following important question: Should a negative or a positive rating outlook for a given issuer be incorporated in assessing PD through a downgrade or an upgrade before it has actually happened? The short answer to this question is no, primarily because estimating credit risk incorporates the probability that the credit rating of issuers can change over time. Forcing a rating change for the issuer before it has actually happened may tend to bias the estimate of credit risk.

**Captive Finance Companies**  Large companies in most industrial sectors have captive finance subsidiaries. The principal function of any financial subsidiary is to support the sales of the parent's products. This function can make the finance company a critical component of the parent's long-term business strategy. In light of this close relationship between the captive finance company and its parent, credit ratings for both are usually identical. However, if the legal clauses guarantee that the parent company's bankruptcy does not automatically trigger the bankruptcy of the financial subsidiary, rating differences may exist between the parent company and its financial subsidiary.[2] For the purpose of quantifying credit risk, I use the actual credit rating of the financial subsidiary in the calculations.

Estimating the probability of default of financial subsidiaries on the basis of Merton's structural model can lead to difficulties. This is because the equity of the financial subsidiary may not be traded. For example, Ford Motor is traded, whereas its financial subsidiary, Ford Credit, is not traded. Considering that the financing arm of major industrial corporates is vital to the survival of both the parent and the subsidiary, one can argue that the equity market takes this relationship into account when valuing the parent company. Under this argument, one can assign the same probability of default to both companies when only one of them is traded in the market.

## Recovery Rate

In the event of default, bondholders do not receive all of the promised coupon and principal payments on the bond. Recovery rate for a bond, which is defined as the percentage of the face value that can be recovered in the event of default, is of natural interest to investors. Considering that credit market convention is to ask how much of promised debt is lost rather than how much of it is recovered, the term loss given default (LGD), which is defined as one minus recovery rate, is also commonly used in the credit risk literature.

In general, estimating the recovery value of a bond in the event of default is rather complex. This is because the payments made to bondholders could take the form of a combination of equity and derivative securities, new debt, or modifications to the terms of the surviving debt. Because there may be no market for some forms of payments, it may not be feasible to measure the recovery value. Moreover, the amount recovered could take several months or even years to materialize and could potentially also depend on the relative strength of the negotiating positions. As a result, estimating historical averages of amounts recovered from defaulted debt requires making some simplifying assumptions.

Moody's, for instance, proxies the recovery rate with the secondary market price of the defaulted instrument approximately 1 month after the time of default.[3] The motivation for such a definition is that many investors may wish to trade out of defaulted bonds and a separate investor clientele may acquire these and pursue the legal issues related to recovering money from defaulted debt instruments. In this context, Moody's recovery rate proxy can be interpreted as a transfer price between these two investor groups.

Empirical research on recovery rates suggests that industrial sector, seniority of the debt, state of the economy, and credit rating of the issuer 1 year prior to default are variables that have significant influence on potential recovery rates.[4] For example, during periods of economic downturns, the recovery rate is usually lower relative to historical averages. This has the consequence that there is also a time dimension to the potential recovery rates. Differences in recovery rates for defaulted debt across industry sectors arise because the recovery amount depends on the net worth of tangible assets the firm has. For instance, firms belonging to industrial sectors with physical assets, such as public utilities, have higher recovery rates than the industrywide average. Empirical results also tend to suggest that issuers that were rated investment grade 1 year prior to default tend to have higher recovery values than issuers that were rated noninvestment grade.

To incorporate the variations in the observed recovery rates over time and between issuers when quantifying credit risk, the standard deviation of recovery rates, denoted $\sigma_{RR}$, is taken into account. Including the uncertainty in recovery rates has the effect of increasing credit risk at the issuer level. Common practice is to use the beta distribution to model the observed variations in recovery rates. The advantage of choosing the beta distribution is that is has a simple functional form, dependent on two parameters, which allows for high recovery rate outliers observed in the empirical data to be modeled. The beta distribution has support on the interval 0 to 1 and its density function is given by

$$f(x, \alpha, \beta) = \begin{cases} \frac{\Gamma(\alpha + \beta)}{\Gamma(\alpha)\Gamma(\beta)} x^{\alpha - 1}(1 - x)^{\beta - 1}, & 0 < x < 1 \\ 0, & \text{otherwise} \end{cases} \quad (5.14)$$

where $\alpha > 0$, $\beta > 0$, and $\Gamma(\cdot)$ is the gamma function. The mean and variance of the beta distribution are given, respectively, by

$$\mu = \frac{\alpha}{\alpha + \beta} \quad (5.15)$$

and

$$\sigma^2 = \frac{\alpha\beta}{(\alpha + \beta)^2(\alpha + \beta + 1)} \quad (5.16)$$

**EXHIBIT 5.2**  Recovery Rate Statistics on Defaulted Securities (1978 to 2001)

| Bond Seniority | Number of Issuers | Median (%) | Mean (%) | Standard Deviation (%) |
|---|---|---|---|---|
| Senior secured | 134 | 57.42 | 52.97 | 23.05 |
| Senior unsecured | 475 | 42.27 | 41.71 | 26.62 |
| Senior subordinated | 340 | 31.90 | 29.68 | 24.97 |
| Subordinated | 247 | 31.96 | 31.03 | 22.53 |

*Source:* E. Altman, A. Resti, and A. Sironi, "Analyzing and Explaining Default Recovery Rates," Report submitted to the International Swaps and Derivatives Association, December 2001.

Exhibit 5.2 shows the empirical estimates of recovery rates on defaulted securities covering the period 1978 to 2001 based on prices at time of default. Note that senior secured debt recovers on average 53 percent of the face value of the debt, whereas senior unsecured debt recovers only around 42 percent of face value. The standard deviation of the recovery rates for all seniority classes is roughly around 25 percent.

The empirical estimates for average recovery rates tend to vary somewhat depending on the data set used and the recovery rate definition. For instance, the study by Moody's using defaulted bond data covering the period 1970 to 2000 suggests that the mean recovery rate for senior secured bonds is 52.6 percent, for senior unsecured bonds is 46.9 percent, and for subordinated bonds is 31.6 percent.

In the numerical examples to be presented in this book, I assume that the bonds under consideration are senior unsecured debt. Furthermore, I assume that the standard deviation of the recovery rate is 25 percent and the average recovery rate is 47 percent, which is closer to Moody's estimate.

## Rating Migrations

The framework for assessing the issuer's PD involves estimating the probability associated with the issuer defaulting on its promised debt payments. In this framework, the issuer is considered to be in one of two states: its current rating or the default state. In practice, default is just one of many states to which the issuer's rating can make a transition. The action of rating agencies can result in the issuer's rating being downgraded or upgraded by one or several notches. One can associate the concept of a state with each rating grade, so that rating actions result in the transition to one of several states. Each rating action can be viewed as a credit event that changes the perceived probability of default of the issuer. In the credit risk terminology, such a multistate credit event process is described as credit or rating migration.

Associated with rating migrations are transition probabilities, which model the relative frequency with which such credit events occur.

Modeling the rating migrations process requires estimating a matrix of transition probabilities, which is referred to as the rating transition matrix. Each cell in the 1-year rating transition matrix corresponds to the probability of an issuer migrating from one rating state to another over the course of a 12-month horizon. Mathematically speaking, a rating transition matrix is a Markov matrix, which has the property that the sum of all cells in any given row of the matrix is equal to one. Incorporating rating migrations into the credit risk-modeling framework provides a much richer picture of changes in the aggregate credit quality of the issuer.

The technique used to estimate transition probabilities is similar in principle to the estimation of probability of default. For instance, computing the 1-year transition probability from the rating Aa1 to Baa1 requires first determining the number of issuers rated Baa1 that had an Aa1 rating 1 year earlier. Dividing this number by the total number of issuers that were rated Aa1 during the previous year gives the 1-year transition probability between these two ratings. Again, if the ratings of some Aa1 issuers are withdrawn during the 1-year period of interest, then the total number of Aa1 issuers is reduced by this number. Annual transition probabilities calculated in this manner are then aggregated over a number of years to estimate the average historical transition probability. Exhibit 5.3 shows the 1-year rating transition matrix estimated by Moody's covering the period 1983 to 2001. In this exhibit, the transition probabilities are expressed in percentages and the column WR refers to the percentage of ratings that were withdrawn.

The interpretation of the numbers in this matrix is the following. The first cell in the matrix refers to the probability (expressed in percentage terms) of remaining in the rating grade Aaa 1 year from now. The estimate of this probability is 85 percent on the basis of historical migration data. The cell under column A3 in the first row of the matrix refers to the probability of an issuer migrating from an Aaa rating to an A3 rating in 1 year. Again, the estimate of this probability on the basis of historical migration data is 0.16 percent. Similarly, the cells in the second row correspond to the 1-year migration probabilities of an issuer that is currently rated Aa1.

Exhibit 5.3 reveals interesting information concerning the relative frequency of rating downgrades and upgrades. For example, the rating transition matrix suggests that higher ratings have generally been less likely than lower ratings to be revised over 1 year. Another observation is that large and sudden rating changes occur infrequently. As one moves down the rating scale, the likelihood of a multinotch rating change increases. The transition matrix also reveals one feature that is somewhat less desirable. This

**EXHIBIT 5.3** Moody's Average One-Year Rating Transition Matrix (1983 to 2001)

| | Aaa | Aa1 | Aa2 | Aa3 | A1 | A2 | A3 | Baa1 | Baa2 | Baa3 | Ba1 | Ba2 | Ba3 | B1 | B2 | B3 | Caa–C | Default | WR |
|---|---|---|---|---|---|---|---|---|---|---|---|---|---|---|---|---|---|---|---|
| Aaa | 85.00 | 5.88 | 2.90 | 0.47 | 0.71 | 0.28 | 0.16 | 0.00 | 0.00 | 0.00 | 0.04 | 0.00 | 0.00 | 0.00 | 0.00 | 0.00 | 0.00 | 0.00 | 4.56 |
| Aa1 | 2.54 | 76.02 | 7.87 | 6.58 | 2.31 | 0.32 | 0.05 | 0.18 | 0.00 | 0.00 | 0.09 | 0.00 | 0.00 | 0.00 | 0.00 | 0.00 | 0.00 | 0.00 | 4.04 |
| Aa2 | 0.70 | 2.90 | 77.00 | 8.39 | 3.93 | 1.35 | 0.58 | 0.16 | 0.00 | 0.00 | 0.00 | 0.00 | 0.05 | 0.08 | 0.00 | 0.00 | 0.00 | 0.00 | 4.85 |
| Aa3 | 0.08 | 0.61 | 3.36 | 77.88 | 8.89 | 3.14 | 0.85 | 0.24 | 0.21 | 0.16 | 0.00 | 0.04 | 0.09 | 0.00 | 0.00 | 0.00 | 0.00 | 0.08 | 4.38 |
| A1 | 0.03 | 0.11 | 0.60 | 5.53 | 77.68 | 7.20 | 2.88 | 0.78 | 0.27 | 0.13 | 0.36 | 0.25 | 0.05 | 0.12 | 0.01 | 0.00 | 0.00 | 0.00 | 3.99 |
| A2 | 0.05 | 0.06 | 0.29 | 0.77 | 5.34 | 77.47 | 7.18 | 2.87 | 0.80 | 0.39 | 0.28 | 0.10 | 0.11 | 0.03 | 0.07 | 0.00 | 0.03 | 0.02 | 4.13 |
| A3 | 0.05 | 0.10 | 0.05 | 0.23 | 1.48 | 8.26 | 71.77 | 6.69 | 3.65 | 1.43 | 0.54 | 0.19 | 0.22 | 0.33 | 0.05 | 0.04 | 0.01 | 0.00 | 4.91 |
| Baa1 | 0.08 | 0.02 | 0.13 | 0.18 | 0.20 | 2.71 | 7.67 | 71.19 | 7.37 | 3.14 | 1.04 | 0.46 | 0.35 | 0.55 | 0.09 | 0.00 | 0.02 | 0.00 | 4.73 |
| Baa2 | 0.07 | 0.10 | 0.12 | 0.17 | 0.17 | 0.87 | 3.67 | 6.90 | 71.50 | 7.02 | 1.68 | 0.52 | 0.65 | 0.48 | 0.45 | 0.23 | 0.03 | 0.08 | 5.30 |
| Baa3 | 0.03 | 0.00 | 0.03 | 0.07 | 0.18 | 0.57 | 0.65 | 3.22 | 9.33 | 67.03 | 6.38 | 2.59 | 1.90 | 0.80 | 0.31 | 0.18 | 0.16 | 0.07 | 6.15 |
| Ba1 | 0.08 | 0.00 | 0.00 | 0.03 | 0.22 | 0.12 | 0.67 | 0.75 | 2.94 | 7.68 | 66.47 | 4.60 | 3.88 | 1.12 | 1.27 | 0.81 | 0.33 | 0.43 | 8.39 |
| Ba2 | 0.00 | 0.00 | 0.00 | 0.03 | 0.04 | 0.15 | 0.13 | 0.35 | 0.70 | 2.30 | 8.35 | 63.96 | 6.20 | 1.67 | 3.70 | 1.35 | 0.53 | 0.62 | 9.88 |
| Ba3 | 0.00 | 0.02 | 0.00 | 0.00 | 0.04 | 0.16 | 0.17 | 0.17 | 0.26 | 0.69 | 2.71 | 5.04 | 66.66 | 4.83 | 5.16 | 2.22 | 0.85 | 0.65 | 8.74 |
| B1 | 0.02 | 0.00 | 0.00 | 0.00 | 0.06 | 0.09 | 0.15 | 0.07 | 0.24 | 0.30 | 0.42 | 2.52 | 5.70 | 66.89 | 5.22 | 4.58 | 1.78 | 2.27 | 8.23 |
| B2 | 0.00 | 0.00 | 0.06 | 0.01 | 0.11 | 0.00 | 0.07 | 0.17 | 0.12 | 0.18 | 0.29 | 1.63 | 2.95 | 5.75 | 61.22 | 7.61 | 3.69 | 3.71 | 8.10 |
| B3 | 0.00 | 0.00 | 0.06 | 0.00 | 0.02 | 0.04 | 0.06 | 0.11 | 0.12 | 0.20 | 0.18 | 0.35 | 1.17 | 4.02 | 3.36 | 62.05 | 6.84 | 8.04 | 8.91 |
| Caa–C | 0.00 | 0.00 | 0.00 | 0.00 | 0.00 | 0.00 | 0.00 | 0.48 | 0.48 | 0.48 | 0.64 | 0.00 | 1.36 | 1.85 | 1.23 | 2.87 | 54.21 | 26.54 | 10.36 |
| Default | 0.00 | 0.00 | 0.00 | 0.00 | 0.00 | 0.00 | 0.00 | 0.00 | 0.00 | 0.00 | 0.00 | 0.00 | 0.00 | 0.00 | 0.00 | 0.00 | 0.00 | 100.0 | 0.00 |

*Source:* Adapted from Exhibit 13 in David T. Hamilton, Richard Cantor, and Sharon Ou, "Default and Recovery Rates of Corporate Issuers," *Moody's Investors Service*, February 2002, p. 14. © Moody's Investors Service, Inc., and/or its affiliates. Reprinted with permission. All rights reserved.

concerns the probability of default for different ratings, which, contrary to expectations, does not increase monotonically as one moves down the rating grade. For example, the probability of default for an Aa3-rated issuer is 0.08 percent, whereas for an A3-rated issuer it is zero and it is only 0.07 percent for a Baa2-rated issuer.

This raises the following important question: Should we be concerned with the empirical observations that Aa3-rated issuers are more likely to default than Baa2-rated issuers and that for some ratings the probability of default is zero? The answer is yes, primarily because this has implications for the calculation of default correlations to be discussed in the next chapter. A PD of zero for A3-rated issuers implies that the probability of contemporaneous defaults of A3-rated issuers and issuers of any other rating is zero. Clearly, a default probability of zero is undesirable because it leads to nonintuitive results when estimating credit risk. Therefore it is necessary to make the following fine tunings to the rating transition matrix shown in Exhibit 5.3:

- Eliminate the column WR in Exhibit 5.3 and normalize each row so that all cells in any given row add up to 100 percent.
- Refine the resulting probabilities under the default column so that they are monotonically increasing, with the implication that probability of default increases as credit rating declines.
- Readjust the probabilities in the remaining columns so that each row represents a valid probability vector.

The process of deleting the WR column and scaling up the transition probabilities so that each row represents a valid probability vector (i.e., all cells in the row sum to 1 or equivalently 100 percent) is called normalization. I refer to the default probabilities for various ratings derived through the normalization process as the normalized PD. For the purpose of refining the normalized probabilities so that they increase monotonically as ratings decline, I take into account both Moody's and Standard & Poor's normalized default probability estimates. Exhibit 5.4 shows the normalized probability of default for various rating grades based on Moody's and Standard & Poor's estimates and the default probabilities to be used when estimating credit risk in the numerical examples.

For issuers in the rating grade Baa1 and lower, the PD values in Exhibit 5.4 are chosen to reflect the maximum of the estimates of Moody's and Standard & Poor's. For issuers with ratings between Aaa and Aa3, I assume the default probability increases by 1 basis point (0.01 percentage point) for every one-notch downgrade. From the grade Aa3 to grade A3, PD is assumed to increase by 2 basis points for every one-notch downgrade.

**EXHIBIT 5.4**  Normalized One-Year Probability of Default for Various Rating Grades

| Rating Grade | Rating Description | Standard & Poor's (%) | Moody's (%) | PD Used (%) |
|---|---|---|---|---|
| 1 | Aaa/AAA | 0.00 | 0.00 | 0.01 |
| 2 | Aa1/AA+ | 0.00 | 0.00 | 0.02 |
| 3 | Aa2/AA | 0.00 | 0.00 | 0.03 |
| 4 | Aa3/AA− | 0.03 | 0.08 | 0.04 |
| 5 | A1/A+ | 0.02 | 0.00 | 0.06 |
| 6 | A2/A | 0.05 | 0.02 | 0.08 |
| 7 | A3/A− | 0.05 | 0.00 | 0.10 |
| 8 | Baa1/BBB+ | 0.13 | 0.08 | 0.13 |
| 9 | Baa2/BBB | 0.23 | 0.07 | 0.23 |
| 10 | Baa3/BBB− | 0.37 | 0.46 | 0.46 |
| 11 | Ba1/BB+ | 0.48 | 0.67 | 0.67 |
| 12 | Ba2/BB | 1.03 | 0.72 | 1.03 |
| 13 | Ba3/BB− | 1.46 | 2.46 | 2.46 |
| 14 | B1/B+ | 3.25 | 3.97 | 3.97 |
| 15 | B2/B | 9.37 | 8.41 | 9.37 |
| 16 | B3/B− | 11.49 | 13.72 | 13.72 |
| 17 | Caa–C/CCC | 25.25 | 29.60 | 29.60 |

With these changes to the default probability estimates, Exhibit 5.5 shows the normalized rating transition matrix used to quantify credit risk in the numerical examples in this book.

## QUANTIFYING CREDIT RISK

In the previous section, I identified the important variables that influence credit risk at the security level. In this section, I will focus on quantifying credit risk at the security level. Most people are familiar with the concept of risk in connection with financial securities. In broad terms, risk is associated with potential financial loss that can arise from holding the security, the exact magnitude of which is difficult to forecast. As a result, it is common to describe the potential loss in value using an appropriate probability distribution whose mean and standard deviation serve as useful measures for risk quantification.

This practice is well known in the equities market, where investors focus on market risk measures that model variations in stock return. This leads to quantifying the market risk measures through expected return and standard deviation of return. Under the assumption that equity returns are normally distributed, the realized return lies within one standard deviation of the expected return with two-thirds probability.

**EXHIBIT 5.5** Normalized One-Year Rating Transition Matrix

| | Aaa | Aa1 | Aa2 | Aa3 | A1 | A2 | A3 | Baa1 | Baa2 | Baa3 | Ba1 | Ba2 | Ba3 | B1 | B2 | B3 | Caa–C | Default |
|---|---|---|---|---|---|---|---|---|---|---|---|---|---|---|---|---|---|---|
| Aaa | 89.06 | 6.16 | 3.04 | 0.49 | 0.74 | 0.29 | 0.17 | 0.00 | 0.00 | 0.00 | 0.04 | 0.00 | 0.00 | 0.00 | 0.00 | 0.00 | 0.00 | 0.01 |
| Aa1 | 2.65 | 79.20 | 8.20 | 6.86 | 2.41 | 0.33 | 0.05 | 0.19 | 0.00 | 0.00 | 0.09 | 0.00 | 0.00 | 0.00 | 0.00 | 0.00 | 0.00 | 0.02 |
| Aa2 | 0.74 | 3.05 | 80.90 | 8.82 | 4.13 | 1.42 | 0.61 | 0.17 | 0.00 | 0.00 | 0.00 | 0.00 | 0.05 | 0.08 | 0.00 | 0.00 | 0.00 | 0.03 |
| Aa3 | 0.08 | 0.64 | 3.52 | 81.48 | 9.30 | 3.28 | 0.89 | 0.25 | 0.22 | 0.17 | 0.00 | 0.04 | 0.09 | 0.00 | 0.01 | 0.00 | 0.00 | 0.04 |
| A1 | 0.03 | 0.11 | 0.62 | 5.76 | 80.88 | 7.50 | 3.00 | 0.81 | 0.28 | 0.14 | 0.37 | 0.26 | 0.05 | 0.12 | 0.01 | 0.00 | 0.00 | 0.06 |
| A2 | 0.05 | 0.06 | 0.30 | 0.80 | 5.57 | 80.75 | 7.48 | 2.99 | 0.83 | 0.41 | 0.29 | 0.11 | 0.12 | 0.03 | 0.07 | 0.03 | 0.03 | 0.08 |
| A3 | 0.05 | 0.11 | 0.05 | 0.24 | 1.55 | 8.68 | 75.40 | 7.03 | 3.83 | 1.50 | 0.57 | 0.20 | 0.23 | 0.35 | 0.05 | 0.05 | 0.01 | 0.10 |
| Baa1 | 0.08 | 0.02 | 0.14 | 0.19 | 0.21 | 2.84 | 8.04 | 74.68 | 7.73 | 3.29 | 1.09 | 0.48 | 0.37 | 0.58 | 0.09 | 0.02 | 0.02 | 0.13 |
| Baa2 | 0.07 | 0.11 | 0.13 | 0.18 | 0.18 | 0.92 | 3.87 | 7.27 | 75.35 | 7.40 | 1.77 | 0.55 | 0.69 | 0.51 | 0.47 | 0.27 | 0.03 | 0.23 |
| Baa3 | 0.03 | 0.00 | 0.03 | 0.08 | 0.19 | 0.61 | 0.69 | 3.42 | 9.92 | 71.29 | 6.79 | 2.76 | 2.02 | 0.85 | 0.33 | 0.36 | 0.17 | 0.46 |
| Ba1 | 0.09 | 0.00 | 0.00 | 0.03 | 0.24 | 0.13 | 0.73 | 0.82 | 3.20 | 8.36 | 72.31 | 5.00 | 4.22 | 1.22 | 1.38 | 1.24 | 0.36 | 0.67 |
| Ba2 | 0.00 | 0.00 | 0.00 | 0.03 | 0.04 | 0.16 | 0.14 | 0.39 | 0.77 | 2.53 | 9.18 | 70.35 | 6.82 | 1.84 | 4.07 | 2.07 | 0.58 | 1.03 |
| Ba3 | 0.00 | 0.02 | 0.00 | 0.00 | 0.04 | 0.17 | 0.19 | 0.19 | 0.28 | 0.75 | 2.94 | 5.47 | 72.38 | 5.25 | 5.60 | 3.34 | 0.92 | 2.46 |
| B1 | 0.02 | 0.00 | 0.00 | 0.00 | 0.06 | 0.10 | 0.16 | 0.08 | 0.26 | 0.32 | 0.45 | 2.69 | 6.09 | 71.52 | 5.58 | 6.80 | 1.90 | 3.97 |
| B2 | 0.00 | 0.00 | 0.06 | 0.01 | 0.11 | 0.00 | 0.07 | 0.18 | 0.12 | 0.19 | 0.30 | 1.69 | 3.05 | 5.95 | 63.38 | 11.70 | 3.82 | 9.37 |
| B3 | 0.00 | 0.00 | 0.07 | 0.00 | 0.02 | 0.04 | 0.07 | 0.12 | 0.13 | 0.22 | 0.20 | 0.38 | 1.28 | 4.41 | 3.69 | 68.14 | 7.51 | 13.72 |
| Caa–C | 0.00 | 0.00 | 0.00 | 0.00 | 0.00 | 0.00 | 0.00 | 0.00 | 0.54 | 0.54 | 0.71 | 0.00 | 1.52 | 2.06 | 1.37 | 3.20 | 60.46 | 29.60 |
| Default | 0.00 | 0.00 | 0.00 | 0.00 | 0.00 | 0.00 | 0.00 | 0.00 | 0.00 | 0.00 | 0.00 | 0.00 | 0.00 | 0.00 | 0.00 | 0.00 | 0.00 | 100.0 |

**EXHIBIT 5.6**   Typical Shape of the Credit Loss Distribution

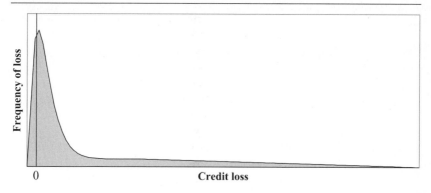

Quantifying credit risk at the security level is similar in principle. Unlike the case for equities, corporate bond investors focus on the distribution of potential losses that can result from the issuer-specific credit events. Borrowing the principle from the equities market, it has become common practice to quantify credit risk at the security level through the mean and the standard deviation of the loss distribution. However, there is an important difference between the two risk measures. This pertains to the distribution of credit loss, which, unlike for market risk, is far from being a normal distribution. Hence, deviations from the expected loss by one standard deviation can occur more frequently than on one in three occasions. Credit market convention is to refer to the standard deviation of loss resulting from credit events as unexpected loss (UL) and the average loss as expected loss (EL). Exhibit 5.6 shows the typical shape of the distribution of credit losses.

In this section, I discuss how expected and unexpected loss as used to quantify credit risk at the security level can be determined. Depending on whether the loss distribution takes into account the changes in security prices resulting from rating migrations or not, we can compute two sets of loss variables, one in the default mode and another in the migration mode. I now discuss quantification of credit risk in both these modes.

## Expected Loss Under Default Mode

Expected loss under the default mode of a bond is defined as the average loss the bondholder can expect to incur if the issuer goes bankrupt. Because default probability estimates are based on a 1-year holding period, expected loss is also expressed over a 1-year period. In practice, the issuer could actually default at any time during the 1-year horizon. Because a bond portfolio manager is usually interested in the worst-case loss scenario, which

**EXHIBIT 5.7**   Bond Price Distribution
Under the Default Mode

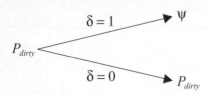

corresponds to the issuer defaulting in the immediate future, I use the 1-year PD to quantify the worst-case loss. This has the implication that one can quantify credit risk using the current trading price for the bond rather than its 1-year forward price. Because the portfolio manager's goal is to manage relative risk versus a benchmark, the use of 1-year PD in conjunction with current trading prices does not bias the relative risk estimates. However, this assumption leads to considerable simplification in quantifying credit risk because deriving forward yield curves for various credit ratings is quite tedious.

The estimate of expected loss for a security depends on three variables: probability of default of the issuer, the average recovery rate, and the nominal exposure (NE) to the security. One can think of the default process $\delta$ as being a Bernoulli random variable that takes the value 0 or 1. The value $\delta = 1$ signals a default and the value $\delta = 0$ signals no default. Conditional upon default, the recovery rate $\psi$ is a random variable whose mean recovery rate is RR. Exhibit 5.7 pictorially depicts the default process and the recovery values. In this exhibit, $P_{\text{dirty}}$ denotes the dirty price (clean price plus accrued interest) for a \$1 face value of the bond.

Exhibit 5.7 indicates that if the issuer defaults, the price of the bond will be equal to its recovery rate $\psi$, which is a random variable. If the issuer does not default, the bond can be sold for a value equal to its current dirty price $P_{\text{dirty}}$. In this default mode framework, the price of the risky debt can be written as

$$\tilde{P} = P_{\text{dirty}} \times I_{[\delta = 0]} + \psi \times I_{[\delta = 1]} \tag{5.17}$$

In equation (5.17), $I$ is the indicator function of the default process. For the purpose of quantifying credit risk, the variable of interest is the credit loss resulting from holding the corporate bond. This is a random variable $\tilde{\ell}$, which is given by

$$\tilde{\ell} = P_{\text{dirty}} - \tilde{P} = P_{\text{dirty}} - P_{\text{dirty}} \times I_{[\delta = 0]} - \psi \times I_{[\delta = 1]} \tag{5.18}$$

Taking expectations on both sides of equation (5.18) makes it possible to compute the expected loss arising from credit risk. This is given by

$$\text{EL} = E(\tilde{\ell}) = P_{\text{dirty}} - P_{\text{dirty}} \times (1 - \text{PD}) - E(\psi \times I_{[\delta=1]}) \qquad (5.19)$$

Note that computing the expected loss requires taking the expectation of the product of two random variables, the recovery rate process and the default process. Knowledge of the joint distribution of these two random variables is required to compute this expectation. Most credit risk models make the simplifying assumption that these two random variables are independent. If one makes this assumption, one gets the following equation for expected loss:

$$\text{EL} = P_{\text{dirty}} \times \text{PD} - \text{RR} \times \text{PD} \qquad (5.20)$$
$$= \text{PD} \times (P_{\text{dirty}} - \text{RR})$$

Recall that $P_{\text{dirty}}$ is the dirty price of the bond for $1 nominal and RR in equation (5.20) is the mean recovery rate, which is expressed as a fraction of the face value of the debt. It is important to note that the quantity $(P_{\text{dirty}} - \text{RR})$ is different from LGD, which is defined as one minus the recovery rate. The loss on default (LD) captures this new quantity:

$$\text{LD} = P_{\text{dirty}} - \text{RR} \qquad (5.21)$$

Note that loss on default is identical to loss given default if the dirty price of the bond is equal to one. In all other circumstances, these two quantities are not the same.

Equation (5.20) was derived under the assumption that the nominal exposure is $1. The expected loss from credit risk for a nominal exposure equal to NE is given by

$$\text{EL} = \text{NE} \times \text{PD} \times \text{LD} \qquad (5.22)$$

The use of the quantity LD rather than LGD in defining expected loss might raise some doubts in the mind of the reader. To clear these doubts, consider the following example, which illustrates why LD is more appropriate than LGD in the context of bond portfolio management.

Consider the case of a bond portfolio manager who has the option to invest $1 million either in a bond with dirty price $100 (issuer A) or in a bond with dirty price $80 (issuer B). In the latter case, the portfolio manager buys $1.25 million nominal value of issuer B's bond to fully invest the $1 million. Assume that both issuers default within the next 1 year and the recovery value is $50 for $100 face value of exposure. If the portfolio manager had invested in issuer A's bond, he or she would recover $500,000 because the nominal exposure is $1 million. On the other hand, if the portfolio manager invested in issuer B's bond, then the amount recovered would be $625,000. This is because the portfolio manager has a nominal exposure of $1.25 million of issuer B's bond. Clearly, from the portfolio manager's perspective, the credit loss resulting from an investment in issuer A's bond is $500,000, whereas the credit loss from an investment in issuer B's bond is only $375,000, although both investments recovered 50 percent of the face value of debt. Use of the quantity LD correctly identifies the losses in both circumstances, whereas the LGD definition indicates that the losses are $500,000 for issuer A's bond and $625,000 for issuer B's bond. In practice, LGD is used in conjunction with the exposure amount of the transaction to identify the expected loss. However, this definition also incorrectly identifies the losses as being identical for both bonds in this example.

## Unexpected Loss Under Default Mode

The expected loss on the bond is the average loss that the investor can expect to incur over the course of a 1-year period. However, the actual loss may well exceed this average loss over certain time periods. The potential deviation from the expected loss that the investor can expect to incur is quantified in terms of the standard deviation of the loss variable defined in equation (5.18). Credit market convention is to refer to the standard deviation of loss as unexpected loss. Hence, to derive the unexpected loss formula, one needs to compute the standard deviation of the random variable $\tilde{\ell}$. To facilitate this computation, one rewrites equation (5.18) as follows:

$$\tilde{\ell} = P_{\text{dirty}} - P_{\text{dirty}} \times (1 - I_{[\delta=1]}) - \psi \times I_{[\delta=1]} \qquad (5.23)$$
$$= I_{[\delta=1]} \times (P_{\text{dirty}} - \psi)$$

Recalling a standard result from probability theory, one can write the variance of any random variable $z$ as the difference between the expected value of the random variable squared minus the square of its expected value. In equation form, this is given by

$$\sigma_z^2 = E(z^2) - [E(z)]^2 \qquad (5.24)$$

Again make the simplifying assumption that the default and recovery rate processes are independent in deriving the unexpected loss formula. Under this assumption, one can write the variance of the random variable $\tilde{\ell}$ as

$$\text{Var}(\tilde{\ell}) = E(I_{[\delta=1]}^2) \times E[(P_{\text{dirty}} - \psi)^2] - [E(I_{[\delta=1]})]^2 \times [E(P_{\text{dirty}} - \psi)]^2$$
$$(5.25)$$

Taking expected values and using the relation (5.24) results in the following simplification of equation (5.25).

$$\text{Var}(\tilde{\ell}) = \left[\sigma_{PD}^2 + PD^2\right] \times \left[\sigma_{RR}^2 + LD^2\right] - PD^2 \times LD^2 \qquad (5.26)$$

In this equation, $\sigma_{PD}^2$ is the variance of the Bernoulli random variable $\delta$, which is given by

$$\sigma_{PD}^2 = PD \times (1 - PD) \qquad (5.27)$$

Simplifying the terms in equation (5.26), it can be shown that unexpected loss, which is the standard deviation of the loss variable, is given by

$$UL = \sqrt{PD \times \sigma_{RR}^2 + LD^2 \times \sigma_{PD}^2} \qquad (5.28)$$

This formula for unexpected loss assumes that the nominal exposure is equal to \$1. For a nominal exposure equal to NE, the unexpected loss at the security level is given by

$$UL = NE \times \sqrt{PD \times \sigma_{RR}^2 + LD^2 \times \sigma_{PD}^2} \qquad (5.29)$$

**On the Independence Assumption**   In deriving the expressions for expected and unexpected losses on a bond resulting from credit risk, I made the simplifying assumption that the default process and the recovery rate process are independent. One needs to ask whether this assumption is reasonable. Examining theoretical models on credit risk does not give a definitive answer to this question. For instance, in Merton's framework, the default process of a firm is driven by the value of the firm's assets. The risk of a firm's default is therefore explicitly linked to the variability in the firm's asset value. In this setup, both the default process and the recovery rate are a function of the structural characteristics of the firm, and one can show that PD and RR are inversely related.

The reduced-form models, unlike the structural models, do not condition default on the value of the firm. The default and recovery processes are modeled independently of the structural features of the firm and are further assumed to be independent of each other. This independence assumption between default and recovery processes, which is fundamental to reduced-form models, is pervasive in credit value at risk models.

Empirical results on the relationship between default and recovery values tend to suggest that these two variables are negatively correlated. The intuition behind this result is that both default rate and recovery rate may depend on certain structural factors. For instance, if a borrower defaults on the debt payments, the recovery rate depends on the net worth of the firm's assets. This net worth, which is usually a function of prevailing economic conditions, is lower during periods of recession. In contrast, during recession, the probability of default of issuers tends to increase. The combination of these two effects results in a negative correlation between default and recovery rates.

More recent empirical research on the relationship between default and recovery rate processes suggests that a simple microeconomic interpretation based on supply and demand tends to drive aggregate recovery rate values.[5] In particular, during high-default years, the supply of defaulted securities tends to exceed demand, which in turn drives secondary market prices down. Because RR values are based on bond prices shortly after default, the observed recovery rates are lower when there is an excess supply of defaulted securities.

To incorporate the empirical evidence that recovery values decrease when default rates are high, one has to identify periods when PD is high relative to normal levels. If PD values are determined on the basis of historical average default rates as is done by rating agencies, it is difficult to distinguish between low- and high-default periods. On the other hand, if a structural approach is used to estimate PD values as is done by KMV Corporation, it is possible to signal periods when PD values are higher than historical average levels. This information can then be incorporated to determine the appropriate recovery rates to be used. Such an approach amounts to the use of a regime-switching model to determine the average recovery rates. Again, empirical estimates tend to suggest that bond recovery rates could decline roughly by 20 percent from historical averages during periods of economic downturn.

In the numerical examples in this book, I estimate the relevant credit risk measures for two different economic regimes: the normal economy and recession. Under recession, I assume that the recovery rates are 20 percent lower than the average recovery rates.

## Expected Loss Under Migration Mode

To derive the formula for expected loss under the default mode, I took into consideration the credit event that results in the issuer defaulting on debt payments. In general, this is not the only credit event the bondholder experiences that influences the market price of the bond. More frequent are credit events that result in rating upgrades or downgrades of the bond issuer. These credit events correspond to a change in the opinion of the rating agencies concerning the creditworthiness of the issuer. Because rating changes are issuer-specific credit events, the associated bond price changes fall under credit risk. Including the price risk resulting from rating migrations in the calculation of potential credit losses is referred to as the credit risk under the migration mode.

In practice, a change in bond price can be either positive or negative depending on whether the rating change results in an upgrade or a downgrade, respectively. However, I use the term credit loss generically to refer to a change in bond price as a result of a credit event. Before proceeding to derive the formula that quantifies expected loss under the migration mode, I indicate how the price change resulting from a credit event can be estimated.

**Estimating Price Changes** Practitioners familiar with the pricing of corporate bonds know that the issuer's rating does not fully explain yield differentials between bonds of similar maturities. Using the Lehman Brothers corporate bond database, Elton, Gruber, Agrawal, and Mann found that pricing errors can vary from 34 cents per $100 for Aa financials to greater than $1.17 per $100 for Baa industrials.[6] Their study suggests that the following factors have an important influence on observed price differentials between corporate bonds:

- The finer rating categories introduced by the major rating agencies when combined with the bonds' maturity.
- Differences between Standard and Poor's and Moody's ratings for the issuers.
- Differences in expected recovery rate for the bonds.
- The coupon on the bonds due to different tax treatment.
- Whether the bonds are new or have traded for more than 1 year.

These observations indicate that one cannot use generic yield curves for various rating grades to reprice bonds when the issuer's rating changes. One has to adopt a different technique to estimate the price risk resulting from rating changes. It is important to bear in mind that in the context of credit risk quantification, the objective is to estimate approximate price changes from rating migrations rather than capture the correct trading price for the bond. To this end, rating migrations should result in a price change that is consistent with perceived change in the creditworthiness of the issuer.

The technique adopted here to estimate the change in bond price due to a rating change uses the current modified duration and convexity of the bond. To determine the change in yield associated with a rating change, I assume that there exists a fixed yield spread between each rating grade that is a function of the debt issue's seniority. These yield spreads are taken relative to the government yield curve. If the modified duration of the bond is denoted by $D$ and the convexity by $C$, then the change in price of the bond due to a change $\Delta y$ in the bond yield as a result of the rating change is given by

$$\text{Price change} = -P_{\text{dirty}} \times D \times \Delta y + 0.5 \times P_{\text{dirty}} \times C \times \Delta y^2 \quad (5.30)$$

Because our interest is in estimating the loss resulting from the rating change to quantify credit risk, the following equation is the one that is relevant:

$$\Delta P = P_{\text{dirty}} \times D \times \Delta y - 0.5 \times P_{\text{dirty}} \times C \times \Delta y^2 \quad (5.31)$$

The advantage of such a technique is that it retains price differentials observed in the market between bonds with similar maturity and credit rating when the issuer migrates to a different rating grade. Exhibit 5.8 shows the indicative yield spreads relative to government bonds for different rating grades as a function of the seniority of the debt issue. These yield spreads are used in conjunction with the current duration and convexity of the bond to estimate the price change resulting from a rating migration.

**EXHIBIT 5.8**   Yield Spreads for Different Rating Grades and Debt Seniority[a]

| Rating Grade | Rating Description | Senior Unsecured (bp) | Subordinated (bp) |
|---|---|---|---|
| 1 | Aaa/AAA | 15 | 20 |
| 2 | Aa1/AA+ | 30 | 40 |
| 3 | Aa2/AA | 45 | 60 |
| 4 | Aa3/AA− | 60 | 80 |
| 5 | A1/A+ | 75 | 100 |
| 6 | A2/A | 90 | 120 |
| 7 | A3/A− | 105 | 140 |
| 8 | Baa1/BBB+ | 130 | 180 |
| 9 | Baa2/BBB | 155 | 220 |
| 10 | Baa3/BBB− | 180 | 260 |
| 11 | Ba1/BB+ | 230 | 330 |
| 12 | Ba2/BB | 280 | 410 |
| 13 | Ba3/BB− | 330 | 480 |
| 14 | B1/B+ | 430 | 610 |
| 15 | B2/B | 530 | 740 |
| 16 | B3/B− | 630 | 870 |
| 17 | Caa–C/CCC | 780 | 1040 |

[a]bp, basis points.

**Deriving Expected Loss**   Unlike in the case of the default mode, the issuer can migrate to one of several rating grades under the migration mode during the course of the year. Associated with these rating migrations are discrete transition probabilities that constitute the rows of the rating transition matrix given in Exhibit 5.5. In the rating migration framework, the transition probabilities represent historical averages and can be treated as deterministic variables. The random variables here are the credit losses that the bondholder incurs when the issuer rating changes. The expected value of the credit loss for a rating change from the $i$th grade to the $k$th grade is given by

$$\Delta P_{ik} = P_{\text{dirty}} \times D \times \Delta y_{ik} - 0.5 \times P_{\text{dirty}} \times C \times \Delta y_{ik}^2 \qquad (5.32)$$

In equation (5.32), $\Delta y_{ik}$ denotes the yield change when the issuer rating changes from grade $i$ to grade $k$. When the issuer migrates to the default state, the credit loss $\Delta P_{ik}$ is equal to the loss on default LD. Considering that there are 18 rating grades including the default state, the expected loss under the rating migration mode for an issuer whose current credit rating is $i$ is given by

$$\text{EL} = \sum_{k=1}^{18} p_{ik} \times \Delta P_{ik} \qquad (5.33)$$

In equation (5.33), $p_{ik}$ denotes the 1-year transition probability of migrating from rating grade $i$ to rating grade $k$. This equation quantifies the expected loss over a 1-year horizon for a nominal exposure of \$1. For a nominal exposure NE, the expected loss under migration mode is given by

$$\text{EL} = \text{NE} \times \sum_{k=1}^{18} p_{ik} \times \Delta P_{ik} \qquad (5.34)$$

**Unexpected Loss Under Migration Mode**

By definition, the unexpected loss under the migration mode is the standard deviation of the credit loss variable. The loss variable under the migration mode is given by

$$\tilde{\ell} = \sum_{k=1}^{18} p_{ik} \times \Delta \tilde{P}_{ik} \qquad (5.35)$$

In equation (5.35), $\Delta \tilde{P}_{ik}$ denotes the credit loss when the credit rating changes from grade $i$ to grade $k$, which is regarded as a random variable. The expected value of this random variable is $\Delta P_{ik}$ and its variance is denoted by $\sigma_{ik}^2$. When $k$ is equal to the default state, $\sigma_{ik}$ is equal to $\sigma_{\text{RR}}$, which is the standard deviation of the recovery rate. Recalling equation

(5.24), one can write the variance of the loss variable as

$$\text{Var}(\tilde{\ell}) = E\left( \sum_{k=1}^{18} p_{ik} \times \Delta\tilde{P}_{ik}^2 \right) - \left[ E\left( \sum_{k=1}^{18} p_{ik} \times \Delta\tilde{P}_{ik} \right) \right]^2 \quad (5.36)$$

Taking expectations and making use of the relation (5.24) once more gives the following expression for the variance of the loss variable:

$$\text{Var}(\tilde{\ell}) = \sum_{k=1}^{18} p_{ik} \times \left( \Delta P_{ik}^2 + \sigma_{ik}^2 \right) - \left( \sum_{k=1}^{18} p_{ik} \times \Delta P_{ik} \right)^2 \quad (5.37)$$

If one assumes that there is no uncertainty associated with the credit losses except in the default state, all $\sigma_{ik}^2$ terms in equation (5.37) drop out other than $\sigma_{RR}^2$. Making this assumption and noting that $p_{ik}$ is equal to PD when $k$ is the default state gives the unexpected loss under the migration mode for a nominal exposure NE:

$$\text{UL} = \text{NE} \times \sqrt{\text{PD} \times \sigma_{RR}^2 + \sum_{k=1}^{18} p_{ik} \times \Delta P_{ik}^2 - \left( \sum_{k=1}^{18} p_{ik} \times \Delta P_{ik} \right)^2} \quad (5.38)$$

## NUMERICAL EXAMPLE

In this section, I give a numerical example to illustrate the computations of expected and unexpected losses under the default mode and the migration mode. The security level details of the example are given in Exhibit 5.9.

Because the mean recovery rate is assumed to be 47 percent, the loss on default for this security is equal to 0.5833 for $1 nominal exposure. The probability of default for this security is equal to 0.10 percent, which

**EXHIBIT 5.9** Security-Level Details of Example Considered

| Description | Value |
| --- | --- |
| Issuer rating grade | A3 |
| Settlement date | 24 April 2002 |
| Bond maturity date | 15 February 2007 |
| Coupon rate | 6.91% |
| Dirty price for $1 nominal | 1.0533 |
| Nominal exposure | $1,000,000 |
| Modified duration | 4.021 |
| Convexity | 19.75 |
| Mean recovery rate | 47% |
| Volatility of RR | 25% |

corresponds to the last column in row A3 of the transition matrix given in Exhibit 5.5. The expected and unexpected losses in the default mode when PD = 0.001 are given as follows:

$$EL = NE \times PD \times LD$$
$$= 1{,}000{,}000 \times 0.001 \times 0.5833 = \$583.3$$

$$UL = NE \times \sqrt{PD \times \sigma_{RR}^2 + LD^2 \times \sigma_{PD}^2}$$
$$= 1{,}000{,}000 \times \sqrt{0.001 \times 0.25^2 + 0.5833^2 \times 0.001 \times (1 - 0.001)}$$
$$= \$20{,}059.88$$

Under the migration mode, the breakdown of the calculations involved in estimating expected and unexpected losses is given in Exhibit 5.10. The expected loss under the migration mode is given by

$$EL = NE \times \sum_{k=1}^{18} p_{ik} \times \Delta P_{ik}$$
$$= 1{,}000{,}000 \times 0.003012 = \$3012$$

**EXHIBIT 5.10** Calculation of Expected Loss and Unexpected Loss Under the Migration Mode

| Grade | $P_{ik}$ (%) | $\Delta y_{ik}$ (%) | $\Delta P_{ik}$ | $p_{ik} \times \Delta P_{ik}$ | $p_{ik} \times \Delta P_{ik}^2$ |
|---|---|---|---|---|---|
| 1 | 0.05 | −0.90 | −0.0390 | −0.000019 | 7.590E − 07 |
| 2 | 0.11 | −0.75 | −0.0323 | −0.000036 | 1.151E − 06 |
| 3 | 0.05 | −0.60 | −0.0258 | −0.000013 | 3.325E − 07 |
| 4 | 0.24 | −0.45 | −0.0193 | −0.000046 | 8.912E − 07 |
| 5 | 1.55 | −0.30 | −0.0128 | −0.000198 | 2.539E − 06 |
| 6 | 8.68 | −0.15 | −0.0064 | −0.000553 | 3.529E − 06 |
| 7 | 75.40 | 0.00 | 0.0000 | 0.000000 | 0.000E + 00 |
| 8 | 7.03 | 0.25 | 0.0105 | 0.000740 | 7.785E − 06 |
| 9 | 3.83 | 0.50 | 0.0209 | 0.000801 | 1.676E − 05 |
| 10 | 1.50 | 0.75 | 0.0312 | 0.000468 | 1.458E − 05 |
| 11 | 0.57 | 1.25 | 0.0513 | 0.000293 | 1.501E − 05 |
| 12 | 0.20 | 1.75 | 0.0709 | 0.000142 | 1.006E − 05 |
| 13 | 0.23 | 2.25 | 0.0900 | 0.000207 | 1.864E − 05 |
| 14 | 0.35 | 3.25 | 0.1267 | 0.000443 | 5.615E − 05 |
| 15 | 0.05 | 4.25 | 0.1612 | 0.000081 | 1.299E − 05 |
| 16 | 0.05 | 5.25 | 0.1937 | 0.000097 | 1.876E − 05 |
| 17 | 0.01 | 6.75 | 0.2385 | 0.000024 | 5.688E − 06 |
| 18 | 0.10 | | 0.5833 | 0.000583 | 3.402E − 04 |
| Sum | | | | 0.003012 | 5.259E − 04 |

The unexpected loss under the migration mode is given by

$$
\begin{aligned}
UL &= NE \times \sqrt{ PD \times \sigma_{RR}^2 + \sum_{k=1}^{18} p_{ik} \times \Delta P_{ik}^2 - \left( \sum_{k=1}^{18} p_{ik} \times \Delta P_{ik} \right)^2 } \\
&= 1{,}000{,}000 \times \sqrt{0.001 \times 0.25^2 + 5.259 \times 10^{-4} - 0.003012^2} \\
&= \$24{,}069.2
\end{aligned}
$$

It is useful to note here that under the migration mode the expected loss is significantly higher. The increase in the unexpected loss in the migration mode is only around 20 percent relative to the unexpected loss under the default mode.

## QUESTIONS

1. The asset value of a firm is \$12 million and the face value of its debt is \$10 million. Assuming the annualized growth rate and the volatility of asset returns are 5 and 10 percent, respectively, compute the 1-year probability of default of the firm using Merton's approach.
2. Explain the practical problems associated with the use of Merton's approach to determine a firm's probability of default. How does the KMV approach resolve these problems?
3. What are the relative merits of the structural and empirical approaches to determining probability of default?
4. How are recovery rates on defaulted bonds estimated? What factors influence the recovery rate on a bond?
5. What are rating outlooks? Do changes in rating outlooks influence bond prices? Explain why or why not.
6. A senior unsecured bond is trading at a dirty price of \$103.50 and the probability of default of the issuer is 20 basis points. Assuming a mean recovery rate of 47 percent and a volatility of recovery rate of 25 percent, compute the expected and unexpected losses under the default mode for a \$10 million nominal amount of the bond held.
7. What is the empirical evidence on the relationship between recovery rates and default rates? Do reduced-form models take this empirical relationship into account in modeling credit risk?
8. Explain the practical difficulties involved in estimating price changes using generic yield curves for different rating categories.
9. Assuming that the rating of the bond in Question 6 is A2, compute the expected and unexpected losses under the migration mode. For the calculations, use the rating transition matrix given in Exhibit 5.5 and the yield spreads for different rating categories given in Exhibit 5.8. The modified duration and convexity of the bond are 4 years and 20, respectively.

## CHAPTER 6

# Portfolio Credit Risk

The focus in the previous chapter was primarily on identifying the elements of credit risk and quantifying credit risk in terms of expected and unexpected losses at the security level. A natural extension of the analysis presented in the previous chapter is to quantify credit risk when an investor holds more than one corporate bond. In this case, one has to model the co-movement of credit migration and defaults between two or more bonds. This leads to the topic of correlated credit events, which are fundamental to the modeling of portfolio credit risk. In practice, measuring these correlations directly is difficult, if not impossible. Standard techniques used to estimate them follow an indirect approach that makes use of the correlation between variables that drive credit events. The variable that is usually considered to drive credit events is the asset returns of the firm. Because asset returns are not directly observable, the method used to estimate asset return correlation between different obligors is a much-debated topic. Furthermore, the choice of the joint distribution function for asset returns of different issuers has a strong influence on the estimate of portfolio credit risk. The appropriate joint distribution function to be used is still a hotly debated topic.

In this chapter I develop the relevant equations for computing portfolio credit risk under both the default mode and the credit migration mode. I indicate how the loss correlation between obligor pairs, which is required to compute portfolio credit risk, can be determined. I also give a simple technique for deriving approximate asset return correlations between obligor pairs. Finally, I provide numerical examples to illustrate the various concepts presented in this chapter.

## QUANTIFYING PORTFOLIO CREDIT RISK

In Chapter 5, credit risk at the security level was quantified in terms of the mean and the standard deviation of the loss distribution resulting from price changes due to credit events. Quantification of credit risk at the portfolio level follows a similar approach. Once again one is interested in the loss distribution of the portfolio due to price changes of individual bonds arising from credit events. The mean and the standard deviation of the portfolio loss distribution, denoted expected portfolio loss ($EL_P$) and unexpected portfolio loss ($UL_P$), are used to quantify portfolio credit risk.

To derive the expressions for expected and unexpected losses for the portfolio, consider a two-obligor portfolio for purposes of illustration. Let $\tilde{\ell}_i$ denote the loss variable for a nominal exposure $NE_i$ to a bond issued by the $i$th obligor in the portfolio that has an expected loss $EL_i$ and unexpected loss $UL_i$. An investor holding the two-obligor portfolio is faced with a loss distribution given by

$$\tilde{\ell}_P = \tilde{\ell}_1 + \tilde{\ell}_2 \tag{6.1}$$

The expected portfolio loss is given by

$$EL_P = E(\tilde{\ell}_1 + \tilde{\ell}_2) = EL_1 + EL_2 \tag{6.2}$$

The variance of the portfolio loss distribution is given by

$$\begin{aligned} Var(\tilde{\ell}_P) &= E\big[(\tilde{\ell}_1 + \tilde{\ell}_2)^2\big] - [E(\tilde{\ell}_1 + \tilde{\ell}_2)]^2 \\ &= E(\tilde{\ell}_1^2) + E(\tilde{\ell}_2^2) + 2E(\tilde{\ell}_1\tilde{\ell}_2) - EL_1^2 - EL_2^2 - 2EL_1 \times EL_2 \end{aligned} \tag{6.3}$$

It is easy to verify that this equation simplifies to the following relation:

$$Var(\tilde{\ell}_P) = UL_1^2 + UL_2^2 + 2E(\tilde{\ell}_1\tilde{\ell}_2) - 2EL_1 \times EL_2 \tag{6.4}$$

Based on a standard result in probability theory, the correlation between the two random variables $\tilde{\ell}_1$ and $\tilde{\ell}_2$, which is referred to as the loss correlation, is given by

$$\rho_{12}^\ell = \frac{E(\tilde{\ell}_1\tilde{\ell}_2) - EL_1 \times EL_2}{UL_1 \times UL_2} \tag{6.5}$$

With the use of equation (6.5), the variance of the portfolio loss distribution simplifies to

$$Var(\tilde{\ell}_P) = UL_1^2 + UL_2^2 + 2 \times \rho_{12}^\ell \times UL_1 \times UL_2 \tag{6.6}$$

Because by definition the unexpected portfolio loss is the standard deviation of the portfolio loss distribution, for the two-obligor portfolio this is given by

$$UL_P = \sqrt{UL_1^2 + UL_2^2 + 2 \times \rho_{12}^\ell \times UL_1 \times UL_2} \qquad (6.7)$$

When an investor is holding bonds issued by $n$ obligors in the portfolio, the expected and the unexpected portfolio loss are given, respectively, by

$$EL_P = \sum_{i=1}^{n} EL_i \qquad (6.8)$$

$$UL_P = \sqrt{\sum_{i=1}^{n} \sum_{k=1}^{n} \rho_{ik}^\ell \times UL_i \times UL_k} \qquad (6.9)$$

In equation (6.9), when $i = k$, one sets $\rho_{ik}^\ell = 1$. Because in practice bond portfolio managers tend to hold more than one bond issued by the same obligor in the portfolio, equation (6.9) must be generalized to include such cases. To do this, it is tempting to apply the constraint $\rho_{ik}^\ell = 1$ when the $i$th bond's issuer is the same as the $k$th bond's issuer in equation (6.9). However, the loss correlation between two bonds of the same issuer is usually not equal to one. In fact, the foregoing equations are equally applicable to any $n$-bond portfolio where the number of obligors is usually less than $n$.

**Remarks**  In deriving the expressions for expected loss and the unexpected loss for the portfolio, I have made no assumption regarding the loss mode under which the portfolio loss distribution is computed. In fact, the equations for expected and unexpected portfolio loss given by (6.8) and (6.9), respectively, are applicable to both the default mode and the credit migration mode. If, for instance, the expected loss and unexpected loss at the security level are computed in the credit migration mode, then equations (6.8) and (6.9) capture the expected loss and the unexpected loss of the portfolio in the credit migration mode.

Readers familiar with Markowitz portfolio theory will immediately recognize some similarities between market risk and credit risk. Whereas in market risk the measures of interest are the expected return and the standard deviation of return of the portfolio, in credit risk the measures of interest are the expected loss and the standard deviation loss of the portfolio. Apart from this conceptual similarity in terms of risk quantification, there are some major differences between market and credit risk. For instance, the distribution of security returns can be closely approximated using a normal distribution function. The distribution of credit loss, however, is far from being a normal distribution function.

The other major difference concerns the complexity involved in computing market and credit risk at the portfolio level. For instance, computing the standard deviation of portfolio returns under market risk requires knowledge of the correlation between security returns. Given historical time series of security returns, it is fairly straightforward to compute the correlation between security returns. Such a simple calculation is not possible for credit risk, where the time series of interest is the credit loss on bonds for various issuers. This is because the occurrence of credit losses is quite infrequent, and, furthermore, certain issuer's bonds may not have suffered a credit loss in recent history. As a consequence, direct estimation of the loss correlation between issuer pairs is seldom possible, and therefore indirect methods are mostly used to infer loss correlation. It is useful to note here that the value of loss correlation computed under the default mode is different from the loss correlation computed under the migration mode for any given obligor pair.

In connection with portfolio credit risk, most readers are familiar with the term default correlation, which is commonly used instead of loss correlation to compute the portfolio's unexpected loss. Although loss correlation and default correlation are closely related, they are not the same. In the next section, I discuss in detail default correlation and derive its relationship to loss correlation under the default mode. Methods for estimating default correlation are also discussed.

## DEFAULT CORRELATION

In broad terms, default correlation measures the strength of the default relationship between two obligors. It answers the important question of how the default by one obligor can influence the contemporaneous default of other obligors. An increase in default correlation between two obligors increases the unexpected loss of a two-bond portfolio assuming all other parameters remain the same.

Formally, default correlation between two obligors is defined as the correlation between the default indicators for these two obligors over some specified interval of time, this being typically 1 year. Denote the default indicator for the $i$th obligor by the Bernoulli random variable $\delta_i$, which takes the value 1 when default occurs and 0 otherwise, over the 1-year horizon. From the standard definition of correlation between random variables, one has the following relation for default correlation between the obligors $i$ and $k$, which is denoted $\rho_{ik}^\delta$:

$$\rho_{ik}^\delta = \frac{E(I_{[\delta_i=1]} \cdot I_{[\delta_k=1]}) - E(I_{[\delta_i=1]})E(I_{[\delta_k=1]})}{\sqrt{\mathrm{Var}(I_{[\delta_i=1]}) \times \mathrm{Var}(I_{[\delta_k=1]})}} \qquad (6.10)$$

Because the default indicator $\delta_i$ is a Bernoulli random variable, one has the following properties:

$$E(I_{[\delta_i=1]}) = PD_i = prob(\delta_i = 1) \tag{6.11}$$

$$Var(I_{[\delta_i=1]}) = \sigma^2_{PD_i} = PD_i \times (1 - PD_i) \tag{6.12}$$

$$E(I_{[\delta_i=1]} \cdot I_{[\delta_k=1]}) = prob(\delta_i = 1, \delta_k = 1) \tag{6.13}$$

Based on these relations, the default correlation between two obligors simplifies to

$$\rho^{\delta}_{ik} = \frac{prob(\delta_i = 1, \delta_k = 1) - PD_i \times PD_k}{\sqrt{PD_i \times (1 - PD_i) \times PD_k \times (1 - PD_k)}} \tag{6.14}$$

Knowledge of the probability of joint default between obligors allows us to compute the default correlation using equation (6.14). Before I discuss various approaches that can be used to do this, I first establish the relationship between default correlation and loss correlation when credit risk is estimated under the default mode.

### Relationship to Loss Correlation

The relationship between default correlation and loss correlation derived here is only applicable to the case where the credit loss is estimated under the default mode. From Chapter 5, the loss variable under the default mode for a nominal exposure $NE_i$ is given by

$$\tilde{\ell}_i = NE_i \times I_{[\delta_i=1]} \times (P_{dirty,i} - \Psi_i) \tag{6.15}$$

Under the assumption that default rate and recovery rate processes are independent, one can derive the following relation for the term $E(\tilde{\ell}_i \tilde{\ell}_k)$:

$$E(\tilde{\ell}_i\tilde{\ell}_k) = NE_i \times NE_k \times E(I_{[\delta_i=1]} \cdot I_{[\delta_k=1]}) \times E[(P_{dirty,i} - \Psi_i) \cdot (P_{dirty,k} - \Psi_k)] \tag{6.16}$$

If one makes the further simplifying assumption that the recovery rates between the $i$th and the $k$th issuer are independent, then one obtains the following relation:

$$E(\tilde{\ell}_i\tilde{\ell}_k) = NE_i \times NE_k \times E(I_{[\delta_i=1]} \cdot I_{[\delta_k=1]}) \times LD_i \times LD_k \tag{6.17}$$

Making use of equations (6.10) and (6.12), one can rewrite equation (6.17) as follows:

$$E(\tilde{\ell}_i \tilde{\ell}_k) = \text{NE}_i \times \text{NE}_k \times (\sigma_{\text{PD}_i} \times \sigma_{\text{PD}_k} \times \rho_{ik}^\delta + \text{PD}_i \times \text{PD}_k) \times \text{LD}_i \times \text{LD}_k \qquad (6.18)$$

Incorporating equation (6.18) into (6.5) and simplifying gives the following relation between loss correlation and default correlation when $i \neq k$:

$$\rho_{ik}^\ell = \frac{\text{NE}_i \times \text{NE}_k \times \sigma_{\text{PD}_i} \times \sigma_{\text{PD}_k} \times \text{LD}_i \times \text{LD}_k}{\text{UL}_i \times \text{UL}_k} \times \rho_{ik}^\delta \qquad (6.19)$$

Under the assumption that recovery rates for bonds issued by two different obligors are independent, equation (6.19) indicates that loss correlation is lower than default correlation. In the general case, loss correlation can be either lower or higher than default correlation depending on the level of correlation between recovery rates for different obligors. The assumption $\rho_{ik}^\ell = \rho_{ik}^\delta$ implicitly postulates that recovery rates for different obligors are positively correlated as follows:

$$\rho_{ik}^r = \frac{\rho_{ik}^\delta \times (\text{UL\%}_i \times \text{UL\%}_k - \sigma_{\text{PD}_i} \times \sigma_{\text{PD}_k} \times \text{LD}_i \times \text{LD}_k)}{\sigma_{\text{RR}_i} \times \sigma_{\text{RR}_k}(\rho_{ik}^\delta \times \sigma_{\text{PD}_i} \times \sigma_{\text{PD}_k} + \text{PD}_i \times \text{PD}_k)} \qquad (6.20)$$

In equation (6.20), the variable UL% is the unexpected loss as a percentage of exposure, which is given by UL% = UL/NE.

### Estimating Default Correlation

I mentioned that estimation of the loss correlation between obligors is usually done through indirect methods. This is also true in the case of default correlation. Because knowledge of default correlation allows one to compute loss correlation and therefore unexpected portfolio loss, I focus on how default correlation can be estimated. The standard technique for estimating default correlation is based on the latent variable approach. In such an approach, default of an obligor is assumed to occur if a latent variable that is considered to play a role in the firm's default falls below a certain threshold value. Correlation between the latent variables of different obligors is then used to infer the default correlation between obligors.

The latent variable that is used in practice is the asset returns of the obligor. The motivation for using asset return as the latent variable is that in Merton's model, a firm's default is driven by changes in its asset value. As a result, the correlation between the asset returns of two obligors can be used to compute the default correlation between them. In practice, one uses the correlation between asset returns for two obligors to estimate the probability of their joint default, which is given by prob($\delta_i = 1$, $\delta_k = 1$). Using this information, one can compute the default correlation between the obligors $i$ and $k$ using equation (6.14).

To illustrate the intuition behind the latent variable approach, recall Merton's structural model for default. The basic premise of Merton's default model, as discussed in Chapter 5, is that when the asset value of the firm falls below outstanding liabilities, the firm will default. In this framework, the joint probability of two firms defaulting within a certain time period is simply the likelihood of both firms' asset values falling below their outstanding liabilities. The joint probability of both firms defaulting can be computed if one knows the joint distribution of asset returns.

At this point it is useful once again to recall the discussion in Chapter 5. Specifically, I showed that under the assumption that asset returns are normally distributed, it is possible to derive a relationship between the probability of default and the default threshold. This threshold, denoted $D_i$ for the $i$th obligor, is obligor specific and depends on asset volatility, leverage, and the outstanding liabilities of the firm. The relationship between default threshold and the obligor's probability of default is given by

$$ \mathrm{PD}_i = \frac{1}{\sqrt{2\pi}} \int\limits_{-\infty}^{D_i} \exp(-0.5z^2)dz \tag{6.21} $$

Estimating the probability of joint defaults between two firms requires making an assumption regarding the joint distribution of asset returns. If one makes the simplifying assumption that the asset returns are jointly normal and the asset return correlation between the $i$th and the $k$th obligor is $\rho_{ik}^\alpha$, then the joint probability of default of the two obligors is given by

$$ \mathrm{prob}(\delta_i = 1, \delta_k = 1) = \frac{1}{2\pi\sqrt{1-(\rho_{ik}^\alpha)^2}} \int\limits_{-\infty}^{D_i} \int\limits_{-\infty}^{D_k} \exp\left(-\frac{x^2 - 2\rho_{ik}^\alpha xy + y^2}{2[1 - (\rho_{ik}^\alpha)^2]}\right) dx\,dy $$

$$ \tag{6.22} $$

The integral limits $D_i$ and $D_k$ can be determined using equation (6.21) if one knows the probability of default of the obligors. Knowledge of the joint probability of default for two obligors then allows computation of the default correlation between the obligors using equation (6.14).

**Remarks** The analysis presented so far in this chapter indicates that there is a considerable degree of subjectivity involved in the quantification of portfolio credit risk. First, loss correlations that are required to compute unexpected portfolio loss need to be estimated using an indirect approach. If one uses default correlation to infer loss correlation, one needs to make further assumptions regarding the correlation between recovery rates of different obligors. Because default correlations themselves are difficult to estimate directly, one needs to identify latent variables that influence defaults. Dependence between latent variables can then be transformed into dependence between default events.

Asset returns were identified as a potential candidate for the latent variable. Because the marginal distribution of asset returns is assumed to be normal, I took this a step further and claimed that the joint distribution of asset returns between obligors can be modeled as being normal. In general, if the joint distribution between two random variables is normal, then it can be shown that the marginal distribution of the two random variables is also normal. However, the converse is not generally true. That is, if the marginal distribution of two random variables is normal, the joint distribution of these two random variables may not be bivariate normal. The assumption that the joint distribution of asset returns of obligors in the bond portfolio is multivariate normal can result in underestimating the probability of joint defaults.

Further simplifications are required in estimating asset return correlations because asset returns are not directly observable. In practice, factor models are used to estimate asset correlation between obligors and this is discussed in the next section. From the practitioner's point of view, it can be seen that the mechanics involved in the process of quantifying portfolio credit risk is susceptible to considerable model risk.

Existing empirical results suggest that most factors that are determinants of default probabilities are positively correlated.[1] This includes asset values, asset volatilities, and debt-to-equity ratios. As a consequence, default correlations across firms are also positively correlated. Default correlations tend to have a time-varying component and are high during periods of economic downturn.

## DEFAULT MODE: TWO-BOND PORTFOLIO

I now present a numerical example comprising a two-bond portfolio to illustrate the various concepts presented so far in this chapter. Using this example, I point out the differences between different correlation measures and the implications for portfolio credit risk under the default mode when different assumptions are made. The bond-level details of the example portfolio considered are given in Exhibit 6.1. I assume that the asset return correlation between the issuers is 30 percent.

**EXHIBIT 6.1**  Bond Level Details of Example Considered

| Description | Bond 1 | Bond 2 |
|---|---|---|
| Bond issuer | Oracle Corp | Alliance Capital |
| Issuer rating grade | A3 | A2 |
| Settlement date | 24 April 2002 | 24 April 2002 |
| Bond maturity date | 15 February 2007 | 15 August 2006 |
| Coupon rate (%) | 6.91 | 5.625 |
| Dirty price for $1 nominal | 1.0533 | 1.0029 |
| Nominal exposure ($) | 1,000,000 | 1,000,000 |
| PD (historical) (bp) | 10 | 8 |
| KMV's EDF (bp) | 58 | 158 |
| Mean recovery rate (%) | 47 | 47 |
| Volatility of RR (%) | 25 | 25 |

Depending on whether the historical PD or KMV's EDF is used in the calculations, the risk measures of interest can be quite different. This is evident on examining the following numerical results:

**Using Historical PD:**

Joint default probability $\text{prob}(\delta_i = 1, \delta_k = 1) = 1.2505 \times 10^{-5}$.

Default correlation $\rho_{ik}^{\delta} = 0.01301$.

Loss correlation $\rho_{ik}^{\ell}$ when recovery rates between issuers are independent is 0.0109.

Recovery rate correlation $\rho_{ik}^{r}$ when the assumption $\rho_{ik}^{\ell} = \rho_{ik}^{\delta}$ is made is 0.9401.

Expected portfolio loss $\text{EL}_P = \$1,010$.

Unexpected portfolio loss $\text{UL}_P$ using loss correlation is $26,205.

Unexpected portfolio loss $\text{UL}_P$ using default correlation is $26,233.

**Using KMV's EDF:**

Joint default probability $\text{prob}(\delta_i = 1, \delta_k = 1) = 5.1096 \times 10^{-4}$.

Default correlation $\rho_{ik}^{\delta} = 0.04428$.

Loss correlation $\rho_{ik}^{\ell}$ when recovery rates between issuers are independent is 0.03678.

Recovery rate correlation $\rho_{ik}^{r}$ when assumption $\rho_{ik}^{\ell} = \rho_{ik}^{\delta}$ is made is 0.83276.

Expected portfolio loss $\text{EL}_P = \$11,803$

Unexpected portfolio loss $\text{UL}_P = $ using loss correlation is $89,379

Unexpected portfolio loss $\text{UL}_P = $ using default correlation is $89,676

It is useful to note here that if default correlation rather than loss correlation is used to aggregate portfolio unexpected loss, one is making the assumption that recovery rates between obligors are highly correlated. When using historical PDs for the issuers in this example, the assumption that default correlation and loss correlation are the same has the implication that recovery rates are almost perfectly correlated. It is also interesting to note here that there is a 350 percent increase in unexpected loss when the EDF estimates of KMV Corporation are used in the calculations instead of historical PDs for the example portfolio.

## ESTIMATING ASSET RETURN CORRELATION

Under the assumption that markets are frictionless, and with no taxes and no bankruptcy costs, the value of the firm's assets is simply the sum of the firm's equity and debt as follows:

$$A_t = S_t + B_t \tag{6.23}$$

Although asset prices are not traded, this equation allows an estimate of the asset value of the firm using traded equity prices and the present value of outstanding debt. Once this is accomplished, estimating asset return correlation between issuers becomes a simple exercise of computing the historical correlation between the asset return time series of various obligors.

From an academic point of view, this task is fairly straightforward. However, in practice, computing the present value of outstanding liabilities is far from being a simple task. This is because firms have multiple liabilities, and corporate loans, which are part of the liabilities, are not traded. To circumvent this problem, practitioners seek to infer the asset return correlation between obligors on the basis of observed equity returns. The intuition behind such an approach is linked to Merton's structural model for valuing risky debt. In Merton's framework, the bondholder can be seen as making a loan maturing at time $T$ to finance the operations of the firm. The risk faced by the bondholder is the risk that the firm cannot repay the face value of the loan at maturity. To hedge this risk, the bondholder can purchase a put option on the asset value of the firm with strike price equal to the face value of debt and option maturity equal to the term of the loan. Because such a strategy is riskless, the return of this hedged portfolio should be equal to the risk-free rate of interest. If $F$ denotes the face value of the debt, $r$ the risk-free interest rate, $p_t$ the value of the put option, and $B_t$ the current value of debt, one has the following relation:

$$B_t + p_t = Fe^{-rT} = F_t \tag{6.24}$$

Equations (6.23) and (6.24) give the following relation:

$$A_t = S_t + F_t - p_t \tag{6.25}$$

Because this relation holds for all $t$, one obtains the following instantaneous relationship:

$$dA_t = dS_t + dF_t - dp_t \tag{6.26}$$

In general, changes in equity prices are closely related to changes in option prices. If this co-movement is exploited, one can approximate the foregoing relation as follows:

$$dA_t = dS_t + dF_t - \kappa dS_t = (1 - \kappa)dS_t + dF_t \tag{6.27}$$

Dividing both sides of equation (6.27) by $A_t$ leads to the following relation:

$$\frac{dA_t}{A_t} = (1 - \kappa)\frac{S_t}{A_t}\frac{dS_t}{S_t} + \frac{F_t}{A_t}\frac{dF_t}{F_t} \tag{6.28}$$

Equation (6.28) shows the relationship between asset returns, equity returns, and risk-free bond returns. With $w = F_t/A_t$, equation (6.28) simplifies to

$$r_A = (1 - w) \times r_S + w \times r_F \tag{6.29}$$

Equation (6.29) is the familiar relation that is exploited to relate the asset return correlation between obligors to the equity return correlation. For instance, the covariance between the asset returns of two obligors $i$ and $k$ using equation (6.29) can be written as

$$\text{cov}(r_A^i, r_A^k) = (1 - w_i) \times (1 - w_k) \times \text{cov}(r_S^i, r_S^k) + (1 - w_i) \times w_k \times \text{cov}(r_S^i, r_F^k)$$

$$+ w_i \times (1 - w_k) \times \text{cov}(r_F^i, r_S^k) + w_i \times w_k \times \text{cov}(r_F^i, r_F^k) \tag{6.30}$$

If it is assumed that $w$ is small and the equity returns and risk-free bond returns are weakly correlated, this equation can be further simplified as follows:

$$\text{cov}(r_A^i, r_A^k) = (1 - w_i) \times (1 - w_k) \times \text{cov}(r_S^i, r_S^k) \tag{6.31}$$

This relationship provides the economic motivation for using equity return correlations to infer the asset return correlation between obligors.

**Remarks**   The quantity $w = F_t/A_t$ is the leverage ratio of the firm. For firms having a relatively low leverage ratio, equity return correlation provides a reasonable approximation to asset return correlation. This is because for such firms one can make use of the approximate relationship given by equation (6.31). On the other hand, for firms having a high leverage ratio, asset returns will be correlated through both equity components and risk-free debt components. For such firms, the asset return correlation is higher than the equity return correlation. To see why this is the case, note that highly leveraged firms have substantial proportions of long-term debt that are sensitive to interest rates. For such firms, the ratios $w_i$ and $w_k$ are large, and $r_F^i$ and $r_F^k$ are highly correlated through their sensitivities to interest rates. As a result, the asset return correlations are higher than their corresponding equity return correlations.

Summarizing the above analysis, economic theory suggests that firms with low leverage ratio have approximately the same levels of asset return and equity return correlation. On the other hand, highly leveraged firms can have significantly higher asset return correlation compared to the equity return correlation between the firms. A recent empirical study conducted by KMV Corporation demonstrates that this is indeed the case.[2] By comparing the relationship between equity return correlation and asset return correlation, KMV concluded that for firms belonging to the financial and utilities sectors, realized asset return correlation is on average 55 percent higher than the corresponding equity return correlation. The reason for this difference is that firms in both these sectors are highly leveraged. Industrial firms, on the other hand, have less leverage. For such firms, equity return correlation can serve as a reasonable approximation to asset return correlation. Again the empirical study of KMV leads to a similar conclusion.

The approach outlined for deriving asset return correlation is based on the assumption that the equity of the firm is traded. This is not always the case. For example, Ford Motor Credit has significant outstanding debt, but only the parent company's equity is traded. In this case, it is not obvious how the asset return correlation between such a firm and other debt issuers can be estimated. Further difficulties can arise with regard to classifying a firm as belonging to the industrial, the utilities, or the financial sector. For instance, should Ford Motor Credit be grouped under the financial sector or the automotive sector? One can avoid addressing these questions directly if a factor-based model is used to estimate asset return correlation. This is taken up in the next section.

## Factor Models

The objective of any risk-modeling exercise is to be able to use the risk model to predict future risk scenarios. To achieve this objective, one needs to find good forward-looking estimates of the input variables that define the risk model. One important input variable for the risk model is the asset return correlation between obligor pairs. In general, the ability to find a good forward-looking estimate of asset or equity return correlation between obligor pairs is the most difficult part of any risk-modeling exercise. This is because historical data have the effect of magnifying firm-specific events that may not be relevant in the future and this can bias correlation estimates. Moreover, a company's business may change over time through acquisitions and mergers. In such cases, historical equity or asset returns of the company may not reflect the true risks inherent in the new business strategy pursued by the company.

One can avoid some of these pitfalls by using a factor model to estimate asset return correlation between different obligors. A factor model relates the systematic or nondiversifiable components of the firm's asset returns to various common factors such as macroeconomic variables or returns on prespecified portfolios, which drive the firm's asset value. Knowledge of the sensitivities to the common factors and the correlation between the common factors then allows an estimate of the asset return correlation between obligors. In the context of estimating asset return correlation, the factors that are commonly used include asset returns of various industry and country groups and macroeconomic factors. In case the business strategy of a company changes, one can immediately infer the impact of this change on the asset return correlation between the company and other firms. This is possible because a change in the business strategy results in a change in the industry or country factor sensitivities to common factors.

For most practical applications, one restricts the factor model to be linear. In its most generic form, such a linear factor model can be written as

$$r_i = \sum_{k=1}^{m} b_{ik} \times f_k + e_i \tag{6.32}$$

In this equation, $r_i$ is the asset return of the $i$th firm, the $f_k$ are the common factors, the $b_{ik}$ are the sensitivities to the common factors, and $e_i$ is the firm-specific or idiosyncratic return. The sensitivity term $b_{ik}$ has the interpretation that it represents the change in the return of the $i$th firm for a unit change in factor $k$. The firm-specific component of the return $e_i$ has the property that it is uncorrelated with each of the factors $f_k$. An additional key assumption of the linear factor model is that the residual return of one firm is uncorrelated with the residual return of any other firm. This has the implication that the only sources of correlation among asset returns of firms are those that arise from their exposures to the common factors and the covariance among the common factors.

Under those assumptions, it is easy to show that the covariance between the return of the $i$th firm and the return of the $k$th firm is

$$\text{cov}(r_i, r_k) = \sum_{k=1}^{m} \sum_{l=1}^{m} b_{ik} \times b_{jl} \times \text{cov}(f_k, f_l) + \text{cov}(e_i, e_k) \tag{6.33}$$

The last term in equation (6.33) is zero when $i \neq k$. Using the factor model, it is easy to derive the correlation between the asset returns of the $i$th firm and the $k$th firm. This is given by

$$\rho_{ik}^{\alpha} = \frac{\text{cov}(r_i, r_k)}{\sigma_i \times \sigma_k} \qquad (6.34)$$

where

$$\sigma_i = \sqrt{\text{cov}(r_i, r_i)} \qquad (6.35)$$

The foregoing factor model concept is exploited by both KMV Corporation and CreditMetrics to derive the asset return correlation between obligors. The important difference between the two is that KMV uses asset returns to construct the factor model, whereas CreditMetrics' implementation is based on equity returns.[3]

For purposes of illustration, I briefly describe the factor model implementation of KMV Corporation for estimating asset return correlation between obligors.[4] Assume a firm's asset return comprises a component that is firm specific and another that is nondiversifiable. The nondiversifiable component of asset return can be considered to comprise a component that is industry specific and another that is country specific. Further subclassification of the industry and country asset returns can be made to increase the granularity of the asset correlation estimates. The mechanics involved in such a decomposition of asset returns is given as follows:

$$\begin{bmatrix} \text{Firm} \\ \text{asset} \\ \text{return} \end{bmatrix} = \begin{bmatrix} \text{Composite} \\ \text{factor} \\ \text{return} \end{bmatrix} + \begin{bmatrix} \text{Firm-} \\ \text{specific} \\ \text{return} \end{bmatrix}$$

$$\begin{bmatrix} \text{Composite} \\ \text{factor} \\ \text{return} \end{bmatrix} = \begin{bmatrix} \text{Country} \\ \text{factor} \\ \text{return} \end{bmatrix} + \begin{bmatrix} \text{Industry} \\ \text{factor} \\ \text{return} \end{bmatrix}$$

$$\begin{bmatrix} \text{Country} \\ \text{factor} \\ \text{return} \end{bmatrix} = \begin{bmatrix} \text{Global} \\ \text{economic} \\ \text{effect} \end{bmatrix} + \begin{bmatrix} \text{Regional} \\ \text{factor} \\ \text{effect} \end{bmatrix} + \begin{bmatrix} \text{Sector} \\ \text{factor} \\ \text{effect} \end{bmatrix} + \begin{bmatrix} \text{Country-} \\ \text{specific} \\ \text{effect} \end{bmatrix}$$

$$\begin{bmatrix} \text{Industry} \\ \text{factor} \\ \text{return} \end{bmatrix} = \begin{bmatrix} \text{Global} \\ \text{economic} \\ \text{effect} \end{bmatrix} + \begin{bmatrix} \text{Regional} \\ \text{factor} \\ \text{effect} \end{bmatrix} + \begin{bmatrix} \text{Sector} \\ \text{factor} \\ \text{effect} \end{bmatrix} + \begin{bmatrix} \text{Industry-} \\ \text{specific} \\ \text{effect} \end{bmatrix}$$

On the basis of this decomposition, asset return correlations are computed from each firm's composite factor return. In KMV's global correlation model, industry and country indices are produced from a global database of market asset values estimated from the traded equity prices together with each firm's outstanding liabilities. These indices are then used to create a composite factor index for each firm depending on its country and industry classification.

## Approximate Asset Return Correlations

The foregoing method of computing asset return correlations between obligors using factor models is fairly complex. When managing large corporate bond portfolios, one may wish to use a data vendor rather than estimate asset return correlations in-house. However, when the costs involved are high relative to the size of the portfolio being managed, one may wish to find reasonable approximations to the asset return correlation. I outline a simple procedure that can be used to compute approximate asset return correlation between obligors.

Earlier in this chapter, I remarked that a study conducted by KMV Corporation suggested that average equity return correlations are 55 percent lower than average asset return correlations for financial institutions and utilities. For industrial corporates, on the other hand, equity return correlations and asset return correlations are approximately the same. The median equity correlations in the KMV study are reported to be 20 percent for financial institutions, 12 percent for utilities, and 18 percent for large industrial corporates. The median asset return correlations, on the other hand, are approximately 34 percent for financial institutions, 20 percent for utilities, and 18 percent for industrials. Making use of this information in conjunction with equation (6.30), it is possible to derive the approximate leverage ratio $w$ for the different industry groupings. Specifically, if one assumes that the leverage ratio is the same across each industry sector and that the outstanding debt has the same maturity for all firms, one can derive the following equation:

$$\rho_{ik}^{\alpha} = (1 - w_i)(1 - w_k) \, \rho_{ik}^{e} + w_i \, w_k \qquad (6.36)$$

In deriving equation (6.36), we have made the assumption that all returns in equation (6.30) are standardized normal variables. The variables in equation (6.36) are the following:

$w_i$ = Leverage ratio for the $i$th industry sector.
$\rho_{ik}^{e}$ = Equity return correlation between the $i$th and the $k$th industry sectors.
$\rho_{ik}^{\alpha}$ = Asset return correlation between the $i$th and the $k$th industry sectors.

Using equation (6.36) and the reported values for equity and asset return correlations, we obtain the following leverage ratios for the various industry sectors:

$$w_{\text{Financial}} = 55 \text{ percent}$$
$$w_{\text{Utility}} = 40 \text{ percent}$$
$$w_{\text{Industrial}} = 30 \text{ percent}$$

To compute approximate asset return correlations between the different industry sectors, assume that the median equity return correlation reported for firms in a given sector can be used. In particular, assume that the equity return correlation between the sectors takes the lower value of the equity return correlation for given sectors. For example, the equity return correlation between the financial sector and the utilities sector is taken to be 12 percent. Given the leverage ratios for each sector and the equity return correlations between the sectors, it is fairly straightforward to compute the asset return correlation using equation (6.36). The asset return correlations obtained from such an exercise for the three major industry sectors are given in Exhibit 6.2.

It is possible to increase the granularity of the these estimates when computing the asset return correlation between two obligors. For instance, obligors could be classified in terms of the actual industry they belong to within the sector. Under such a classification, one can assume that the asset return correlation between two obligors in the same industry group is higher than the value at the sector level. Furthermore, one could also incorporate the empirical evidence that the asset return correlations between lower rated firms are higher. Possible subclassifications within the sectors are as follows:

**Industrial Sector:**

- Consumer noncyclical (CNC)
- Consumer cyclical (CCL)
- Basic industries and chemicals (BAC)
- Communication and technology (COT)
- Energy (ENE)
- Transportation (TRA)

**EXHIBIT 6.2** Approximate Asset Return Correlations for Major Industry Sectors

|  | Financials (%) | Utilities (%) | Industrials (%) |
|---|---|---|---|
| Financials | 34 | 25 | 22 |
| Utilities | 25 | 20 | 17 |
| Industrials | 22 | 17 | 18 |

### Financial Sector:

- Banks (BNK)
- Brokerage (BRO)
- Financial services (FIN)
- Insurance and reits (INR)

### Utilities Sector:

- Utilities (UTL)

The total asset return correlation between two obligors can then be assumed to consist of three components:

$$\rho_{ik}^{\alpha} = \rho_{ik}^{\alpha}(\text{sector}) + \rho_{ik}^{\alpha}(\text{industry}) + \rho_{ik}^{\alpha}(\text{rating}) \qquad (6.37)$$

A suggested value for the component of the asset return correlation arising from the industry and rating categories is 10% of the sector component. For the component of the asset return correlation arising from ratings, one considers an increased contribution only if both firms are rated below A3. Incorporating these values into equation (6.37) results in the following equation, which captures the total asset return correlation between two obligors:

$$\rho_{ik}^{\alpha} = \rho_{ik,S}^{\alpha} + 0.10 \times \rho_{ik,S}^{\alpha} \,(\text{if industry}_i = \text{industry}_k)$$
$$+ 0.10 \times \rho_{ik,S}^{\alpha} \,(\text{if rating}_i \textit{ and } \text{rating}_k < \text{A3}) \qquad (6.38)$$

In this equation, $\rho_{ik,S}^{\alpha}$ is the component of the asset return correlation from the sector exposure, which is given in Exhibit 6.2.

## CREDIT RISK UNDER MIGRATION MODE

I have discussed how loss correlation between obligor pairs can be estimated under the default mode. I showed how loss correlation is related to default correlation under the default mode and further established the link between asset return correlation and default correlation. When portfolio credit risk is computed in the migration mode, the estimate of loss correlation between obligor pairs is different. Because loss correlation is difficult to estimate directly, asset return correlations are again used to derive the loss correlation between obligors under the migration mode. In this section, I indicate how loss correlation under the migration mode can be determined using asset return correlation information.

Earlier in this chapter I showed that to determine the loss correlation between two obligors, one has to compute the term $E(\tilde{\ell}_1 \tilde{\ell}_2)$. This quantity is the expected value of the joint distribution of credit loss of a two-obligor portfolio. Under the migration mode, any obligor can migrate to one of 18 states (including the current state). In this model, state 1 corresponds to an Aaa rating and state 18 corresponds to the default state. Clearly, the joint distribution for a two-obligor portfolio in this framework is a discrete distribution that can take 324 states ($18 \times 18$). If the probability of occupying each of these states and the credit loss in each state is known, the expected value of the joint credit loss can be computed.

Computing the probabilities associated with each of the states in the joint distribution requires modeling correlated rating migrations. Because asset returns of a firm influence rating migrations, the asset return correlation between obligors can be used to compute the probability of occupying different states in the joint distribution. Essentially the approach to estimating the probabilities requires extending Merton's framework to include rating migrations. The generalization involves including thresholds for rating migrations in addition to the default threshold to trigger credit events using the firm's asset returns. This makes it possible to build a link between the firm's underlying value and its credit rating to determine the joint probabilities of the two obligors in different states.

For purpose of illustration, consider an obligor that has a current credit rating of A1. Let $p_{A1,Aaa}$ denote the probability of transitioning to the credit rating Aaa. Under the assumption that the asset returns of the obligor is normally distributed, the credit event that signals the obligor rating migration from A1 to Aaa occurs when the standardized asset returns of the obligor exceeds the threshold $z_{A1,Aaa}$. This threshold can be determined by solving the following integral equation:

$$P_{A1,Aaa} = \frac{1}{\sqrt{2\pi}} \int_{z_{A1,Aaa}}^{\infty} \exp(-0.5x^2)dx \qquad (6.39)$$

A rating transition of this obligor from A1 to Aa1 occurs if the asset return falls between the thresholds $z_{A1,Aaa}$ and $z_{A1,Aa1}$. The threshold $z_{A1,Aa1}$ can be determined by solving the following integral equation:

$$P_{A1,Aa1} = \frac{1}{\sqrt{2\pi}} \int_{z_{A1,Aa1}}^{z_{A1,Aaa}} \exp(-0.5x^2)dx \qquad (6.40)$$

One can extend this sequential rule to determine the thresholds for migrating to other rating grades. Note that these $z$-thresholds are a function of the current credit rating of the obligor. Exhibit 6.3 shows the $z$-thresholds computed using the normalized rating transition probabilities given in Exhibit 5.5 in Chapter 5.

**EXHIBIT 6.3**  z-Thresholds for Various Rating Grades

| | Aaa | Aa1 | Aa2 | Aa3 | A1 | A2 | A3 | Baa1 | Baa2 | Baa3 | Ba1 | Ba2 | Ba3 | B1 | B2 | B3 | Caa | Def |
|---|---|---|---|---|---|---|---|---|---|---|---|---|---|---|---|---|---|---|
| Aaa | -1.229 | -1.666 | -2.109 | -2.239 | -2.567 | -2.849 | -3.280 | -3.280 | -3.280 | -3.280 | -3.719 | -3.719 | -3.719 | -3.719 | -3.719 | -3.719 | -3.719 | -1000 |
| Aa1 | 1.936 | -0.910 | -1.284 | -1.867 | -2.464 | -2.694 | -2.746 | -3.052 | -3.052 | -3.052 | -3.540 | -3.540 | -3.540 | -3.540 | -3.540 | -3.540 | -3.540 | -1000 |
| Aa2 | 2.439 | 1.776 | -1.023 | -1.515 | -1.984 | -2.348 | -2.712 | -2.935 | -2.935 | -2.935 | -2.935 | -2.935 | -3.051 | -3.432 | -3.432 | -3.432 | -3.432 | -1000 |
| Aa3 | 3.143 | 2.446 | 1.724 | -1.067 | -1.646 | -2.119 | -2.403 | -2.534 | -2.703 | -2.918 | -2.918 | -3.002 | -3.353 | -3.353 | -3.353 | -3.353 | -3.353 | -1000 |
| A1 | 3.421 | 2.977 | 2.423 | 1.512 | -1.145 | -1.634 | -2.031 | -2.227 | -2.320 | -2.373 | -2.571 | -2.810 | -2.886 | -3.193 | -3.239 | -3.239 | -3.239 | -1000 |
| A2 | 3.279 | 3.049 | 2.638 | 2.251 | 1.492 | -1.152 | -1.646 | -2.054 | -2.269 | -2.429 | -2.600 | -2.686 | -2.811 | -2.855 | -2.983 | -3.058 | -3.156 | -1000 |
| A3 | 3.277 | 2.953 | 2.863 | 2.611 | 2.052 | 1.244 | -1.084 | -1.484 | -1.872 | -2.154 | -2.329 | -2.412 | -2.535 | -2.854 | -2.942 | -3.060 | -3.090 | -1000 |
| Baa1 | 3.142 | 3.076 | 2.819 | 2.628 | 2.489 | 1.814 | 1.199 | -1.089 | -1.548 | -1.914 | -2.122 | -2.254 | -2.390 | -2.787 | -2.925 | -2.966 | -3.011 | -1000 |
| Baa2 | 3.179 | 2.913 | 2.742 | 2.586 | 2.476 | 2.149 | 1.603 | 1.140 | -1.179 | -1.693 | -1.919 | -2.014 | -2.166 | -2.323 | -2.552 | -2.792 | -2.834 | -1000 |
| Baa3 | 3.415 | 3.415 | 3.221 | 2.993 | 2.717 | 2.351 | 2.138 | 1.640 | 1.038 | -1.092 | -1.480 | -1.729 | -2.019 | -2.220 | -2.329 | -2.495 | -2.605 | -1000 |
| Ba1 | 3.131 | 3.131 | 3.131 | 3.036 | 2.688 | 2.583 | 2.251 | 2.047 | 1.623 | 1.099 | -1.076 | -1.335 | -1.658 | -1.793 | -2.001 | -2.316 | -2.473 | -1000 |
| Ba2 | 1000 | 1000 | 1000 | 3.406 | 3.167 | 2.818 | 2.665 | 2.423 | 2.160 | 1.743 | 1.115 | -0.978 | -1.305 | -1.422 | -1.789 | -2.141 | -2.315 | -1000 |
| Ba3 | 1000 | 3.518 | 3.518 | 3.518 | 3.215 | 2.822 | 2.633 | 2.507 | 2.370 | 2.135 | 1.687 | 1.278 | -0.932 | -1.159 | -1.497 | -1.827 | -1.967 | -1000 |
| B1 | 3.522 | 3.522 | 3.522 | 3.522 | 3.136 | 2.908 | 2.704 | 2.638 | 2.471 | 2.328 | 2.185 | 1.735 | 1.268 | -0.906 | -1.142 | -1.566 | -1.754 | -1000 |
| B2 | 1000 | 1000 | 3.229 | 3.185 | 2.900 | 2.900 | 2.796 | 2.624 | 2.537 | 2.435 | 2.310 | 1.922 | 1.573 | 1.188 | -0.678 | -1.117 | -1.318 | -1000 |
| B3 | 1000 | 1000 | 3.212 | 3.212 | 3.129 | 3.007 | 2.882 | 2.728 | 2.612 | 2.473 | 2.379 | 2.241 | 1.954 | 1.480 | 1.246 | -0.798 | -1.093 | -1000 |
| Caa | 1000 | 1000 | 1000 | 1000 | 1000 | 1000 | 1000 | 1000 | 2.552 | 2.301 | 2.100 | 2.100 | 1.838 | 1.610 | 1.496 | 1.285 | -0.536 | -1000 |
| Def | 1000 | 1000 | 1000 | 1000 | 1000 | 1000 | 1000 | 1000 | 1000 | 1000 | 1000 | 1000 | 1000 | 1000 | 1000 | 1000 | 1000 | -1000 |

## Computing Joint Migration Probabilities

Having determined the various thresholds for credit migration of any obligor, one can compute the joint migration probabilities of two obligors. Computing these joint migration probabilities, however, requires knowledge of the joint probability distribution of the asset returns of the two obligors and the correlation between them. Standard practice is to model the joint distribution to be bivariate normal. Once again, for purpose of illustration, let the current credit rating of obligor 1 be A1 and the credit rating of obligor 2 be A3. Let $\rho$ denote the asset return correlation between the two obligors. The joint probability that obligor 1 migrates to a B2 rating and obligor 2 migrates to an Aaa rating is given by the following integral equation:

$$h_{B2,Aaa} = \frac{1}{2\pi\sqrt{1-\rho^2}} \int_{z_{A1,B2}}^{z_{A1,B1}} \int_{z_{A3,Aaa}}^{\infty} \exp\left(-\frac{x^2 - 2\rho xy + y^2}{2(1-\rho^2)}\right) dx\, dy \quad (6.41)$$

In equation (6.41), $z_{A1,B1}$ is the threshold corresponding to the row A1 and column B1 in Exhibit 6.3. The other $z$-thresholds can be similarly determined from Exhibit 6.3. Following this approach, it is fairly straightforward to compute the joint migration probabilities $h_{ik}$ to any of 324 discrete states for a two-obligor portfolio. The probability $h_{64}$, for instance, denotes the joint probability that after 1 year obligor 1 has an A2 rating and obligor 2 has an Aa3 rating.

## Computing Joint Credit Loss

To compute the expected value of the joint loss distribution, one needs to determine the credit loss associated with each state of the discrete joint probability distribution. Assume that the initial credit rating of obligor 1 is $u$ and that of obligor 2 is $v$. After 1 year, let the credit ratings of these two obligors be $i$ and $k$, respectively. The joint credit loss as a result of the rating migration of obligor 1 to state $i$ and that of obligor 2 to state $k$ is given by

$$g_{ik} = NE_1 \times NE_2 \times \Delta P_{ui,1} \times \Delta P_{vk,2} \quad (6.42)$$

In equation (6.42), $\Delta P_{ui,1}$ is the credit loss when obligor 1 migrates from grade $u$ to grade $i$. This can be determined using equation (5.32) given in Chapter 5. One can similarly determine the credit loss resulting from obligor 2 migrating from grade $v$ to grade $k$, which is given by $\Delta P_{vk,2}$. If the obligor migrates to the default state, then the corresponding credit loss is equal to loss on default LD. I make the assumption that the loss on default of each obligor is independent of that of the other so that the expected value of joint credit loss when both obligors default is simply the product of the individual losses at default of the obligors.

## Portfolio Credit Risk

Once the joint probabilities of being in each of the states and the corresponding credit losses have been determined, it is fairly simple to compute the expected value of the joint distribution of credit loss. This is given by

$$E(\tilde{\ell}_1 \tilde{\ell}_2) = \sum_{i=1}^{18} \sum_{k=1}^{18} h_{ik} \times g_{ik} \qquad (6.43)$$

One now has all the quantities that are required to compute the loss correlation between the two obligors under the migration mode using equation (6.5). Once the loss correlation between the obligors is computed, the unexpected loss for a two-bond portfolio can be computed using equation (6.7). For a general portfolio having $n$ bonds, the loss correlation under the migration mode can be computed following the foregoing approach for any obligor pair. Letting $EL_i$ and $UL_i$ denote, respectively, the expected loss and unexpected loss of the $i$th bond in the portfolio under the migration mode, one can compute the expected and unexpected loss of the portfolio using equations (6.8) and (6.9).

## Migration Mode: Two-Bond Portfolio

I now consider the two-bond portfolio given in Exhibit 6.1 and compute the portfolio credit risk under the migration mode. As a first step, one needs to compute the joint rating migration probabilities in each of the 324 states and the corresponding joint credit losses to determine the loss correlation. The joint rating migration probabilities and joint credit loss in each of the 324 states of the discrete probability distribution for the two-bond portfolio are given in Exhibits 6.4 and 6.5, respectively.

The various credit risk parameters of interest for this two-bond portfolio are as follows:

- The loss correlation $\rho_{ik}^{\ell}$ under the migration mode is 0.06334.
- The expected portfolio loss $EL_P$ under the migration mode is \$4,740.
- The unexpected portfolio loss $UL_P$ under the migration mode = \$31,610.

*(text continued on page 118)*

**EXHIBIT 6.4** Joint Rating Migration Probabilities for 30% Asset Return Correlation

| | Aaa | Aa1 | Aa2 | Aa3 | A1 | A2 | A3 | Baa1 | Baa2 | Baa3 | Ba1 | Ba2 | Ba3 | B1 | B2 | B3 | Caa-C | Def |
|---|---|---|---|---|---|---|---|---|---|---|---|---|---|---|---|---|---|---|
| Aaa | 0.0005 | 0.0007 | 0.0003 | 0.0012 | 0.0051 | 0.0143 | 0.0293 | 0.0004 | 0.0001 | 0.0000 | 0.0000 | 0.0000 | 0.0000 | 0.0000 | 0.0000 | 0.0000 | 0.0000 | 0.0000 |
| Aa1 | 0.0005 | 0.0007 | 0.0003 | 0.0011 | 0.0052 | 0.0159 | 0.0380 | 0.0007 | 0.0002 | 0.0001 | 0.0000 | 0.0000 | 0.0000 | 0.0000 | 0.0000 | 0.0000 | 0.0000 | 0.0000 |
| Aa2 | 0.0016 | 0.0025 | 0.0011 | 0.0045 | 0.0213 | 0.0708 | 0.1939 | 0.0044 | 0.0016 | 0.0004 | 0.0001 | 0.0000 | 0.0000 | 0.0000 | 0.0000 | 0.0000 | 0.0000 | 0.0000 |
| Aa3 | 0.0030 | 0.0048 | 0.0022 | 0.0092 | 0.0466 | 0.1693 | 0.5438 | 0.0150 | 0.0057 | 0.0016 | 0.0005 | 0.0001 | 0.0002 | 0.0002 | 0.0000 | 0.0000 | 0.0000 | 0.0000 |
| A1 | 0.0115 | 0.0204 | 0.0096 | 0.0418 | 0.2304 | 0.9631 | 4.0379 | 0.1546 | 0.0635 | 0.0191 | 0.0060 | 0.0019 | 0.0020 | 0.0026 | 0.0003 | 0.0003 | 0.0001 | 0.0004 |
| A2 | 0.0348 | 0.0743 | 0.0381 | 0.1790 | 1.2059 | 7.0429 | 61.9039 | 5.3813 | 2.8154 | 1.0554 | 0.3877 | 0.1333 | 0.1518 | 0.2200 | 0.0322 | 0.0313 | 0.0062 | 0.0555 |
| A3 | 0.0004 | 0.0012 | 0.0007 | 0.0035 | 0.0312 | 0.2734 | 5.3686 | 0.8220 | 0.5054 | 0.2172 | 0.0874 | 0.0316 | 0.0374 | 0.0584 | 0.0093 | 0.0094 | 0.0019 | 0.0188 |
| Baa1 | 0.0001 | 0.0003 | 0.0002 | 0.0009 | 0.0083 | 0.0809 | 2.0409 | 0.3700 | 0.2410 | 0.1089 | 0.0454 | 0.0168 | 0.0201 | 0.0324 | 0.0053 | 0.0054 | 0.0011 | 0.0116 |
| Baa2 | 0.0000 | 0.0001 | 0.0000 | 0.0002 | 0.0017 | 0.0179 | 0.5456 | 0.1113 | 0.0756 | 0.0354 | 0.0151 | 0.0057 | 0.0069 | 0.0113 | 0.0019 | 0.0020 | 0.0004 | 0.0044 |
| Baa3 | 0.0000 | 0.0000 | 0.0000 | 0.0001 | 0.0007 | 0.0076 | 0.2578 | 0.0562 | 0.0391 | 0.0187 | 0.0081 | 0.0031 | 0.0037 | 0.0062 | 0.0011 | 0.0011 | 0.0002 | 0.0025 |
| Ba1 | 0.0000 | 0.0000 | 0.0000 | 0.0000 | 0.0004 | 0.0048 | 0.1797 | 0.0415 | 0.0295 | 0.0144 | 0.0063 | 0.0024 | 0.0029 | 0.0050 | 0.0009 | 0.0009 | 0.0002 | 0.0021 |
| Ba2 | 0.0000 | 0.0000 | 0.0000 | 0.0000 | 0.0001 | 0.0016 | 0.0631 | 0.0152 | 0.0110 | 0.0055 | 0.0024 | 0.0009 | 0.0011 | 0.0019 | 0.0003 | 0.0004 | 0.0001 | 0.0008 |
| Ba3 | 0.0000 | 0.0000 | 0.0000 | 0.0000 | 0.0001 | 0.0016 | 0.0679 | 0.0170 | 0.0124 | 0.0062 | 0.0028 | 0.0011 | 0.0013 | 0.0023 | 0.0004 | 0.0004 | 0.0001 | 0.0010 |
| B1 | 0.0000 | 0.0000 | 0.0000 | 0.0000 | 0.0000 | 0.0004 | 0.0185 | 0.0048 | 0.0035 | 0.0018 | 0.0008 | 0.0003 | 0.0004 | 0.0007 | 0.0001 | 0.0001 | 0.0000 | 0.0003 |
| B2 | 0.0000 | 0.0000 | 0.0000 | 0.0000 | 0.0001 | 0.0009 | 0.0416 | 0.0110 | 0.0082 | 0.0042 | 0.0019 | 0.0007 | 0.0009 | 0.0016 | 0.0003 | 0.0003 | 0.0001 | 0.0007 |
| B3 | 0.0000 | 0.0000 | 0.0000 | 0.0000 | 0.0000 | 0.0003 | 0.0176 | 0.0048 | 0.0037 | 0.0019 | 0.0009 | 0.0003 | 0.0004 | 0.0007 | 0.0001 | 0.0001 | 0.0000 | 0.0003 |
| Caa-C | 0.0000 | 0.0000 | 0.0000 | 0.0000 | 0.0000 | 0.0003 | 0.0174 | 0.0049 | 0.0037 | 0.0020 | 0.0009 | 0.0003 | 0.0004 | 0.0008 | 0.0001 | 0.0001 | 0.0000 | 0.0004 |
| Def | 0.0000 | 0.0000 | 0.0000 | 0.0000 | 0.0000 | 0.0007 | 0.0411 | 0.0128 | 0.0102 | 0.0055 | 0.0026 | 0.0010 | 0.0013 | 0.0024 | 0.0004 | 0.0005 | 0.0001 | 0.0013 |

**EXHIBIT 6.5**  Joint Credit Loss Distribution in Million USD

| | Aaa | Aa1 | Aa2 | Aa3 | A1 | A2 | A3 | Baa1 | Baa2 | Baa3 | Ba1 | Ba2 | Ba3 | B1 | B2 | B3 | Caa–C | Def |
|---|---|---|---|---|---|---|---|---|---|---|---|---|---|---|---|---|---|---|
| Aaa | 0.0011 | 0.0009 | 0.0007 | 0.0006 | 0.0004 | 0.0002 | 0.0000 | −0.0003 | −0.0006 | −0.0009 | −0.0015 | −0.0020 | −0.0026 | −0.0036 | −0.0046 | −0.0056 | −0.0068 | −0.0167 |
| Aa1 | 0.0009 | 0.0007 | 0.0006 | 0.0004 | 0.0003 | 0.0002 | 0.0000 | −0.0002 | −0.0005 | −0.0007 | −0.0012 | −0.0016 | −0.0021 | −0.0029 | −0.0037 | −0.0044 | −0.0055 | −0.0133 |
| Aa2 | 0.0007 | 0.0006 | 0.0004 | 0.0003 | 0.0002 | 0.0001 | 0.0000 | −0.0002 | −0.0004 | −0.0005 | −0.0009 | −0.0012 | −0.0015 | −0.0022 | −0.0028 | −0.0033 | −0.0041 | −0.0100 |
| Aa3 | 0.0004 | 0.0004 | 0.0003 | 0.0002 | 0.0002 | 0.0001 | 0.0000 | −0.0001 | −0.0002 | −0.0004 | −0.0006 | −0.0008 | −0.0010 | −0.0014 | −0.0018 | −0.0022 | −0.0027 | −0.0066 |
| A1 | 0.0002 | 0.0002 | 0.0002 | 0.0001 | 0.0001 | 0.0000 | 0.0000 | −0.0001 | −0.0001 | −0.0002 | −0.0003 | −0.0004 | −0.0005 | −0.0007 | −0.0009 | −0.0011 | −0.0014 | −0.0033 |
| A2 | 0.0000 | 0.0000 | 0.0000 | 0.0000 | 0.0000 | 0.0000 | 0.0000 | 0.0000 | 0.0000 | 0.0000 | 0.0000 | 0.0000 | 0.0000 | 0.0000 | 0.0000 | 0.0000 | 0.0000 | 0.0000 |
| A3 | −0.0002 | −0.0002 | −0.0001 | −0.0001 | −0.0001 | −0.0001 | 0.0000 | 0.0001 | 0.0001 | 0.0002 | 0.0003 | 0.0004 | 0.0005 | 0.0007 | 0.0009 | 0.0011 | 0.0013 | 0.0033 |
| Baa1 | −0.0006 | −0.0005 | −0.0004 | −0.0003 | −0.0002 | −0.0001 | 0.0000 | 0.0002 | 0.0003 | 0.0005 | 0.0008 | 0.0011 | 0.0013 | 0.0019 | 0.0024 | 0.0029 | 0.0036 | 0.0087 |
| Baa2 | −0.0009 | −0.0008 | −0.0006 | −0.0005 | −0.0003 | −0.0002 | 0.0000 | 0.0003 | 0.0005 | 0.0008 | 0.0012 | 0.0017 | 0.0022 | 0.0031 | 0.0039 | 0.0047 | 0.0057 | 0.0140 |
| Baa3 | −0.0013 | −0.0011 | −0.0009 | −0.0006 | −0.0004 | −0.0002 | 0.0000 | 0.0004 | 0.0007 | 0.0010 | 0.0017 | 0.0024 | 0.0030 | 0.0042 | 0.0053 | 0.0064 | 0.0079 | 0.0193 |
| Ba1 | −0.0020 | −0.0017 | −0.0013 | −0.0010 | −0.0007 | −0.0003 | 0.0000 | 0.0005 | 0.0011 | 0.0016 | 0.0026 | 0.0036 | 0.0046 | 0.0065 | 0.0082 | 0.0099 | 0.0121 | 0.0297 |
| Ba2 | −0.0027 | −0.0022 | −0.0018 | −0.0013 | −0.0009 | −0.0004 | 0.0000 | 0.0007 | 0.0014 | 0.0021 | 0.0035 | 0.0048 | 0.0062 | 0.0087 | 0.0110 | 0.0132 | 0.0163 | 0.0398 |
| Ba3 | −0.0033 | −0.0028 | −0.0022 | −0.0016 | −0.0011 | −0.0005 | 0.0000 | 0.0009 | 0.0018 | 0.0027 | 0.0044 | 0.0061 | 0.0077 | 0.0108 | 0.0137 | 0.0165 | 0.0203 | 0.0497 |
| B1 | −0.0046 | −0.0038 | −0.0030 | −0.0023 | −0.0015 | −0.0008 | 0.0000 | 0.0012 | 0.0025 | 0.0037 | 0.0061 | 0.0084 | 0.0106 | 0.0149 | 0.0190 | 0.0228 | 0.0281 | 0.0687 |
| B2 | −0.0058 | −0.0048 | −0.0038 | −0.0029 | −0.0019 | −0.0010 | 0.0000 | 0.0016 | 0.0031 | 0.0046 | 0.0076 | 0.0106 | 0.0134 | 0.0189 | 0.0240 | 0.0288 | 0.0355 | 0.0867 |
| B3 | −0.0069 | −0.0058 | −0.0046 | −0.0034 | −0.0023 | −0.0011 | 0.0000 | 0.0019 | 0.0037 | 0.0056 | 0.0091 | 0.0126 | 0.0160 | 0.0226 | 0.0287 | 0.0345 | 0.0425 | 0.1038 |
| Caa–C | −0.0085 | −0.0071 | −0.0056 | −0.0042 | −0.0028 | −0.0014 | 0.0000 | 0.0023 | 0.0046 | 0.0068 | 0.0112 | 0.0155 | 0.0197 | 0.0277 | 0.0353 | 0.0424 | 0.0522 | 0.1275 |
| Def | −0.0208 | −0.0173 | −0.0138 | −0.0103 | −0.0068 | −0.0034 | 0.0000 | 0.0056 | 0.0112 | 0.0166 | 0.0274 | 0.0378 | 0.0480 | 0.0676 | 0.0860 | 0.1033 | 0.1272 | 0.3108 |

Note that under the migration mode, both expected and unexpected portfolio losses of the two-bond portfolio are higher than under the default mode using historical default probabilities. The loss correlation under the migration mode is also significantly higher than under the default mode.

## NUMERICAL EXAMPLE

I now consider a more general portfolio to illustrate the portfolio credit risk concepts covered in this chapter. The specific portfolio comprises 23 bonds with issuer credit ratings varying from A1 to Ba3. It is assumed that the nominal exposure is $20 million in each bond. The traded prices for these bonds were captured as of 24 April 2002. The details of individual bonds held in the portfolio are given in Exhibit 6.6. All bonds in the portfolio are noncallable and are treated as senior unsecured debt. The recovery rates for the bonds are assumed to be 47 percent of face value and the standard deviation of recovery rates to be 25 percent.

To compute the portfolio credit loss, one requires values for asset return correlation between the issuers in the portfolio. I consider two cases: one where the asset return correlation is assumed to be 30 percent between every issuer pair and the other where the asset return correlation is computed on the basis of equation (6.38). The asset return correlation between the issuers for this portfolio is given in Exhibit 6.7.

In the context of bond portfolio management, it is customary to report various risk quantities relative to the current mark-to-market value of the portfolio. In accordance with this practice, I introduce two additional risk terms, percentage portfolio expected loss ($\%\mathrm{EL}_P$) and percentage portfolio unexpected loss ($\%\mathrm{UL}_P$). If $M_P$ denotes the mark-to-market value of the portfolio, the two additional risk terms are

$$\%\mathrm{EL}_P = \frac{\mathrm{EL}_P}{M_P} \tag{6.44}$$

and

$$\%\mathrm{UL}_P = \frac{\mathrm{UL}_P}{M_P} \tag{6.45}$$

The portfolio credit risk quantities of interest under the default mode are given in Exhibits 6.8 and 6.9. Exhibits 6.10 gives the portfolio credit risk quantities of interest under the migration mode.

**EXHIBIT 6.6**  Composition of Bond Portfolio as of 24 April 2002

| S. No. | Issuer | Ticker | Industry | Issuer Rating | Nominal USD mn | Dirty Price | Maturity | Coupon (%) | KMV's EDF (bp) |
|---|---|---|---|---|---|---|---|---|---|
| 1 | Health Care Reit | HCN | INR | Ba1 | 20.0 | 99.91 | 15 Aug 07 | 7.500 | 3 |
| 2 | Hilton Hotels | HLT | CCL | Ba1 | 20.0 | 104.13 | 15 May 08 | 7.625 | 29 |
| 3 | Apple Computer | AAPL | COT | Ba2 | 20.0 | 100.97 | 15 Feb 04 | 6.500 | 144 |
| 4 | Delta Air Lines | DAL | TRA | Ba3 | 20.0 | 99.42 | 15 Dec 09 | 7.900 | 147 |
| 5 | Alcoa Inc | AA | BAC | A1 | 20.0 | 105.24 | 01 Jun 06 | 5.875 | 21 |
| 6 | ABN Amro Bank | AAB | BNK | Aa3 | 20.0 | 109.18 | 31 May 05 | 7.250 | 10 |
| 7 | Abbey Natl Plc | ABBEY | BNK | Aa3 | 20.0 | 108.43 | 17 Nov 05 | 6.690 | 33 |
| 8 | Alliance Capital | AC | FIN | A2 | 20.0 | 100.29 | 15 Aug 06 | 5.625 | 158 |
| 9 | Aegon Nv | AGN | INR | A1 | 20.0 | 110.42 | 15 Aug 06 | 8.000 | 10 |
| 10 | Abbott Labs | ABT | CNC | Aa3 | 20.0 | 104.54 | 01 Jul 06 | 5.625 | 7 |
| 11 | Caterpillar Inc | CAT | BAC | A2 | 20.0 | 105.98 | 01 May 06 | 5.950 | 24 |
| 12 | Coca Cola Enter | CCE | CNC | A2 | 20.0 | 102.04 | 15 Aug 06 | 5.375 | 88 |
| 13 | Countrywide Home | CCR | FIN | A3 | 20.0 | 101.25 | 01 Aug 06 | 5.500 | 149 |
| 14 | Colgate-Palm Co | CL | CNC | Aa3 | 20.0 | 101.43 | 29 Apr 05 | 3.980 | 4 |
| 15 | Hershey Foods Co | HSY | CNC | A1 | 20.0 | 105.61 | 01 Oct 05 | 6.700 | 2 |
| 16 | IBM Corp | IBM | COT | A1 | 20.0 | 99.66 | 01 Oct 06 | 4.875 | 26 |
| 17 | Johnson Controls | JCI | COT | A3 | 20.0 | 100.30 | 15 Nov 06 | 5.000 | 24 |
| 18 | JP Morgan Chase | JPM | BNK | Aa3 | 20.0 | 108.62 | 01 Jun 05 | 7.000 | 42 |
| 19 | Bank One NA ILL | ONE | BNK | Aa3 | 20.0 | 101.50 | 26 Mar 07 | 5.500 | 19 |
| 20 | Oracle Corp | ORCL | COT | A3 | 20.0 | 105.33 | 15 Feb 07 | 6.910 | 58 |
| 21 | Pub Svc EL & Gas | PEG | UTL | A3 | 20.0 | 104.94 | 01 Mar 06 | 6.750 | 39 |
| 22 | Procter & Gamble | PG | CNC | Aa3 | 20.0 | 101.76 | 30 Apr 05 | 4.000 | 4 |
| 23 | PNC Bank NA | PNC | BNK | A3 | 20.0 | 102.26 | 01 Aug 06 | 5.750 | 24 |

**EXHIBIT 6.7**  Indicative Asset Return Correlation Matrix for Example Portfolio

| Ticker | HCN | HLT | AAPL | DAL | AA | AAB | ANL | AC | AGN | ABT | CAT | CCE | CCR | CL | HSY | IBM | JCI | JPM | ONE | ORCL | PEG | PG | PNC |
|---|---|---|---|---|---|---|---|---|---|---|---|---|---|---|---|---|---|---|---|---|---|---|---|
| HCN | 1.000 | 0.242 | 0.242 | 0.242 | 0.220 | 0.340 | 0.340 | 0.340 | 0.374 | 0.220 | 0.220 | 0.220 | 0.374 | 0.220 | 0.220 | 0.220 | 0.242 | 0.340 | 0.340 | 0.242 | 0.275 | 0.220 | 0.374 |
| HLT | 0.242 | 1.000 | 0.198 | 0.198 | 0.180 | 0.220 | 0.220 | 0.220 | 0.220 | 0.180 | 0.180 | 0.180 | 0.242 | 0.180 | 0.180 | 0.180 | 0.198 | 0.220 | 0.220 | 0.198 | 0.187 | 0.180 | 0.242 |
| AAPL | 0.242 | 0.198 | 1.000 | 0.198 | 0.180 | 0.220 | 0.220 | 0.220 | 0.220 | 0.180 | 0.180 | 0.180 | 0.242 | 0.180 | 0.198 | 0.180 | 0.216 | 0.220 | 0.220 | 0.216 | 0.187 | 0.180 | 0.242 |
| DAL | 0.242 | 0.198 | 0.198 | 1.000 | 0.180 | 0.220 | 0.220 | 0.220 | 0.220 | 0.180 | 0.180 | 0.180 | 0.242 | 0.180 | 0.180 | 0.180 | 0.198 | 0.220 | 0.220 | 0.198 | 0.187 | 0.180 | 0.242 |
| AA | 0.220 | 0.180 | 0.180 | 0.180 | 1.000 | 0.220 | 0.374 | 0.340 | 0.220 | 0.180 | 0.198 | 0.180 | 0.220 | 0.180 | 0.180 | 0.180 | 0.180 | 0.220 | 0.220 | 0.180 | 0.170 | 0.180 | 0.220 |
| AAB | 0.340 | 0.220 | 0.220 | 0.220 | 0.220 | 1.000 | 0.374 | 0.340 | 0.340 | 0.220 | 0.220 | 0.220 | 0.340 | 0.220 | 0.220 | 0.220 | 0.220 | 0.374 | 0.374 | 0.220 | 0.250 | 0.220 | 0.374 |
| ABBEY | 0.340 | 0.220 | 0.220 | 0.220 | 0.374 | 0.374 | 1.000 | 0.340 | 0.340 | 0.220 | 0.220 | 0.220 | 0.340 | 0.220 | 0.220 | 0.220 | 0.220 | 0.374 | 0.374 | 0.220 | 0.250 | 0.220 | 0.374 |
| AC | 0.340 | 0.220 | 0.220 | 0.220 | 0.340 | 0.340 | 0.340 | 1.000 | 0.340 | 0.220 | 0.220 | 0.220 | 0.374 | 0.220 | 0.220 | 0.220 | 0.220 | 0.340 | 0.340 | 0.220 | 0.250 | 0.220 | 0.340 |
| AGN | 0.374 | 0.220 | 0.220 | 0.220 | 0.220 | 0.340 | 0.340 | 0.340 | 1.000 | 0.220 | 0.220 | 0.220 | 0.340 | 0.220 | 0.220 | 0.220 | 0.220 | 0.340 | 0.340 | 0.220 | 0.250 | 0.220 | 0.340 |
| ABT | 0.220 | 0.180 | 0.180 | 0.180 | 0.180 | 0.220 | 0.220 | 0.220 | 0.220 | 1.000 | 0.180 | 0.198 | 0.220 | 0.198 | 0.198 | 0.180 | 0.180 | 0.220 | 0.220 | 0.180 | 0.170 | 0.198 | 0.220 |
| CAT | 0.220 | 0.180 | 0.180 | 0.180 | 0.198 | 0.220 | 0.220 | 0.220 | 0.220 | 0.180 | 1.000 | 0.180 | 0.220 | 0.180 | 0.180 | 0.180 | 0.180 | 0.220 | 0.220 | 0.180 | 0.170 | 0.180 | 0.220 |
| CCE | 0.220 | 0.180 | 0.180 | 0.180 | 0.180 | 0.220 | 0.220 | 0.220 | 0.220 | 0.198 | 0.180 | 1.000 | 0.220 | 0.198 | 0.198 | 0.180 | 0.180 | 0.220 | 0.220 | 0.180 | 0.170 | 0.198 | 0.220 |
| CCR | 0.374 | 0.242 | 0.242 | 0.242 | 0.220 | 0.340 | 0.340 | 0.374 | 0.340 | 0.220 | 0.220 | 0.220 | 1.000 | 0.220 | 0.220 | 0.220 | 0.242 | 0.340 | 0.340 | 0.242 | 0.275 | 0.220 | 0.374 |
| CL | 0.220 | 0.180 | 0.180 | 0.180 | 0.180 | 0.220 | 0.220 | 0.220 | 0.220 | 0.198 | 0.180 | 0.198 | 0.220 | 1.000 | 0.198 | 0.180 | 0.180 | 0.220 | 0.220 | 0.180 | 0.170 | 0.198 | 0.220 |
| HSY | 0.220 | 0.180 | 0.198 | 0.180 | 0.180 | 0.220 | 0.220 | 0.220 | 0.220 | 0.198 | 0.180 | 0.198 | 0.220 | 0.198 | 1.000 | 0.180 | 0.180 | 0.220 | 0.220 | 0.180 | 0.170 | 0.198 | 0.220 |
| IBM | 0.220 | 0.180 | 0.180 | 0.180 | 0.180 | 0.220 | 0.220 | 0.220 | 0.220 | 0.180 | 0.180 | 0.180 | 0.220 | 0.180 | 0.180 | 1.000 | 0.198 | 0.220 | 0.220 | 0.198 | 0.170 | 0.180 | 0.220 |
| JCI | 0.242 | 0.198 | 0.216 | 0.198 | 0.180 | 0.220 | 0.220 | 0.220 | 0.220 | 0.180 | 0.180 | 0.180 | 0.242 | 0.180 | 0.180 | 0.198 | 1.000 | 0.220 | 0.220 | 0.216 | 0.187 | 0.180 | 0.242 |
| JPM | 0.340 | 0.220 | 0.220 | 0.220 | 0.220 | 0.374 | 0.374 | 0.340 | 0.340 | 0.220 | 0.220 | 0.220 | 0.340 | 0.220 | 0.220 | 0.220 | 0.220 | 1.000 | 0.374 | 0.220 | 0.250 | 0.220 | 0.374 |
| ONE | 0.340 | 0.220 | 0.220 | 0.220 | 0.220 | 0.374 | 0.374 | 0.340 | 0.340 | 0.220 | 0.220 | 0.220 | 0.340 | 0.220 | 0.220 | 0.220 | 0.220 | 0.374 | 1.000 | 0.220 | 0.250 | 0.220 | 0.374 |
| ORCL | 0.242 | 0.198 | 0.216 | 0.198 | 0.180 | 0.220 | 0.220 | 0.220 | 0.220 | 0.180 | 0.180 | 0.180 | 0.242 | 0.180 | 0.180 | 0.198 | 0.216 | 0.220 | 0.220 | 1.000 | 0.187 | 0.180 | 0.242 |
| PEG | 0.275 | 0.187 | 0.187 | 0.187 | 0.170 | 0.250 | 0.250 | 0.250 | 0.250 | 0.170 | 0.170 | 0.170 | 0.275 | 0.170 | 0.170 | 0.170 | 0.187 | 0.250 | 0.250 | 0.187 | 1.000 | 0.170 | 0.275 |
| PG | 0.220 | 0.180 | 0.180 | 0.180 | 0.180 | 0.220 | 0.220 | 0.220 | 0.220 | 0.198 | 0.180 | 0.198 | 0.220 | 0.198 | 0.198 | 0.180 | 0.180 | 0.220 | 0.220 | 0.180 | 0.170 | 1.000 | 0.220 |
| PNC | 0.374 | 0.242 | 0.242 | 0.242 | 0.220 | 0.374 | 0.374 | 0.340 | 0.340 | 0.220 | 0.220 | 0.220 | 0.374 | 0.220 | 0.220 | 0.220 | 0.242 | 0.374 | 0.374 | 0.242 | 0.275 | 0.220 | 1.000 |

**EXHIBIT 6.8**  Portfolio Credit Risk Under Default Mode Using Constant Asset Return Correlation of 30 percent

| Description | EL$_P$ (mn \$) | UL$_P$ (mn \$) | %EL$_P$ (bp) | %UL$_P$ (bp) |
|---|---|---|---|---|
| Using historical PD and $\rho_{ik}^{\ell}$ | 0.660 | 3.268 | 13.8 | 68.6 |
| Using historical PD and $\rho_{ik}^{\delta}$ | 0.660 | 3.334 | 13.8 | 69.9 |
| Using KMV's EDF and $\rho_{ik}^{\ell}$ | 1.175 | 4.725 | 24.7 | 99.1 |
| Using KMV's EDF and $\rho_{ik}^{\delta}$ | 1.175 | 4.869 | 24.7 | 102.2 |

**EXHIBIT 6.9**  Portfolio Credit Risk Under Default Mode Using Indicative Asset Return Correlation Matrix

| Description | EL$_P$ (mn \$) | UL$_P$ (mn \$) | %EL$_P$ (bp) | %UL$_P$ (bp) |
|---|---|---|---|---|
| Using historical PD and $\rho_{ik}^{\ell}$ | 0.660 | 3.136 | 13.8 | 65.8 |
| Using historical PD and $\rho_{ik}^{\delta}$ | 0.660 | 3.177 | 13.8 | 66.7 |
| Using KMV's EDF and $\rho_{ik}^{\ell}$ | 1.175 | 4.489 | 24.7 | 94.2 |
| Using KMV's EDF and $\rho_{ik}^{\delta}$ | 1.175 | 4.593 | 24.7 | 96.4 |

**EXHIBIT 6.10**  Portfolio Credit Risk Under Migration Mode

| Description | EL$_P$ (mn \$) | UL$_P$ (mn \$) | %EL$_P$ (bp) | %UL$_P$ (bp) |
|---|---|---|---|---|
| Using constant asset return correlation of 30 percent | 1.622 | 4.603 | 34.0 | 96.6 |
| Using indicative asset return correlation matrix | 1.622 | 4.233 | 34.0 | 88.8 |

## QUESTIONS

1. What are the similarities and differences between aggregation of credit risk and market risk at the portfolio level?
2. Explain the differences between asset return correlation, default correlation, and loss correlation.
3. What is model risk? In connection with the quantification of credit risk, is the model risk high or low? Justify your answer.
4. It was assumed that recovery rates between two obligors are independent when the expression for loss correlation was derived. If recovery rates on bonds issued by different obligors are assumed to be positively correlated, will loss correlation be higher or lower? Justify your answer.
5. For the two-bond portfolio example given in Exhibit 6.1, compute the expected and unexpected losses of the portfolio under the default mode

using (a) default correlation to aggregate portfolio credit risk, and (b) loss correlation to aggregate portfolio credit risk. Use historical default probabilities in the calculations and assume that the asset return correlation between obligors is 20 percent.

6. How is the leverage ratio of a firm defined? Discuss why equity return correlation is not a good approximation for asset return correlation if the firm has a high leverage ratio.

7. Discuss the motivation for the use of factor models to derive asset return correlation between obligors.

8. When computing the $z$-thresholds to determine rating transitions, it was assumed that asset returns are standardized normal random variables. Will the $z$-threshold values differ if the true mean and variance of the asset returns are used in the calculations? Justify your answer.

9. For the two-bond portfolio example given in Exhibit 6.1, compute the loss correlation, expected loss, and unexpected loss of the portfolio under the migration mode. Assume that the asset return correlation between the bond obligors is 20 percent.

## CHAPTER 7

# Simulating the Loss Distribution

The previous chapter dealt with portfolio credit risk quantification using an analytical approach. Portfolio credit risk was quantified using the first two moments of the loss distribution, namely expected loss and unexpected loss (or equivalently the standard deviation of loss). Although these two measures are useful, they do not fully model the inherent risks in a credit portfolio. This is because the distribution of credit losses is highly skewed and has a long, fat tail. As a result, it is difficult to make an estimate of the credit loss in the tail part of the loss distribution for a given confidence level using only standard deviation information. To compute credit loss at higher confidence levels, one has to resort to simulating the loss distribution using Monte Carlo techniques. The advantage of performing a simulation is that different tail risk measures can be computed from the simulated loss distribution. When managing a corporate bond portfolio, computing tail risk measures are extremely important if one wishes to avoid concentration risk arising from insufficient credit diversification.

In this chapter, I provide a brief introduction to Monte Carlo methods and describe the computational process involved in performing a Monte Carlo simulation to generate the distribution of credit losses. I then introduce the tail risk measures of interest when managing a corporate bond portfolio and indicate how these risk measures can be computed. The example portfolio comprising 23 bonds presented in the previous chapter is used to illustrate the concepts presented in this chapter.

## MONTE CARLO METHODS

Numerical methods known as Monte Carlo methods can be loosely described as statistical simulation methods that make use of sequences of random numbers to perform the simulation. The first documented account of Monte Carlo simulation dates to the 18th century, when a simulation technique was used to estimate the value $\pi$. However, it is only since the digital computer era that this technique has gained scientific acceptance for solving complex numerical problems in various disciplines. The name "Monte Carlo" was coined by Nicholis Metropolis while working on the Manhattan Project during World War II, because of the similarity of statistical simulation to games of chance symbolized by the capital of Monaco. John von Neumann laid much of the early foundations of Monte Carlo simulation, which requires the use of pseudo-random number generators and inverse cumulative distribution functions. The application of Monte Carlo simulation techniques to finance was pioneered by Phelim Boyle in 1977 in connection with the pricing of options.[1]

It is tempting to think of Monte Carlo methods as a technique for simulating random processes that are described by a stochastic differential equation. This belief stems from the option pricing applications of Monte Carlo methods in finance, where the underlying variable of interest is the evolution of stock prices, which is described by a stochastic differential equation. However, this description is too restrictive because many Monte Carlo applications have no apparent stochastic content, such as the evaluation of a definite integral or the inversion of a system of linear equations. In many applications of Monte Carlo methods, the only requirement is that the physical or mathematical quantity of interest can be described by a probability distribution function.

Monte Carlo methods have become a valuable computational tool in modern finance for pricing complex derivative securities and for performing value at risk calculations. An important advantage of Monte Carlo methods is that they are flexible and easy to implement. Furthermore, the increased availability of powerful computers has enhanced the efficiency of these methods. Nonetheless, the method can still be slow and standard errors of estimates can be large when applied to high-dimensional problems or if the region of interest is not around the mean of the distribution. In such cases, a large number of simulation runs is required to estimate the variable of interest with reasonable accuracy. The standard errors on the estimated parameters can be reduced using conventional variance reduction procedures such as the control variate technique or the antithetic sampling approach.

More recent techniques to speed up the convergence of Monte Carlo methods for high-dimensional problems use deterministic sequences rather than random sequences. These sequences are known as quasi-random sequences in contrast to pseudo-random sequences commonly used in standard Monte Carlo methods. The advantage of using quasi-random sequences is that they generate sequences of $n$-tuples that fill $n$-dimensional space more uniformly than uncorrelated points generated by pseudo-random sequences. However, the computational advantage of quasi-random sequences diminishes as the number of variables increases beyond 30.

An important advantage of Monte Carlo methods is that the computational complexity increases linearly with the number of variables. In contrast, the computational complexity increases exponentially in the number of variables for discrete probability tree approaches for solving similar kinds of problems. This point is best illustrated by considering the problem of credit loss simulation. One approach to computing the loss distribution of a two-bond portfolio is to enumerate all possible combinations of credit states this portfolio can be in after 1 year. Because there are 18 possible credit states that each bond can be in, the two-bond portfolio could take one of 324 (18 times 18) credit states. Valuing the credit loss associated with each one of the 324 states allows one to derive the credit loss distribution of the two-bond portfolio. If the number of bonds in the portfolio increases to 10, the total number of possible credit states is equal to 18 to the power 10, which is equal to $3.57 \times 10^{12}$ credit states. Clearly, even with such a small portfolio, it is practically impossible to enumerate all the states and compute the credit loss distribution.

If one uses Monte Carlo simulation, on the other hand, the problem complexity remains the same irrespective of whether the portfolio comprises 2, 10, or more bonds. In each of these cases, one can run several scenarios, each of which corresponds to a simulation run, and under each scenario compute the credit loss associated with the portfolio. Performing many simulation runs makes it possible to compute the credit loss distribution of the bond portfolio. As the number of bonds in the portfolio increases, the computational effort involved increases linearly in the number of bonds in the portfolio.

The basic building blocks for performing Monte Carlo simulation require a scheme to generate uniformly distributed random numbers and a suitable transformation algorithm if the probability distribution of the variable simulated is different from a uniform distribution. Most applications in finance require the generation of a normally distributed random variable. To simulate such a random variable, the standard transformation techniques used are either the Box–Muller method or the inverse cumulative normal method.[2] If the simulated random variables are greater than one, we need methods to generate correlated random numbers that model the relationship between the variables.

## CREDIT LOSS SIMULATION

In Chapter 6, I introduced the notion of latent variables and discussed how they can be used as a signaling variable for credit events. In particular, I considered the asset return of a firm as a latent variable candidate and indicated how asset return thresholds for rating migrations can be determined. Computing portfolio credit risk requires modeling joint rating migrations, which in turn requires modeling the co-movement of asset returns of different obligors. Considering that the marginal distribution of asset returns is assumed to be normal in Merton's framework, I made the assumption that the joint distribution of asset returns is multivariate normal. The joint evolution of the asset returns of the obligors under the multivariate normal distribution signal how the value of the portfolio evolves, or equivalently, what the credit loss on the portfolio will be. The distribution of obligor asset returns under the multivariate normal distribution can be generated using Monte Carlo simulation. This allows the subsequent computation of the loss distribution of the bond portfolio resulting from credit events.

The foregoing description provides the basic intuition behind the use of Monte Carlo simulation for computing the credit loss distribution. In the context of its intended use here, the Monte Carlo simulation technique can be described as a computational scheme that utilizes sequences of random numbers generated from a given probability distribution function to derive the distribution of portfolio credit loss. The distribution of portfolio credit loss can be computed both under the default mode and under the migration mode. To compute the credit loss under the default mode, one only needs to consider the loss resulting from obligor default. Under the migration mode, one has to compute the credit loss associated with rating migrations in addition to the credit loss resulting from obligor default.

To generate the credit loss for one run of the Monte Carlo simulation, three computational steps are followed:

1. Simulate the correlated random numbers that model the joint distribution of asset returns of the obligors in the portfolio.
2. Infer the implied credit rating of each obligor based on simulated asset returns.
3. Compute the potential loss in value based on the implied credit rating, and in those cases where the asset return value signals an obligor default, compute a random loss on default value by sampling from a beta distribution function.

Repeating this simulation run many times and computing the credit loss under each simulation run makes it possible to generate the distribution of portfolio credit loss under the migration mode. If one is only interested in the credit loss distribution under the default mode, one can compute this by setting the credit loss associated with rating migrations to zero in the simulation run. In the following sections, I briefly describe the computational steps required to generate the credit loss distribution.

## Generating Correlated Asset Returns

I briefly described the steps involved in simulating the credit loss distribution for a bond portfolio. As the first step, I mentioned that correlated random numbers that model the joint distribution of asset returns have to be simulated. An immediate question is whether the obligor-specific means and standard deviations of asset returns have to be taken into account in the simulations. The simple answer to this questions is no. This is because the simulated asset returns will be compared against the rating migration thresholds, which were computed under the assumption that asset returns are standardized normal random variables. As a result, the obligor-specific mean and standard deviation of asset returns are not required for simulating the loss distribution. Hence, I assume that obligor asset returns are standard normal random variables (having mean zero and standard deviation equal to one). Under this assumption, the Monte Carlo simulation method requires generating a sequence of random vectors that are sampled from a standardized multivariate normal distribution.

Many standard numerical packages provide routines to generate sequences of random vectors sampled from a multivariate normal distribution. Although the details of the implementation are beyond the scope of this book, I briefly outline the numerical procedure commonly used to generate sequences of multivariate normal random vectors. Assume that the multivariate normal random vector has a mean vector $\vec{a}$ and covariance matrix $C$. Covariance matrices have the property that they are symmetric and positive definite (meaning all their eigenvalues are greater than zero).[3] Given such a matrix, it is possible to find a unique lower triangular matrix $L$ such that

$$LL^T = C \qquad (7.1)$$

The matrix $L$ is referred to as the Cholesky factor corresponding to the positive-definite matrix $C$. Once the Cholesky factor is determined, generating a sequence of random vectors with the desired multivariate distribution only requires generating a sequence of independent standard normal random variables. If $\vec{x}$ denotes the vector of independent standard normal random variables, the vector $\vec{r}$ with the desired multivariate normal distribution can be constructed as follows:

$$\vec{r} = \vec{a} + L\vec{x} \qquad (7.2)$$

It is easy to verify from this equation that the sequence of random vectors $\vec{r}$ that is generated will have the property that the joint distribution is multinormal with mean vector $\vec{a}$ and covariance matrix $C$.

It is useful to note here that by setting the mean vector $\vec{a}$ to zero and the covariance matrix equal to the correlation matrix, one can generate a sequence of random vectors whose joint distribution is standardized multivariate normal. Because the joint distribution of obligor asset returns was assumed to be standardized multivariate normal, this sequence of random vectors is the one of interest.

### Inferring Implied Credit Rating

The next step in the credit loss simulation process is to infer the credit rating of the various obligors in the portfolio as implied by the simulated asset return vector. In order to do this, one needs to generalize Merton's model to include thresholds for credit rating changes in addition to the default threshold. The implied credit rating can then be derived on the basis of the asset return value relative to these thresholds. Again, in Chapter 6 I derived these $z$-thresholds for different credit ratings under the assumption that the asset returns are normally distributed. These $z$-threshold values are given in Exhibit 6.3 in Chapter 6.

For purposes of illustration, consider the two-bond portfolio given in Exhibit 6.1 in Chapter 6. Assume that for one draw from a bivariate normal distribution, the random asset returns are respectively 2.5 for bond 1 and −3.5 for bond 2. Given the initial issuer rating of A3 for bond 1, one can infer from the $z$-threshold values for A3-rated issuers in Exhibit 6.3 in Chapter 6 that an asset return value of 2.5 implies a credit rating change of the issuer to an A1 rating. Similarly, one can infer from Exhibit 6.3 in Chapter 6 that an asset return value of −3.5 for an A2-rated issuer implies that the issuer defaults on the outstanding debt. Proceeding in this manner, one can derive the implied credit rating of the debt issuers in the two-bond portfolio for every simulation run on the basis of the $z$-threshold values in Exhibit 6.3 in Chapter 6.

For a general $n$-bond portfolio, the implied credit rating of the debt issuers for each simulation run can be similarly determined. It is important to note that the number of obligors in an $n$-bond portfolio will be less than or equal to $n$. In the case where there are fewer than $n$ obligors, credit rating changes should be identical for all bonds issued by the same obligor in any simulation run. This has the implication that the dimension of the simulated asset return vector should be equal to the number of obligors or debt issuers in the bond portfolio.

### Computing Credit Loss

Once the implied rating changes for the obligors are determined for the simulated asset return vector, the corresponding credit loss associated with such implied rating changes could be determined. It is important to note that the price change resulting from a rating change is generically referred to as a loss even though a credit improvement of the obligor results in a price appreciation for the bond. The price change of a bond as a result of a rating change for the bond issuer is a function of the change in the yield spreads and the maturity of the bond. Considering that our interest is to estimate the credit loss due to a change in the bond's mark-to-market value as a result of the rating change, we want to know at what time horizon the bond's price has to be marked to market. In Chapter 5, I argued for the case where the worst-case loss scenario is computed, which corresponds to a rating change of the obligor during the next trading day. In this case, the current trading price of the bond together with its risk parameters duration and convexity serve to characterize the credit loss. The credit loss resulting from a rating change from the $i$th grade to the $k$th grade is a function of the change in the bond yield and is given by equation (5.32) in Chapter 5.

To illustrate the credit loss computation, again focus on the two-bond portfolio example. In this example, the asset return value signaled an upgrade to an A1 rating from the current rating of A3 for bond 1. The change in the yield spread associated with this rating change is $-30$ basis points, using the yield spread information given in Exhibit 5.8 in Chapter 5. Substituting the various parameter values into equation (5.32) in Chapter 5 gives the credit loss for a \$1 million notional amount held of bond 1 as

$$
\begin{aligned}
\text{Credit loss} &= 1,000,000 \times [1.0533 \times 4.021 \times (-0.003) \\
&\quad - 0.5 \times 1.0533 \times 19.75 \times (-0.003)^2] \\
&= -\$12,799.6
\end{aligned}
$$

Note that the negative sign associated with the credit loss indicates that this rating change results in a profit rather than a loss.

For bond 2, the simulated asset return value of $-3.5$ implies default of the obligor. In this case, one must find a random loss on default, which is a function of the assumed recovery rate distribution. In Chapter 5, the recovery rate process was assumed to have a beta distribution whose mean $\mu$ and standard deviation $\sigma$ are given by equations (5.15) and (5.16), respectively. Given the values for $\mu$ and $\sigma$, the parameters $\alpha$ and $\beta$ that define the beta distribution with the desired mean and standard deviation can be computed as follows:

$$
\alpha = \frac{\mu^2(1 - \mu)}{\sigma^2} - \mu \tag{7.3}
$$

$$
\beta = \frac{\alpha}{\mu} - \alpha \tag{7.4}
$$

For the bond in question, the mean recovery rate is $\mu = 47$ percent and the standard deviation of the recovery rate is $\sigma = 25$ percent. Corresponding to these recovery rate values, the parameters of the beta distribution function are $\alpha = 1.403$ and $\beta = 1.582$.

The random recovery rate for bond 2 for the simulation run is determined by drawing a random number from a beta distribution with the $\alpha$ and $\beta$ parameter values as just given. Assume that the simulated recovery value is 40 percent for bond 2. The implied loss on default for the bond can now be computed using equation (5.21) in Chapter 5, which is equal to 0.6533.

The credit loss arising from bond 2 for this simulation run is equal to the nominal exposure times the loss on default, which is equal to $653,300.

For the two-bond portfolio, the total credit loss for this simulation run is the sum of the two losses. If this simulation run corresponds to the $i$th run, the portfolio credit loss under the $i$th simulation run, denoted $\ell_i$, is given by

$$\ell_i = -\$12,799.6 + \$653,300 = \$640,500.4$$

It is important to emphasize that for a general $n$-bond portfolio, all bonds of a particular issuer should have the same recovery value for any one simulation run if they have the same seniority. This information must be taken into account when simulating the credit loss distribution of a general $n$-bond portfolio.

**Remarks**    When simulating a random recovery amount from a beta distribution, it can happen that this recovery amount is close to the nominal value of the bond. Considering that recovery values tend to be lower than the nominal value (typically less than 90 percent of the nominal value), one may wish to put an upper bound for the recovery amount. In performing the loss simulation for an example bond portfolio presented later in this chapter, a maximum recovery rate of 90 percent of the nominal value of the bond is imposed. In general, assuming recovery rates to be uniformly distributed is a better approach to restricting recovery rates to lie within a specific range. The parameters of the uniform distribution having a specified mean and standard deviation can be computed as indicated in Chapter 2.

## Computing Expected Loss and Unexpected Loss

The foregoing procedure outlined how the portfolio credit loss can be computed for one simulation run. By repeating the simulation run $N$ times where $N$ is sufficiently large, the distribution of the credit losses can be generated. Given the simulated loss distribution, one can compute various risk measures of interest. For instance, the expected and the unexpected credit loss using the simulated loss data can be computed as follows:

$$\text{EL}_P = \frac{1}{N}\sum_{i=1}^{N}\ell_i \qquad (7.5)$$

$$\text{UL}_P = \sqrt{\frac{1}{N-1}\sum_{i=1}^{N}(\ell_i - \text{EL}_P)^2} \qquad (7.6)$$

To reduce the standard error of the estimated portfolio expected loss, it is common practice to perform antithetic sampling when performing the

Monte Carlo simulation. The idea behind antithetic sampling is that when random samples are drawn from a symmetric distribution, sampling errors can be avoided if the antithetic or symmetric part of the random sample is also drawn. This ensures that the empirical mean of the random samples is equal to the mean of the distribution function from which the samples are drawn. Including the antithetic part of the samples doubles the total number of simulation runs. All numerical examples presented in this book that use simulation are generated using antithetic sampling. In general, if the number of simulation runs is equal to $N$ in the numerical examples, one half of the simulation runs use antithetic samples.

## Importance Sampling

The Monte Carlo simulation technique described so far is based on random sampling. In such a sampling process, the probability of any value being generated is proportional to the probability density at that point. This property has the effect of generating asset return values in the simulations that tend to cluster around the mean of the normal distribution function. Rating migrations and obligor defaults, however, are events that are driven by asset return values that deviate significantly from the mean of the normal distribution. The implication is that a significant proportion of the simulation runs will not trigger any credit events. If one's intention is to compute the expected and the unexpected loss of the portfolio from the simulations, random sampling will be the appropriate method to use. If, on the other hand, one expects to compute risk measures associated with tail events from the simulated data, random sampling will be inefficient.

If one's primary intention of performing Monte Carlo simulations is to compute tail risk measures (to be discussed in the next section), one can improve the simulation efficiency through importance sampling.[4] Simulation efficiency in the present context refers to the number of simulation runs required to compute the risk measure of interest for a specified standard error of the estimate. Importance sampling artificially inflates the probability of choosing random samples from those regions of the distribution that are of most interest. This means that the sampling process is biased in such a manner that a large number of credit events are simulated relative to what would occur in practice. In the Monte Carlo simulation terminology, the adjustment made to the probability of a particular point being sampled is referred to as its importance weight. To estimate the true probability distribution of the simulated losses when performing importance sampling, one has to restore the actual probability of each sample by multiplying it by the inverse of its importance weight. The numerical results presented in this book are based only on the standard Monte Carlo simulation technique. In practice, when the number of obligors in the portfolio is large (this is usually true for a benchmark portfolio), performing importance sampling leads to improved computational efficiency.

## TAIL RISK MEASURES

The discussions so far in this book focused on the mean and the standard deviation of the credit loss distribution as appropriate risk measures for a corporate bond portfolio. In the credit risk measurement framework, these measures were referred to as expected loss and unexpected loss, respectively. If the distribution of credit losses is normally distributed, the standard deviation can be interpreted as the maximum deviation around the mean that will not be exceeded with a 66 percent level of confidence. Because the credit loss distribution is not normal, a similar interpretation to the standard deviation of credit loss does not hold. In most cases, computing the probability of incurring a large credit loss on a corporate bond portfolio using unexpected loss information is usually not possible.

In general, a major preoccupation of most corporate bond portfolio managers is to structure the portfolio so as to minimize the probability of large losses. To do this, an estimate of the potential downside risk of the portfolio becomes a key requirement. Computing any downside risk measure requires an estimate of the probability mass associated with the tail of the loss distribution. If the simulated credit loss distribution is available, it is quite easy to derive appropriate tail risk measures of interest. For a corporate bond portfolio, the tail risk measures of interest are credit value at risk and expected shortfall risk. Both these risk measures are discussed in what follows, and the method for computing these measures using the simulated credit loss data is also indicated.

### Credit Value at Risk

Credit value at risk (CrVaR) is a tail risk measure that quantifies the extreme losses arising from credit events that can occur at a prespecified level of confidence over a given time horizon. In practical terms, CrVaR provides an estimate of the maximum credit loss on a portfolio that could be exceeded with a probability $p$. It is assumed here that $p$ is expressed in percentage. If the probability $p$ is chosen to be sufficiently small, one can expect that the credit loss will not exceed the CrVaR amount at a high confidence level given by $(100 - p)$ percent. Stated differently, CrVaR at a confidence level of $(100 - p)$ percent refers to the maximum dollar value of loss that will only be exceeded $p$ percent of the time over the given time horizon. Because losses from credit risk are measured over a 1-year horizon, the CrVaR measure to be computed here also relates to a 1-year time horizon.

To compute CrVaR to quantify the tail risk of the credit loss distribution in a corporate bond portfolio, one needs to specify the confidence level at which it should be determined. Within the framework of economic capital allocation, CrVaR is usually measured at a confidence level that reflects the solvency standard of the institution in question. For instance, the solvency standard of an AA-rated institution is typically 99.97 percent, and hence CrVaR is computed at this confidence level. From a portfolio management perspective, however, the confidence level of interest for a CrVaR estimate would typically be much lower. The motivation for this is that portfolio managers have to provide monthly performance reports to clients and return deviations over this period need to be explained. In this case, estimating CrVaR at a confidence level of 91.6 percent would imply that the underperformance relative to the benchmark exceeds the monthly CrVaR estimate once during the year on average if monthly performance reporting is used. In this case, the a CrVaR estimate provides useful information to the portfolio manager and the client in terms of the return surprises one could expect and also what actually happens.

Motivated by the this observation, I choose the confidence level for the CrVaR estimate to be 90 percent. At this level of confidence, the portfolio manager can expect the credit losses to exceed the monthly CrVaR estimate for one reporting period during the year. Once the confidence level for CrVaR is specified, estimating CrVaR from the simulated loss distribution is quite simple. If, for instance, the number of simulation runs is equal to 10,000, then the 90 percent CrVaR is equal to the 1,000th worst-case credit loss. Assuming that the simulated credit losses are sorted in an ascending order of magnitude, the credit loss corresponding to the 9,000th row in the sorted data is the CrVaR at 90 percent confidence level for 10,000 simulation runs.

Considering that standard practice in portfolio management is to report risk measures relative to the current market value of the portfolio, I introduce the term percentage credit value at risk. If $M_P$ denotes the current mark-to-market value of the portfolio, the percentage CrVaR at 90 percent confidence level is defined as

$$\% \, \mathrm{CrVaR}_{90\%} = \frac{\mathrm{CrVaR}_{90\%}}{M_P} \tag{7.7}$$

## Expected Shortfall Risk

Although CrVaR is a useful tail risk measure, it fails to reflect the severity of loss in the worst-case scenarios in which the loss exceeds CrVaR. In other words, CrVaR fails to provide insight as to how far the tail of the loss distribution extends. This information is critical if the portfolio manager is

**EXHIBIT 7.1**    Credit Loss Distribution for Two Portfolios

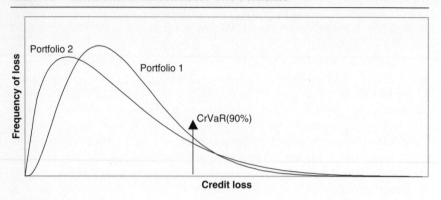

interested in restricting the severity of the losses in the worst-case scenarios under which losses exceed CrVaR. In order to better motivate this point, Exhibit 7.1 shows the credit loss distribution for two portfolios that have identical CrVaR at the 90 percent level of confidence.

Examining Exhibit 7.1, it is clear that although both portfolios have identical CrVaR at the 90 percent confidence level, the severity of the worst-case losses that exceed the 90 percent confidence level are lower for portfolio 1 than portfolio 2. This example suggests that to investigate whether portfolio credit risk is well diversified, it is not sufficient to only examine the tail probability at some confidence level. Examining the loss exceedence beyond the desired confidence level at which CrVaR is esti-mated is important to gauge the loss severity in the tail part of the loss dis-tribution.

One such risk measure that provides an estimate of the loss severity in the tail part of the loss distribution is the expected shortfall risk (ESR), which is sometimes also referred to as conditional VaR.[5] Similar to CrVaR, expected shortfall risk requires specifying a confidence level and a time horizon. Considering that ESR is usually used in conjunction with CrVaR, the confidence level should be chosen as 90 percent and the time horizon 1 year. A simple interpretation of ESR is that it measures the average loss in the worst $p$ percent of scenarios, where $(100 - p)$ percent denotes the con-fidence level at which CrVaR is estimated. In mathematical terms, expected shortfall risk can be defined as the conditional expectation of that part of the credit loss that exceeds the CrVaR limit. The interpretation of ESR as conditional VaR follows from this definition. If $\tilde{\ell}$ denotes the loss variable, ESR can be defined as

$$ESR = E[\tilde{\ell} | \tilde{\ell} > CrVaR] \tag{7.8}$$

**EXHIBIT 7.2**   Various Risk Measures for Portfolio Credit Risk

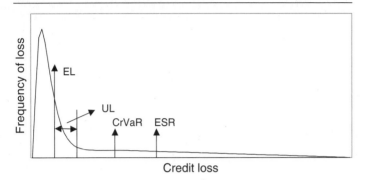

Given the simulated loss distribution of the portfolio, computing expected shortfall risk is quite simple. Let $\ell_i$ denote the simulated credit loss for the $i$th simulation run and assume that the losses are sorted in ascending order. If the number of simulation runs is equal to $N$, the relevant equation to compute ESR at the 90 percent confidence level from the simulations is

$$\mathrm{ESR}_{90\%} = \frac{1}{(1 - 0.9)N} \times \sum_{i=0.9\,N+1}^{N} \ell_i \tag{7.9}$$

The percentage ESR at 90 percent confidence level is defined as

$$\%\,\mathrm{ESR}_{90\%} = \frac{\mathrm{ESR}_{90\%}}{M_P} \tag{7.10}$$

Exhibit 7.2 shows the various credit risk measures presented here that can be computed from the simulated loss data. In the next section, I compute these risk measures by doing a Monte Carlo simulation to generate the loss distribution for an example corporate bond portfolio.

## NUMERICAL RESULTS

In this section, I again consider the bond portfolio comprising 23 bonds shown in Exhibit 6.6 in Chapter 6 to compute the various credit risk measures of interest under both the default mode and the migration mode. Because the expected and the unexpected loss of the portfolio can also be computed directly from the simulated loss data, it will be useful to compare these values with those obtained using an analytical expression. In performing the loss simulation for the bond portfolio, the asset return correlation matrix given in Exhibit 6.7 in Chapter 6 was used. The simulations were

**EXHIBIT 7.3**    Simulated Loss Distribution Under the Migration Mode

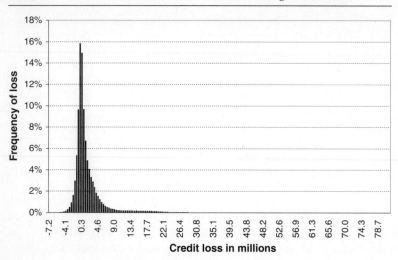

performed using antithetic sampling and the total number of simulations runs was 500,000. Exhibit 7.3 shows the simulated loss distribution for this 23-bond portfolio under the migration mode.

In Exhibit 7.3, the negative credit loss refers to an increase in the mark-to-market value of the portfolio resulting from rating upgrades for some obligors in the portfolio. The simulated loss distribution around the tail region for this portfolio is shown in Exhibit 7.4.

**EXHIBIT 7.4**    Simulated Loss Distribution Around the Tail Region

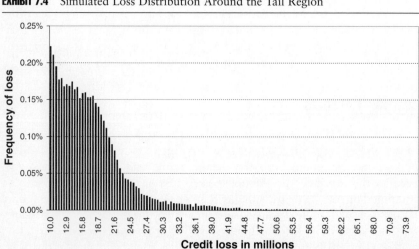

**Exhibit 7.5** Portfolio Credit Risk Measures Under Default Mode Based on
Simulated Loss Distribution

| Description | Amount (million $) | Relative to Portfolio Size (bp) |
|---|---|---|
| Expected loss | 0.662 | 13.9 |
| Unexpected loss | 3.139 | 65.9 |
| CrVaR at 90 percent confidence | 0.0 | 0.0 |
| ESR at 90 percent confidence | 6.624 | 139.0 |

The various portfolio credit risk measures of interest under the default
mode and the migration mode are presented in Exhibits 7.5 and 7.6, respectively. Under the default mode, the probability of default for the obligors in
the portfolio was chosen to be equal to the historical PD.

It is of interest that the expected and unexpected loss figures computed
using the simulated loss distribution are almost identical to the corresponding figures computed using the analytical formula presented in Chapter 6.
The simulation results confirm that under the default mode, loss correlation
between obligors should be used to aggregate portfolio credit risk. It is also
interesting to note that under the default mode the CrVaR at 90 percent
confidence level is zero. This is because the probability of obligor defaults
for this portfolio is much lower. Under the migration mode, the portfolio
has a CrVaR of $4.905 million at the 90 percent confidence level. This has
the interpretation that there is a 90 percent chance that the credit losses will
not exceed $4.905 million on the portfolio over a 1-year time period.

Expected shortfall as a risk measure provides a much better estimate
of the tail risk under both the default mode and the migration mode. For
instance, under the default mode, the portfolio manager can expect to
lose on average $6.624 million on the portfolio if credit events that have
10 percent probability occur. Similarly, under the migration mode, the
portfolio manager can expect to lose on average $11.452 million on the

**Exhibit 7.6** Portfolio Credit Risk Measures Under Migration Mode Based on
Simulated Loss Distribution

| Description | Amount (million $) | Relative to Portfolio Size (bp) |
|---|---|---|
| Expected loss | 1.626 | 34.1 |
| Unexpected loss | 4.238 | 88.9 |
| CrVaR at 90 percent confidence | 4.905 | 102.9 |
| ESR at 90 percent confidence | 11.452 | 240.3 |

portfolio over a 1-year time period if credit events considered having 10 percent probability of occurrence happen.

## QUESTIONS

1. Discuss the different techniques available to speed up Monte Carlo simulation.
2. What is the motivation for performing a Monte Carlo simulation of the credit loss distribution?
3. What are the main computational steps involved in performing a Monte Carlo simulation of the loss distribution?
4. A beta distribution was used to generate random recovery rates of defaulted bonds in the simulations. If a uniform distribution with the same mean and standard deviation is used instead, will the expected and unexpected losses of the portfolio be different? Justify your answer.
5. One of the assumptions made when simulating the loss distribution is that recovery rates of different obligors are independent. If this assumption is relaxed, what changes are needed in the Monte Carlo setup to simulate the loss distribution?
6. If the distribution of credit loss is assumed to be normally distributed, would it be necessary to do a Monte Carlo simulation to compute tail risk measures? Justify your answer assuming that you have computed the mean and the standard deviation of this loss distribution using an analytical approach.
7. Imagine a box to be filled with 50 red balls, 30 green balls, 15 white balls, and 5 black balls. The payoff for drawing a red ball is $6, a green ball is $5, a white ball is $3, and a black ball is $1. The expected payoff when a ball is drawn at random from the box is $5. Will you be willing to pay $5 to play the game? Is this a fair game?
8. In Question 7, assume that two balls of each color have a zero payoff but the expected payoffs when different-colored balls are drawn are, respectively, $6 for red, $5 for green, $3 for white, and $1 for black. This will ensure that the expected payoff on a ball drawn at random is still $5. Will you still pay $5 to play the game? Justify why or why not.
9. Compute the mean, the standard deviation, the value at risk at 90 percent confidence level, and the expected shortfall risk at 90 percent confidence level of the loss variable (initial investment minus the payoff from a single random draw) assuming that the payoffs for the balls are as given in Question 7. Compute the same statistical parameters for Question 8.

## CHAPTER 8

# Relaxing the Normal
# Distribution Assumption

The credit risk analysis presented so far in this book is based on the assumption that asset returns of firms are normally distributed. In contrast, virtually most empirical studies report systematic deviation from normality in market data. One of the most pervasive features observed across equity, foreign exchange, and interest rate markets is excess kurtosis. The implication is that, compared to a normal distribution with the same mean and standard deviation, the true distribution assigns greater probability to extreme market moves. Modeling the observed excess kurtosis in a financial time series requires relaxing the normal distribution assumption. The implications of relaxing the normal distribution assumption for obligor asset returns on various portfolio credit risk measures are the main focus of this chapter.

At the obligor level, relaxing the assumption that distribution of asset returns of firms is normal will not change the expected and unexpected losses. In a portfolio context, however, relaxing the assumption that joint distribution of asset returns is multivariate normal can have a significant impact on the aggregate portfolio credit risk. In fact, the aggregate portfolio credit risk is usually very sensitive to the exact nature of the joint distribution of asset returns. In practice, there is no compelling reason, other than possibly for computational simplicity, to assume that the joint distribution of asset returns of firms is multivariate normal. The extent to which the computational overheads increase will depend on the choice of the alternative distribution function.

In this chapter, I discuss methods for computing the various portfolio credit risk measures of interest when the asset returns of firms are assumed to have a Student's $t$ distribution. The reason for choosing the Student's $t$ distribution is that it exhibits the property of leptokurtosis, which is commonly observed in financial time series data. A distribution function is said to be leptokurtic if the excess kurtosis (relative to a normal distribution) is positive. Distributions that are leptokurtic have a higher peak, a narrower midrange, and fatter tails than a normal distribution function when properly normalized. Another reason for the choice of the Student's $t$ distribution is that the increase in computational overhead is minimal relative to a normal distribution function. Numerical results are presented at the end of the chapter to provide a comparison of portfolio credit risk measures obtained under the two different distribution assumptions for asset returns that drive credit events.

## MOTIVATION

A growing body of empirical studies conducted on financial time series data suggests that returns on traded financial instruments exhibit volatility clustering and extreme movements that are not representative of a normally distributed random variable. Another commonly observed property of financial time series is that during times of large market moves, there is greater degree of co-movement of returns across many firms compared to those observed during normal market conditions. This property, usually referred to as tail dependence, captures the extent to which the dependence (or correlation) between random variables arises from extreme observations. Stated differently, for a given level of correlation between the random variables, a multivariate distribution with tail dependence has a much greater tendency to generate simultaneous extreme values for the random variables than do those distributions that do not have this property.

A multivariate normal distribution does not exhibit tail dependence. The dependence or correlation structure exhibited between the random variables in a multivariate normal distribution arises primarily from co-movements of the variables around the center of the distribution. As a consequence, contagion or herding behavior commonly observed in financial markets is difficult to model within the framework of multivariate normal distributions. To capture contagion and herding behavior in financial markets, distributions that exhibit tail dependence should be used to model financial variables of interest. In the context of credit risk modeling, contagion effects result in greater co-movement of asset returns across firms during periods of recession, leading to higher probability of joint defaults. If one models the joint distribution of asset returns to be multivariate normal, one will fail to capture the effects of contagion in the computed aggregate portfolio credit risk measures.[1]

### Student's *t* distribution

Among the class of distribution functions that exhibit tail dependence, the family of multivariate normal mixture distributions, which includes the

Student's $t$ distribution and the generalized hyperbolic distribution, is an interesting alternative. This is because normal mixture distributions inherit the correlation matrix of the multivariate normal distribution. Hence, correlation matrices for normal mixture distributions are easy to calibrate.[2]

Formally, a member of the $m$-dimensional family of variance mixtures of normal distributions is equal in distribution to the product of a scalar random variable $s$ and a normal random vector $\vec{u}$ having zero mean and covariance matrix $\Sigma$. The scalar random variable $s$ is assumed to be positive with finite second moment and independent of $\vec{u}$. If $\vec{x}$ denotes a random vector having a multivariate normal mixture distribution, then the definition leads to the following equation:

$$\vec{x} = s \cdot \vec{u} \tag{8.1}$$

Because normal mixture distributions inherit the correlation matrix of the multivariate normal distribution, one has the following relationship:

$$\text{Corr}(x_i, x_k) = \text{Corr}(u_i, u_k) \tag{8.2}$$

The random vector $\vec{x}$ has a multivariate $t$ distribution with $v$ degrees of freedom if the scalar random variable $s$ is defined as follows:

$$s = \sqrt{\frac{v}{\omega}} \tag{8.3}$$

In equation (8.3), $\omega$ is a chi-square distributed random variable with $v$ degrees of freedom. For $v > 2$, the resulting Student's $t$ distribution has zero mean vector and covariance matrix $[v/(v - 2)]\Sigma$. Exhibit 8.1 shows

**EXHIBIT 8.1**  Probability Density Functions of Normal and $t$ Distributions

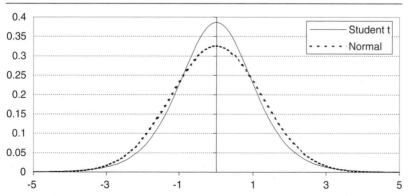

a normal distribution and a Student's $t$ distribution (with $v = 8$) having identical means and variances.

The Student's $t$ distribution has the property that as $v$ increases, the distribution approaches a normal distribution. In fact, for values of $v$ greater than 25, it is difficult to distinguish between a normal distribution and a $t$ distribution. In a multivariate setting, as $v$ decreases, the degree of tail dependence between the random variables increases. Although the choice of an appropriate $v$ is an open problem in finance, $v$ is typically in the range between 5 and 10. In the numerical examples presented in this book, I choose 8 degrees of freedom for the $t$ distribution.

An important distinction between the $t$ distribution and the normal distribution is that uncorrelated multinormal random variables are mutually independent, whereas the components of multivariate $t$ are in general dependent even if they are uncorrelated. In modeling credit risk, this property makes it possible to capture co-movements of asset returns between firms in extreme market situations even if the asset returns exhibit little or no correlation under normal market conditions.

## Probability Density Function

In the univariate case, the probability density function of the Student's $t$ distribution with $v$ degrees of freedom has the following functional form:

$$f_v(x) = \frac{\Gamma((v + 1)/2)}{\sqrt{v\pi} \times \Gamma(v/2)} \times \left(1 + \frac{x^2}{v}\right)^{-(v+1)/2} \tag{8.4}$$

In equation (8.4), $\Gamma(\cdot)$ is the gamma function, which is given by

$$\Gamma(\alpha) = \int_0^\infty x^{\alpha-1} e^{-x} dx \tag{8.5}$$

The probability density function of a bivariate $t$ distribution with $v$ degrees of freedom and correlation $\rho$ between the two random variables is given by

$$f_v(x_1, x_2) = \frac{1}{2\pi\sqrt{1 - \rho^2}} \left(1 + \frac{x_1^2 + x_2^2 - 2\rho x_1 x_2}{(1 - \rho^2)v}\right)^{-(v+2)/2} \tag{8.6}$$

## PORTFOLIO CREDIT RISK

In this section, I revisit the computation of the expected and the unexpected loss of the portfolio using an analytical approach when the joint distribution of asset returns has a $t$ distribution. As mentioned earlier, expected and unexpected loss at the obligor level will not change when asset returns are assumed to be $t$ distributed rather than normally distributed. To see why this is the case, recall that the approach to quantifying credit risk at the obligor level presented in Chapter 5 required estimating rating migration and default probabilities for the obligor among other variables. The approach followed by rating agencies to compute these probabilities is based on historically observed rating migrations of obligor pools. As such, empirical estimation of these probabilities does not require knowledge of the default drivers. In the KMV framework, the actual PD estimates for different obligors is based on empirical data although the approach has the theoretical underpinnings of the Merton framework. Considering that the actual functional form for the asset return distribution of the obligor does not enter into the rating migration and default probability estimates, the assumption that asset returns have a $t$ distribution has no impact on these probabilities. As a result, the expected and the unexpected loss at the obligor level are invariant under a different distributional assumption for obligor asset returns.

At the portfolio level, assuming that the joint distribution of asset returns is multivariate $t$ rather than multivariate normal affects the computed portfolio credit risk measures. This is because the loss correlation between obligors changes as a result of a change in the joint distribution assumption. It is useful to note that the asset return correlation between obligor pairs is the same as in the multivariate normal distribution case because the multivariate $t$ distribution inherits this correlation matrix structure. The change in loss correlation arises primarily from the fact that joint migration probabilities and joint default probabilities change when the joint distribution of asset returns is assumed to have a multivariate $t$ distribution.

The foregoing discussion suggests that the portfolio credit risk measures differ due to a change in the loss correlation between obligor pairs when asset returns have a multivariate $t$ distribution. Considering that the loss correlation parameter does not enter into the portfolio expected loss calculation, the portfolio expected loss would be invariant to a change in the joint distribution of asset returns. Hence, in this section I focus only on the portfolio unexpected loss calculation under the default and migration modes.

## Default Mode

Recall that the analytical formula for computing portfolio unexpected loss is given by equation (6.9) in Chapter 6. Under the multivariate $t$ distribution assumption for asset returns, the loss correlation $\rho_{ik}^{\ell}$ between the $i$th and the $k$th obligor is different from that under the multivariate normal distribution assumption. If one follows the same approach as outlined in Chapter 6 to estimate loss correlation between any two obligors, one needs to compute the default correlation between the obligors to infer loss correlation. Default correlation between obligor pairs can be computed given the joint probability of default between the obligors using equation (6.14) in Chapter 6.

The probability of joint default of two obligors, when asset returns are assumed to be jointly bivariate $t$ distributed, is given by

$$\text{prob}(\delta_i = 1, \delta_k = 1) = \frac{1}{2\pi\sqrt{1-(\rho_{ik}^\alpha)^2}} \int_{-\infty}^{D_i} \int_{-\infty}^{D_k} \left(1 + \frac{x^2 + y^2 - 2\rho_{ik}^\alpha xy}{[1 - (\rho_{ik}^\alpha)^2]\nu}\right)^{-(\nu+2)/2} dx\,dy$$

(8.7)

In equation (8.7), $\rho_{ik}^\alpha$ is the asset return correlation between the two obligors $i$ and $k$. The integral limits $D_i$ and $D_k$ are the default thresholds for obligors $i$ and $k$, respectively, under the assumption that the asset returns have a Student's $t$ distribution. These values can be computed given the probability of default for each obligor. For instance, if $PD_i$ denotes the probability of default of the $i$th obligor, $D_i$ is the solution to the following integral equation:

$$PD_i = \frac{\Gamma((\nu + 1)/2)}{\sqrt{\nu\pi} \times \Gamma(\nu/2)} \int_{-\infty}^{D_i} \left(1 + \frac{x^2}{\nu}\right)^{-(\nu+1)/2} dx$$

(8.8)

Most standard software routines provide implementations to compute the deviate $D_i$ associated with the lower tail probability $PD_i$ of a Student's $t$ distribution with $\nu$ degrees of freedom. On the other hand, many software vendors do not provide routines for computing bivariate $t$ probabilities. However, it is fairly straightforward to compute this using the algorithm developed by Dunnett and Sobel.[3] A computer program based on this algorithm for evaluating the bivariate $t$ probability given by equation (8.7) is included in the appendix to this chapter.

Once the probability of joint default under the bivariate $t$ distribution is evaluated, default correlation between the two obligors can be determined using equation (6.14) in Chapter 6. Then the loss correlation between the obligors can be determined using equation (6.19) in Chapter 6. Based on the two-bond portfolio example considered in Exhibit 6.1 in Chapter 6, the various credit risk quantities of interest computed under the assumption that asset returns have a Student's $t$ distribution are given as follows. The asset return correlation between the obligors is again assumed to be 30 percent.

### Using Historical PD:

- Joint default probability $\text{prob}(\delta_i = 1, \delta_k = 1) = 7.538 \times 10^{-5}$.
- Default correlation $\rho_{ik}^{\delta} = 0.08346$.
- Loss correlation $\rho_{ik}^{\ell}$ when recovery rates between issuers are independent is 0.06943.
- Expected portfolio loss $EL_P = \$1,010$.
- Unexpected portfolio loss $UL_P$ using loss correlation is $26,940.
- Unexpected portfolio loss $UL_P$ using default correlation is $27,113.

### Using KMV's EDF:

- Joint default probability $\text{prob}(\delta_i = 1, \delta_k = 1) = 1.1184 \times 10^{-3}$.
- Default correlation $\rho_{ik}^{\delta} = 0.10843$.
- Loss correlation $\rho_{ik}^{\ell}$ when recovery rates between issuers are independent is 0.09006.
- Expected portfolio loss $EL_P = \$11,803$.
- Unexpected portfolio loss $UL_P$ using loss correlation is $91,467.
- Unexpected portfolio loss $UL_P$ using default correlation is $92,177.

Examining the results, we note that default and loss correlations are considerably higher under the joint $t$-distribution assumption for asset returns. For instance, there is almost a sevenfold increase in loss correlation when the joint distribution of asset returns is $t$ distributed rather than normally distributed. As a consequence, the estimate of the unexpected loss under the $t$ distribution is higher than what was obtained assuming joint normality for asset returns.

### Migration Mode

The steps involved in computing the unexpected loss under the migration mode under the multivariate $t$ distribution assumption for asset returns follows closely the procedure outlined in Chapter 6. The only difference is that the relevant integral relations to be used to compute the $z$-thresholds and the joint migration probabilities are different. Specifically, the integrand for computing the $z$-thresholds are the Student's $t$ density function and the integrand for computing the joint migration probabilities is the density function of a bivariate $t$ distribution.

For purpose of illustration, consider an obligor that has a current credit rating of A1. Let $P_{A1,Aaa}$ denote the probability of transitioning to the credit rating Aaa. Under the assumption that the asset returns of the obligor is $t$ distributed, the credit event that signals the obligor rating migration from A1 to Aaa occurs when the asset returns of the obligor exceeds the threshold $z_{A1,Aaa}$. This threshold can be determined by solving the following integral equation:

$$P_{A1,Aaa} = \frac{\Gamma((\nu + 1)/2)}{\sqrt{\nu\pi} \times \Gamma(\nu/2)} \int\limits_{z_{A1,Aaa}}^{\infty} \left(1 + \frac{x^2}{\nu}\right)^{-(\nu+1)/2} dx \qquad (8.9)$$

A rating transition of this obligor from A1 to Aa1 occurs if the asset return falls between the thresholds $z_{A1,Aaa}$ and $z_{A1,Aa1}$. The threshold $z_{A1,Aa1}$ can be determined by solving the following integral equation:

$$P_{A1,Aa1} = \frac{\Gamma((\nu + 1)/2)}{\sqrt{\nu\pi} \times \Gamma(\nu/2)} \int\limits_{z_{A1,Aa1}}^{z_{A1,Aaa}} \left(1 + \frac{x^2}{\nu}\right)^{-(\nu+1)/2} dx \qquad (8.10)$$

One can extend this sequential rule to determine the thresholds for migrating to other rating grades. Again, it is useful to note here that these $z$-thresholds are a function of the current credit rating of the obligor. Exhibit 8.2 shows the $z$-threshold values computed using the normalized rating transition probabilities when asset returns are $t$ distributed.

Having determined the $z$-threshold values that are used to determine whether rating transitions have occurred, the next step is to compute the joint migration probabilities. Once again, for purpose of illustration, consider the case where the current credit rating of obligor 1 is A1 and the credit rating of obligor 2 is A3. Let $\rho$ denote the asset return correlation between the two obligors. The joint probability that obligor 1 migrates to a B2 rating and obligor 2 migrates to an Aaa rating assuming the joint distribution of asset returns to be bivariate $t$ is given by

$$h_{B2,Aaa} = \frac{1}{2\pi\sqrt{1 - \rho^2}} \int\limits_{z_{A1,B2}}^{z_{A1,B1}} \int\limits_{z_{A3,Aaa}}^{\infty} \left(1 + \frac{x^2 + y^2 - 2\rho xy}{(1 - \rho^2)\nu}\right)^{-(\nu+2)/2} dx\,dy \quad (8.11)$$

This integral can be computed once it is transformed into a form that will allow the use of the computer code given in the appendix. To do this, use the following integral relation:

$$\int\limits_{l_1}^{u_1}\int\limits_{l_2}^{u_2} f(x,y)dx\,dy = \int\limits_{-\infty}^{l_1}\int\limits_{-\infty}^{l_2} f(x,y)dx\,dy + \int\limits_{-\infty}^{u_1}\int\limits_{-\infty}^{u_2} f(x,y)dx\,dy - \int\limits_{-\infty}^{l_1}\int\limits_{-\infty}^{u_2} f(x,y)dx\,dy - \int\limits_{-\infty}^{u_1}\int\limits_{-\infty}^{l_2} f(x,y)dx\,dy$$

$$(8.12)$$

In equation (8.12), the integral limits $l_1$, $l_2$, $u_1$, and $u_2$ can be either finite or infinite. Making use of such a transformation, one can compute numerically

**EXHIBIT 8.2** $z$-Thresholds Under the $t$ Distribution for Various Rating Grades

| | Aaa | Aa1 | Aa2 | Aa3 | A1 | A2 | A3 | Baa1 | Baa2 | Baa3 | Ba1 | Ba2 | Ba3 | B1 | B2 | B3 | Caa | Def |
|---|---|---|---|---|---|---|---|---|---|---|---|---|---|---|---|---|---|---|
| Aaa | -1.334 | -1.889 | -2.538 | -2.752 | -3.342 | -3.923 | -5.041 | -5.041 | -5.041 | -5.041 | -6.442 | -6.442 | -6.442 | -6.442 | -6.442 | -6.442 | -6.442 | -1000 |
| Aa1 | 2.269 | -0.965 | -1.400 | -2.170 | -3.150 | -3.598 | -3.705 | -4.429 | -4.429 | -4.429 | -5.811 | -5.811 | -5.811 | -5.811 | -5.811 | -5.811 | -5.811 | -1000 |
| Aa2 | 3.094 | 2.039 | -1.093 | -1.688 | -2.343 | -2.937 | -3.639 | -4.152 | -4.152 | -4.152 | -4.152 | -4.152 | -4.429 | -5.462 | -5.462 | -5.462 | -5.462 | -1000 |
| Aa3 | 4.671 | 3.112 | 1.967 | -1.144 | -1.862 | -2.553 | -3.034 | -3.279 | -3.618 | -4.108 | -4.108 | -4.304 | -5.222 | -5.222 | -5.222 | -5.222 | -5.222 | -1000 |
| A1 | 5.462 | 4.250 | 3.076 | 1.685 | -1.235 | -1.847 | -2.418 | -2.731 | -2.890 | -2.988 | -3.355 | -3.861 | -4.028 | -4.775 | -4.896 | -4.896 | -4.896 | -1000 |
| A2 | 5.041 | 4.429 | 3.490 | 2.773 | 1.659 | -1.242 | -1.861 | -2.449 | -2.794 | -3.076 | -3.397 | -3.579 | -3.861 | -3.956 | -4.250 | -4.429 | -4.671 | -1000 |
| A3 | 5.041 | 4.152 | 3.956 | 3.427 | 2.449 | 1.351 | -1.163 | -1.649 | -2.176 | -2.609 | -2.903 | -3.051 | -3.279 | -3.956 | -4.152 | -4.429 | -4.501 | -1000 |
| Baa1 | 4.671 | 4.501 | 3.861 | 3.457 | 3.190 | 2.094 | 1.298 | -1.169 | -1.733 | -2.238 | -2.557 | -2.773 | -3.011 | -3.805 | -4.108 | -4.199 | -4.304 | -1000 |
| Baa2 | 4.775 | 4.067 | 3.682 | 3.369 | 3.160 | 2.596 | 1.802 | 1.227 | -1.274 | -1.925 | -2.245 | -2.388 | -2.630 | -2.896 | -3.316 | -3.805 | -3.891 | -1000 |
| Baa3 | 5.462 | 5.462 | 4.896 | 4.250 | 3.639 | 2.937 | 2.580 | 1.853 | 1.110 | -1.172 | -1.643 | -1.974 | -2.397 | -2.716 | -2.903 | -3.201 | -3.412 | -1000 |
| Ba1 | 4.581 | 4.581 | 4.581 | 4.364 | 3.579 | 3.369 | 2.767 | 2.436 | 1.829 | 1.180 | -1.154 | -1.462 | -1.877 | -2.063 | -2.368 | -2.877 | -3.160 | -1000 |
| Ba2 | 1000 | 1000 | 1000 | 5.462 | 4.775 | 3.891 | 3.560 | 3.076 | 2.621 | 1.995 | 1.199 | -1.041 | -1.426 | -1.570 | -2.058 | -2.588 | -2.877 | -1000 |
| Ba3 | 1000 | 5.811 | 5.811 | 5.811 | 4.896 | 3.891 | 3.473 | 3.222 | 2.973 | 2.576 | 1.917 | 1.393 | -0.989 | -1.251 | -1.665 | -2.113 | -2.316 | -1000 |
| B1 | 5.811 | 5.811 | 5.811 | 4.775 | 4.671 | 4.067 | 3.618 | 3.473 | 3.150 | 2.896 | 2.656 | 1.982 | 1.381 | -0.960 | -1.231 | -1.755 | -2.009 | -1000 |
| B2 | 1000 | 1000 | 4.896 | 4.775 | 4.067 | 4.067 | 3.832 | 3.457 | 3.291 | 3.094 | 2.871 | 2.250 | 1.765 | 1.285 | -0.710 | -1.202 | -1.442 | -1000 |
| B3 | 1000 | 1000 | 4.775 | 4.775 | 4.581 | 4.304 | 3.991 | 3.660 | 3.427 | 3.160 | 2.988 | 2.752 | 2.298 | 1.644 | 1.354 | -0.841 | -1.173 | -1000 |
| Caa | 1000 | 1000 | 1000 | 1000 | 1000 | 1000 | 1000 | 1000 | 3.304 | 2.846 | 2.520 | 2.520 | 2.126 | 1.813 | 1.663 | 1.401 | -0.558 | -1000 |
| Def | 1000 | 1000 | 1000 | 1000 | 1000 | 1000 | 1000 | 1000 | 1000 | 1000 | 1000 | 1000 | 1000 | 1000 | 1000 | 1000 | 1000 | -1000 |

the joint migration probability $h_{B2,Aaa}$ given by equation (8.11). One can follow this procedure to compute the joint migration probabilities $h_{ik}$ to any of 324 discrete states for a two-obligor portfolio.

The next step in the process is to compute the credit loss $g_{ik}$ associated with each state of the discrete joint probability distribution. Here, $g_{ik}$ denotes the credit loss due to the rating migration of obligor 1 from state $u$ to state $i$ and of obligor 2 from state $v$ to state $k$. Because this credit loss is not dependent on the asset return distribution, one can compute this using equation (6.42) in Chapter 6.

Once the joint probabilities of being in each of the states and the corresponding credit losses have been determined, it is fairly simple to compute the expected value $E(\tilde{\ell}_1 \tilde{\ell}_2)$ of the joint distribution of credit loss using equation (6.43) in Chapter 6. Inserting this value into equation (6.5) in Chapter 6 allows one to compute the loss correlation between the two obligors under the migration mode when the joint distribution of asset returns is bivariate $t$ distributed. Once the loss correlation between the obligors is determined, computing the unexpected loss of the portfolio is straightforward.

Again it is instructive to compare the expected and the unexpected loss of the two-bond portfolio when asset returns are assumed to be $t$ distributed. The various credit risk measures computed using the analytical approach presented here for the two-bond portfolio example considered in Exhibit 6.1 in Chapter 6 with 30 percent asset return correlation are as follows:

- The loss correlation $\rho_{ik}^{\ell}$ under the migration mode is 0.14905.
- The expected portfolio loss $EL_P$ under the migration mode is \$4,740.
- The unexpected portfolio loss $UL_P$ under the migration mode is \$32,770.

As one might expect, the unexpected loss of the portfolio increases due to an increase in the loss correlation between the obligors.

To provide further comparisons for the credit risk measures obtained when the joint normality of asset returns is relaxed, Exhibit 8.3 shows the risk measures computed for the 23-bond portfolio considered in Exhibit 6.6 in Chapter 6 assuming a multivariate $t$ distribution for asset returns. In computing the expected and unexpected losses for the portfolio, the indicative

**EXHIBIT 8.3** Portfolio Credit Risk Using Indicative Asset Return Correlation Matrix

| Description | $EL_P$ (mn \$) | $UL_P$ (mn \$) | %$EL_P$ (bp) | %$UL_P$ (bp) |
|---|---|---|---|---|
| Under default mode | 0.660 | 3.783 | 13.8 | 79.4 |
| Under migration mode | 1.622 | 5.034 | 34.0 | 105.6 |

asset return correlation matrix given in Exhibit 6.7 in Chapter 6 has been used. The results again show an increase in the portfolio unexpected loss relative to the multivariate normal distribution assumption for asset returns. For example, the percentage portfolio unexpected loss under the migration mode increases roughly by 17 basis points when the joint distribution of asset returns is assumed to be multivariate $t$ rather than multivariate normal.

## LOSS SIMULATION

Under the assumption that the joint distribution of asset returns is multivariate $t$, I outlined a computational procedure for evaluating portfolio unexpected loss using an analytical approach. To compute the tail risk measures, it is necessary to perform a simulation to generate the credit loss distribution of the portfolio. The steps involved in simulating the loss distribution are almost identical to the ones presented in Chapter 7 except for one difference. Instead of generating the sequence of correlated asset returns from a multivariate normal distribution, it is now necessary to generate this sequence from a multivariate $t$ distribution. In this section, I briefly discuss the procedure for generating a sequence of random vectors from a multivariate $t$ distribution. Subsequently, I indicate how the credit loss distribution can be generated under the multivariate $t$ distribution for asset returns.

Earlier in this chapter, I made the observation that a random vector with multivariate $t$ distribution having $v$ degrees of freedom can be derived from a chi-square random variable with $v$ degrees of freedom and a random vector that is normally distributed and independent of the chi-square random variable. This suggests that by appropriately combining a sequence of multivariate normal random vectors and a sequence of chi-square distributed random variables with $v$ degrees of freedom, a sequence of multivariate $t$-distributed random vectors with $v$ degrees of freedom can be simulated.

The procedure for generating a sequence of random vectors from a multivariate normal distribution was discussed in Chapter 7. Hence, I do not purse this further in this section. To generate a sequence of chi-square distributed random variables, the standard procedure is to use the relationship between a chi-square distribution and a gamma distribution. A random variable $x$ is said to have a gamma distribution if its density function is defined as follows:

$$f(x) = \begin{cases} \frac{1}{\Gamma(\alpha)\beta^{\alpha}} x^{\alpha-1} e^{-x/\beta}, & x > 0 \\ 0, & x \leq 0 \end{cases} \qquad (8.13)$$

In equation (8.13), $\alpha > 0$ and $\beta > 0$ are the parameters of the gamma distribution and $\Gamma(\alpha)$ is the gamma function given by equation (8.5). The chi-square distribution with $v$ degrees of freedom is a special case of the gamma distribution with parameter values $\alpha = v/2$ and $\beta = 2$.

Given the foregoing relationship between a gamma and a chi-square distribution, a sequence of random variables having a chi-square distribution with $v$ degrees of freedom can be generated by sampling from a gamma distribution with parameter values $\alpha = v/2$ and $\beta = 2$. Most standard software packages provide routines for generating random sequences from a gamma distribution. Hence, I do not discuss the details concerned with generating such a sequence of random variables.

To summarize, the following are the steps involved in generating an $n$-dimensional sequence of multivariate $t$ distributed random variables with $v$ degrees of freedom:

*Step 1.* Compute the Cholesky factor $L$ of the matrix $C$, where $C$ is the $n \times n$ asset return correlation matrix.

*Step 2.* Simulate $n$ independent standard normal random variates $z_i, z_2, \ldots, z_n$ and set $\vec{u} = L\vec{z}$.

*Step 3.* Simulate a random variate $\omega$ from a chi-square distribution with $v$ degrees of freedom that is independent of the normal random variates and set $S = \sqrt{v}/\sqrt{\omega}$.

*Step 4.* Set $\vec{x} = s \cdot \vec{u}$, which represents the desired $n$-dimensional $t$ variate with $v$ degrees of freedom and correlation matrix $C$.

Repeating steps 2 to 4 allows one to generate the sequence of multivariate $t$-distributed random variables.

Computing the credit loss under each simulation run will require comparing the asset return values against the $z$-thresholds given in Exhibit 8.2 to trigger rating migrations and defaults for the obligors in the portfolio. On the basis of the implied rating changes for the obligors using simulated asset returns, the credit loss for each simulation run can be calculated. The rest of the steps involved in computing the credit risk measures of interest from the simulated loss distribution are identical to the ones outlined in Chapter 7.

Exhibits 8.4 and 8.5 show the various portfolio credit risk measures evaluated for the 23-bond portfolio given in Exhibit 6.6 in Chapter 6 under

**EXHIBIT 8.4** Portfolio Credit Risk Measures Under Default Mode Based on Simulated Loss Distribution and Historical PD

| Description | Amount (million $) | Relative to Portfolio Size (bp) |
|---|---|---|
| Expected loss | 0.659 | 13.8 |
| Unexpected loss | 3.750 | 78.7 |
| CrVaR at 90 percent confidence | 0.0 | 0.0 |
| ESR at 90 percent confidence | 6.593 | 138.3 |

**EXHIBIT 8.5** Portfolio Credit Risk Measures Under Migration Mode Based on Simulated Loss Distribution

| Description | Amount (million $) | Relative to Portfolio Size (bp) |
|---|---|---|
| Expected loss | 1.621 | 34.0 |
| Unexpected loss | 5.009 | 105.1 |
| CrVaR at 90 percent confidence | 4.602 | 96.6 |
| ESR at 90 percent confidence | 12.211 | 256.2 |

the default mode and the migration mode, respectively. These measures were computed with eight degrees of freedom for the multivariate $t$ distribution, and the indicative asset return correlation matrix given in Exhibit 6.7 in Chapter 6 was used to generate correlated asset returns. The simulations were performed using antithetic sampling and the total number of simulation runs was 500,000.

In comparing the credit risk measures shown in Exhibit 7.5 in Chapter 7 against those in Exhibit 8.4, one can make the interesting observation that there is a marginal reduction in the ESR at the 90 percent confidence level under the default mode when the joint distribution of asset returns is assumed to be $t$ distributed with eight degrees of freedom. Under the migration mode, however, ESR at the 90 percent confidence level is roughly 16 basis points higher when the joint distribution of asset returns is assumed to be $t$ distributed with eight degrees of freedom. The credit VaR at the 90 percent confidence level, on the other hand, is lower when asset returns have a multivariate $t$ distribution. This observation once again illustrates that CrVaR as a tail risk measure needs to be used with some caution because it does not reflect the potential losses when losses exceed this amount.

## APPENDIX

The following C program implementation for computing the bivariate $t$ probability given by equation (8.7) uses finite sums of incomplete beta functions:

```
Description:    Function for computing the bivariate t
                  probability
Arguments:      nu is the number of degrees of freedom
                dh is the upper limit of the first
                  integral
                dk is the upper limit of the second
                  integral
```

|  |  |
|---|---|
|  | rho is the correlation between two *t* random variables |
| Return value: | Bivariate probability as a double |
| Reference: | This algorithm is based on the method described by C. W. Dunnett and M. Sobel (1954), "A Bivariate General-ization of Student's *t*-Distribution with Tables for Certain Special Cases," *Biometrika*, vol. 41, pp. 153–169 |
| Remarks: | The C implementation is based on a FORTRAN code provided by Alan Genz at the following Web site: www.sci.wsu.edu/math/faculty/genz/homepage |

```
double bivariate_t_probability (double nu, double dh,
  double dk, double rho)
{
int i, k;
double pi, ors, hrk, krh, bvt, snu, hs, ks;
double gmph, gmpk, xnkh, xnhk, qhrk, hkn, hpk, hkrn;
double btnckh, btnchk, btpdkh, btpdhk, idouble, intpart;
if ((nu < 1.0) || fabs(rho) > 0.9999)
  return (-1.0); /* signal an error */
pi = acos(-1.0);
snu = sqrt(nu);
ors = 1.0 - rho*rho;
hrk = dh - rho*dk;
krh = dk - rho*dh;
if ((fabs(hrk) + ors) > 0.0)
{
  xnhk = hrk*hrk/(hrk*hrk + ors*(nu + dk*dk));
  xnkh = krh*krh/(krh*krh + ors*(nu + dh*dh));
}
else
{
  xnhk = 0.0;
  xnkh = 0.0;
}
hs = ((dh-rho*dk) < 0.0)? -1.0:1.0;
ks = ((dk-rho*dh) < 0.0)? -1.0:1.0;
if (modf(nu/2.0, &intpart) <1.0e-8)
```

```
{
bvt = atan2(sqrt(ors), -rho)/(2.0*pi);
gmph = dh/sqrt(16.0*(nu + dh*dh));
gmpk = dk/sqrt(16.0*(nu + dk*dk));
btnckh = 2.0*atan2(sqrt(xnkh), sqrt(1.0 - xnkh))/pi;
btpdkh = 2.0*sqrt(xnkh*(1.0 - xnkh))/pi;
btnchk = 2.0*atan2(sqrt(xnhk), sqrt(1.0 - xnhk))/pi;
btpdhk = 2.0*sqrt(xnhk*(1.0 - xnhk))/pi;
k = (int) (nu/2.0);
for (i=1; i<=k; i++)
{
idouble = (double) (2*i);
bvt = bvt + gmph*(1.0 + ks*btnckh);
bvt = bvt + gmpk*(1.0 + hs*btnchk);
btnckh = btnckh + btpdkh;
btpdkh = idouble*btpdkh*(1.0 - xnkh)/(idouble + 1.0);
btnchk = btnchk + btpdhk;
btpdhk = idouble*btpdhk*(1.0 - xnhk)/(idouble + 1.0);
gmph = gmph*(idouble - 1.0)/(idouble*(1.0 + dh*dh/nu));
gmpk = gmpk*(idouble - 1.0)/(idouble*(1.0 + dk*dk/nu));
 }
}
else
{
qhrk = sqrt(dh*dh + dk*dk - 2.0*rho*dh*dk + nu*ors);
hkrn = dh*dk + rho*nu;
hkn = dh*dk - nu;
hpk = dh + dk;
bvt = atan2(-snu*(hkn*qhrk+hpk*hkrn), (hkn*hkrn-
  nu*hpk*qhrk))/(2.0*pi);
if (bvt < -1.0e-14)
  bvt = bvt + 1.0;
gmph = dh/(2.0*pi*snu*(1.0 + dh*dh/nu));
gmpk = dk/(2.0*pi*snu*(1.0 + dk*dk/nu));
btnckh = sqrt(xnkh);
btpdkh = btnckh;
btnchk = sqrt(xnhk);
btpdhk = btnchk;
k = (int) ((nu - 1.0)/2.0);
for (i=1; i<=k; i++)
{
idouble = (double) (2*i);
bvt = bvt + gmph*(1.0 + ks*btnckh);
```

```
bvt = bvt + gmpk*(1.0 + hs*btnchk);
btpdkh = (idouble - 1.0)*btpdkh*(1.0 - xnkh)/(idouble);
btnckh = btnckh + btpdkh;
gmph = idouble*gmph/((idouble + 1.0)*(1.0 + dh*dh/nu));
gmpk = idouble*gmpk/((idouble + 1.0)*(1.0 + dk*dk/nu));
 }
}
return(bvt);
}
```

## QUESTIONS

1. What are the drawbacks of modeling the joint distribution of asset returns as a multivariate normal?
2. Discuss the motivation for using Student's $t$ distribution to model the joint distribution of asset returns.
3. How will the credit loss distribution of a portfolio be affected as the number of degrees of freedom of the multivariate $t$ distribution used to model the joint distribution of asset returns is reduced?
4. Assuming that the probability of default of an obligor is 50 basis points, compute the $z$-threshold value that will trigger a default when the obligor's asset returns are modeled as (a) normally distributed and (b) Student's $t$ distributed with eight degrees of freedom.
5. Assuming that the joint distribution of asset returns is bivariate $t$ distributed with eight degrees of freedom, compute the unexpected loss of the two-bond portfolio example given in Exhibit 6.1 in Chapter 6 under the default mode using (a) default correlation to aggregate portfolio credit risk and (b) loss correlation to aggregate portfolio credit risk. Use historical default probabilities in the calculations and assume that the asset correlation between obligors is 20 percent.
6. Describe the steps involved in simulating a sequence of a multivariate $t$-distributed random vector.

## CHAPTER 9

# Risk Reporting and Performance Attribution

**P**ortfolio management is concerned with the process of managing the risk of a portfolio relative to a benchmark with the purpose of either tracking or adding value. In order to manage the risks relative to a benchmark, a framework for risk measurement has to be established. In Chapters 4 to 8, I discussed how market risk and credit risk in a corporate bond portfolio could be quantified, which in turn established the framework for risk measurement. For market risk measurement, I introduced the concept of tracking error to measure the market risk of a portfolio relative to a benchmark. The credit risk measures I introduced, on the other hand, are primarily absolute risk measures for the portfolio.

When portfolios are managed on behalf of clients, communicating the risks of the portfolio relative to the benchmark becomes a requirement. To meet this requirement, one needs to develop a framework for risk reporting. In developing the risk-reporting framework, it is important to keep in mind that the risk reports that are generated should be simple and intuitive so that they improve the effectiveness of risk communication. For instance, the risk report should be able to provide insight on potential return deviations that can arise due to mismatches in risk exposures between the portfolio and the benchmark. In particular, the risk report should be able to identify risk sources that can lead to an underperformance against the benchmark. The usefulness of the risk report is further enhanced if, on the basis of the information it contains, one can quantify the magnitude of potential underperformance and its associated probability. Finally, it is important to ensure that the risk report offers drill-down capability. Drill-down capability is a jargon that is used to refer to the ability of a risk report to provide different levels of granularity to meet the reporting requirements of different interest groups.

A related and equally important requirement in the portfolio management business is to report the performance of the portfolio and explain the factors that led to differences in return versus the benchmark. This process, which involves analyzing the portfolio performance and its relative performance against the benchmark in terms of the decisions that led to differences in returns, is usually referred to as performance attribution. Together, risk reporting and performance attribution constitute the focal point in the relationship between the manager and the fiduciary overseeing the prudent management of the assets.

In this chapter, I develop a framework for reporting the credit risk and market risk of a corporate bond portfolio that is managed against a benchmark. To emphasize the point that the risk estimates presented in the risk report are subject to model risk, I present the credit risk report under both multivariate normal distribution and multivariate $t$-distribution assumptions for the asset returns. I also briefly mention the types of risk guidelines a client can enforce when a corporate bond portfolio mandate is awarded. Finally, I discuss performance attribution and develop a simple performance attribution model for identifying the sources for excess returns against the benchmark for corporate bond portfolios.

## RELATIVE CREDIT RISK MEASURES

Standard industry practice is to quantify the risk of a portfolio against a benchmark in terms of tracking error. Tracking error is a statistical measure of risk that indicates the range of possible outcomes surrounding mean value. Formally, tracking error is the annualized standard deviation of the difference between portfolio return and benchmark return. If it is assumed that the returns are normally distributed, then there is an equal probability of returns being higher or lower than the average outperformance. There is also approximately a 1 in 3 chance of returns being greater than one standard deviation from the mean value. From a downside risk perspective, tracking error for normally distributed returns can be interpreted as the magnitude of underperformance that will be exceeded only on 1 in 6 occasions. Equivalently, tracking error can be interpreted as the relative value at risk of a portfolio against its benchmark at 83 percent confidence level. Such an interpretation is based on the assumption that returns are normally distributed with a zero mean value.

In general, tracking error as a risk measure can be used to substantiate past performance or to predict future performance. Historical tracking errors are based on observed excess returns between the portfolio and the benchmark. Computing future or ex ante tracking errors, on the other hand, requires estimating a risk model. To estimate such a risk model, one needs to specify a set of risk factors that captures the exposure to different sources of risk.[1] Such an approach, although appropriate for quantifying market risk relative to the benchmark, will fail to adequately reflect the true level of credit risk. This is because the risk model is merely a representation of market-driven volatility and correlation observed among the risk factors and is estimated using daily or weekly time series data. Credit events, on the contrary, are events that occur infrequently and hence will not be captured when daily or weekly time series data are collected over a limited time frame, a practice that is common for market risk measurement. Hence, presenting a risk report for a corporate bond portfolio on the basis of tracking error will fail to capture the true risks arising from credit events.

In order to properly quantify and report credit risk relative to a benchmark, one needs to move away from the tracking error framework. Before doing this, however, it is useful to reflect upon the philosophy behind the approach used to compute ex ante tracking error. In broad terms, the approach identifies common risk factors between the portfolio and the benchmark and then uses the difference in exposures to these risk factors as a means of computing ex ante tracking error. The difficulty in trying to extend this approach to compute relative credit risk is that the notion of common risk factors was not included in credit risk. Instead, every obligor in a certain sense qualified to be a risk factor. In the absence of common factors, one alternative to quantifying relative risk would be to compute the difference between the absolute risk measures for the portfolio and the benchmark. The main drawback with the quantification of relative risk in this manner is that one cannot estimate the magnitude of potential underperformance and its associated probability. In this section, I develop a method to compute a relative measure of credit risk that meets this requirement.

The composition of any portfolio that intends to replicate a benchmark can be seen as comprising long and short positions against the benchmark weights for the constituent bonds in the benchmark portfolio. When there are no long or short positions versus the constituent bonds in the benchmark, there will be no residual risk and hence the relative credit and market risk between the portfolio and benchmark will be zero. The relative credit risk between the portfolio and the benchmark can be seen as the credit risk of a portfolio that has net long and short positions in the respective bonds that constitute the benchmark. For those bonds held in the portfolio not contained in the benchmark, one simply extends the composition of the benchmark by including these bonds with a zero weight.

To derive the relative credit risk measure, assume the benchmark comprises $n$ bonds. The portfolio that is set up to replicate the risks of the benchmark will, in general, comprise only a subset of the bonds in the benchmark. However, for mathematical exposition one can consider the portfolio to also comprise $n$ bonds with zero nominal exposures for those bonds that are not held in the portfolio. For the portfolio, let the nominal exposure to the $i$th bond be $NE_{i,P}$ and let $M_P$ be the mark to market value of the portfolio. Let the corresponding values for the benchmark be $NE_{i,B}$ and $M_B$, respectively. The relative credit risk between the portfolio and the benchmark can be seen as the credit risk of an active portfolio, whose nominal exposure to the $i$th bond is given by

$$\mathrm{NE}_{i,A} = \left( \mathrm{NE}_{i,P} - \mathrm{NE}_{i,B} \times \frac{M_P}{M_B} \right) \qquad (9.1)$$

Note that by construction some of the nominal exposures of the active portfolio will be positive and others negative. Given the nominal exposure $\mathrm{NE}_{i,A}$ for $i$th bond in the active portfolio, it is easy to compute the unexpected loss of the $i$th bond and hence the unexpected loss of the active portfolio using equation (6.9) in Chapter 6. The unexpected loss of the active portfolio provides useful information concerning the relative credit risk between the portfolio and the benchmark. However, because the distribution of relative credit losses between two portfolios is not normal, it is difficult to provide a probabilistic interpretation to the level of underperformance against the benchmark based on this risk measure.

I indicated that the relative risk measure would be useful under the condition that it captures both the magnitude and the probability of underperformance. In the absence of information concerning the shape of the credit loss distribution of the portfolio with nominal exposures give by equation (9.1), the approach to measuring relative risk that meets this objective requires simulating the relative credit loss distribution. This makes it possible to compute relative credit risk measures that reflect both the magnitude of underperformance and its associated probability.

Generating the loss distribution for a portfolio with nominal exposures given by equation (9.1) is fairly straightforward if one follows the approach outlined in Chapter 7 or Chapter 8. Once the loss distribution is simulated, credit value at risk and expected shortfall risk at 90 percent confidence level can be computed as indicated in Chapter 7. Considering that this loss distribution is associated with a portfolio that captures the relative credit risk arising from taking long and short positions against the bonds constituting the benchmark, I refer to these risk measures as relative CrVaR and relative ESR, both estimated at a 90 percent level of confidence.

To illustrate the relative credit risk measures defined here, I present a numerical example. Specifically, the portfolio comprising 23 bonds given in Exhibit 6.6 in Chapter 6 is considered to represent the benchmark portfolio. Assume that the actual portfolio held to replicate the benchmark consists of 7 bonds and residual cash (Exhibit 9.1). The holdings of this portfolio are given in Exhibit 9.1, and the mark to market value of the portfolio is equal to USD 73.0 million.

Under the assumption that the asset returns of obligors are multivariate normal, the simulated loss distribution of the relative credit risk between

**EXHIBIT 9.1**   Composition of Portfolio Held as of 24 April 2002

| S. No. | Issuer | Ticker | Industry | Issuer Rating | Nominal USD mn | Dirty Price | Maturity | Coupon (%) |
|---|---|---|---|---|---|---|---|---|
| 1 | Health Care Reit | HCN | INR | Ba1 | 10.0 | 99.91 | 15 Aug 07 | 7.500 |
| 2 | Alcoa Inc | AA | BAC | A1 | 10.0 | 105.24 | 1 Jun 06 | 5.875 |
| 3 | Abbey Natl Plc | ABBEY | BNK | Aa3 | 10.0 | 108.43 | 17 Nov 05 | 6.690 |
| 4 | Countrywide Home | CCR | FIN | A3 | 10.0 | 101.25 | 1 Aug 06 | 5.500 |
| 5 | Colgate-Palm Co | CL | CNC | Aa3 | 10.0 | 101.43 | 29 Apr 05 | 3.980 |
| 6 | Oracle Corp | ORCL | COT | A3 | 10.0 | 105.33 | 15 Feb 07 | 6.910 |
| 7 | Pub Svc EL & Gas | PEG | UTL | A3 | 10.0 | 104.94 | 1 Mar 06 | 6.750 |
| 8 | Cash (1.75% p.a.) | | | | 0.35 | 100.00 | 30 Apr 02 | 1.750 |

the portfolio held and the benchmark is shown in Exhibit 9.2. The simulations were performed under the migration mode using the indicative asset return correlation matrix given in Exhibit 6.7 in Chapter 6. In Exhibit 9.2, negative losses correspond to a profit, which arises primarily from the short positions held in many bonds. These short positions are measured relative to the benchmark weights for these bonds. One can see from Exhibit 9.2 that there is scope for both underperformance and outperformance relative to the benchmark. To highlight the loss distribution in the tail regions, Exhibit 9.3 shows the simulated losses with the peak of the distribution clipped.

It is interesting to note from Exhibit 9.3 that the magnitude of potential underperformance (right tail region) is greater than the potential outperformance that can be generated against the benchmark. Although the probability of small outperformance is large, there is a small probability of

**EXHIBIT 9.2**   Relative Credit Loss Distribution Under the Migration Mode

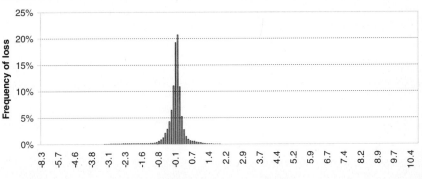

**EXHIBIT 9.3**  Relative Credit Loss Distribution Under the Migration Mode

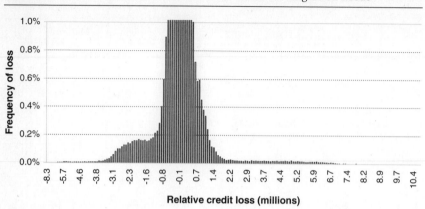

large underperformance against the benchmark. Quantifying relative credit risk in terms of tracking error fails to pick up these differences.

From the simulated losses, the relative credit risk measures of interest can be easily computed. These are shown in Exhibit 9.4. The unexpected loss of the active portfolio computed using equation (6.9) in Chapter 6 is also shown in this exhibit. The relative CrVaR measure in Exhibit 9.4 suggests that there is a 10 percent chance over a 1-year period that the portfolio will underperform the benchmark by more than 38 basis points. The average underperformance in the worst-case 10 percent scenarios is roughly equal to 126 basis points.

## MARGINAL CREDIT RISK CONTRIBUTION

In the previous section, I showed how the relative credit risk of the portfolio against the benchmark can be quantified. Although useful, such a risk measure does not identify the sources that contribute to the relative credit risk. Portfolio managers entrusted with the task of managing the risks relative to a given benchmark need to have the relative credit risk disaggregated

**EXHIBIT 9.4**  Relative Credit Risk Measures Under the Migration Mode

| Description | Amount ($) | Relative to Portfolio Size (bp) |
|---|---|---|
| UL of active portfolio | 653,000 | 89.5 |
| Relative CrVaR at 90 percent confidence | 282,000 | 38.6 |
| Relative ESR at 90 percent confidence | 918,000 | 125.8 |

so that the main risk drivers can be identified. This is necessary to make informed decisions on what bonds to buy and sell in order to mitigate risk concentrations. This leads to the topic of marginal credit risk contribution.

In broad terms, the marginal contribution to total risk from a bond can be defined as the rate of change in risk with respect to a small percentage change in the bond holding. If the risk measure in question is the unexpected loss of the portfolio, the marginal risk measure is referred to as the unexpected loss contribution (ULC). The unexpected loss contribution of the $i$th bond identifies the total amount of risk in the portfolio that is attributable to the $i$th bond. Formally, the ULC of the $i$th bond in the portfolio is defined as

$$\mathrm{ULC}_i = \mathrm{UL}_i \times \frac{\partial \mathrm{UL}_P}{\partial \mathrm{UL}_i} \tag{9.2}$$

By performing the differentiation, one can show that the unexpected loss contribution arising from the $i$th bond in the portfolio is given by

$$\mathrm{ULC}_i = \frac{\mathrm{UL}_i \times \sum_{k=1}^{n} \mathrm{UL}_k \times \rho_{ik}^{\ell}}{\mathrm{UL}_P} \tag{9.3}$$

An attractive feature of ULC as a marginal risk contribution measure is that the sum of the risk contributions of the individual bonds is equal to the total unexpected loss of the portfolio. In other words, the following relation holds:

$$\mathrm{UL}_P = \sum_{i=1}^{n} \mathrm{ULC}_i \tag{9.4}$$

This additivity property ensures that one can correctly identify the diversification effects of individual bonds held in the portfolio. If one works directly with the unexpected loss of the active portfolio, the unexpected loss contribution will identify the sources that contribute to the relative credit risk between the portfolio and the benchmark. I denote the unexpected loss of the active portfolio by $\mathrm{UL}_A$ and the unexpected loss contribution arising from the $i$th bond in the active portfolio by $\mathrm{ULC}_{i,A}$.

A risk report that identifies the risk contribution arising from every bond in the benchmark is not very useful. Typically this could be several thousands for an investment-grade corporate bond benchmark. To make the risk report meaningful, one has to group the bonds into subsets that have certain attributes. These attributes should be chosen such that they have an intuitive interpretation. The aggregated risk contribution arising from such groupings then provides a more meaningful risk report.

Potential attributes on which such groupings can be done are the industrial sector and the credit rating of the bond obligor. Computing the marginal risk contribution based on such groupings to the total relative credit risk enhances the usefulness of the risk report considerably. For instance, if one wishes to calculate the unexpected loss contribution of Aa1-rated obligors to the unexpected loss of the active portfolio, one needs to sum the unexpected loss contributions of all bonds that have this obligor rating in the active portfolio. Similarly, to compute the unexpected loss contribution of bonds that belong to the utilities sector in the active portfolio, one needs to sum the unexpected loss contributions of all bonds that belong to this sector. If the unexpected loss contribution of each bond is indexed by the obligor rating $R$ and the industrial sector $I$ of the bond, computing the unexpected loss contribution from Aa1-rated obligors to the unexpected loss of the active portfolio boils down to evaluating the following summation:

$$\mathrm{ULC}_A(\mathrm{Aa1}) = \sum_{\substack{i=1 \\ R=\mathrm{Aa1}}}^{n} \mathrm{ULC}_{i,A}(R,I) \qquad (9.5)$$

In practice, the unexpected loss contributions will be more informative if they are reported relative to the portfolio size. This requires dividing the unexpected loss contributions in equation (9.5) by the mark to market value of the actual portfolio held. In the next section, I present a sample credit risk report where the benchmark is taken to be the list of bonds given in Exhibit 6.6 in Chapter 6 and the actual portfolio held is taken to be the one given in Exhibit 9.1.

## PORTFOLIO CREDIT RISK REPORT

Active portfolio management focuses on outperforming the return of a specified benchmark without taking undue risks while achieving this objective. Several industrywide standards, such as the Global Industry Performance Standards or Standards of the Association for Investment Management and Research, exist on how to measure and report the added value relative to a benchmark. On the contrary, standards for measuring and reporting portfolio risk relative to a benchmark are practically nonexistent even for market risk. Part of the reason for this is that to measure risk, one has to choose a risk model in the first place. The choice of the appropriate risk factors that govern the risk model influence how well the risk model is able to capture the inherent risks. One could argue that there are broad guidelines as to how these risk factors could be chosen for measuring market risk. For measuring portfolio credit risk relative to a benchmark, on the

**EXHIBIT 9.5** Credit Risk Measures Under Migration Mode and Multinormal Distribution for Asset Returns

| Description | Portfolio Held (bp) | Benchmark (bp) | Active Portfolio (bp) |
|---|---|---|---|
| %EL | 27.1 | 34.0 | −7.0 |
| %UL | 112.7 | 88.8 | 89.5 |
| %CrVaR$_{90\%}$ | 85.2 | 102.9 | 38.6 |
| %ESR$_{90\%}$ | 247.7 | 240.3 | 125.8 |

other hand, there are no clear guidelines as to what these risk factors should be. As a result, there are no guiding principles for best practices in reporting credit risk. In this section, I present a credit risk report that would be a step in this direction.

Earlier in this chapter, I argued why an approach based on tracking error is not appropriate for measuring the credit risk of a portfolio relative to its benchmark. This led me to define the relative credit risk by setting up an active portfolio comprising long and short positions in the bonds that constitute the benchmark. The nominal exposures of the bonds in the active portfolio are given by equation (9.1). The credit risk measures introduced in earlier chapters can then be computed for all relevant portfolios. To ensure that the risk measures are comparable across portfolios, these should be reported as a percentage of the market value of the portfolios. Exhibit 9.5 shows a credit risk report that provides a comparison of various credit risk measures evaluated for three portfolios: the portfolio held, the benchmark portfolio, and the active portfolio.

One can infer from Exhibit 9.5 that the scope for underperformance is quite significant as indicated by the risk measures computed for the active portfolio. Notice that although the ESRs at 90 percent confidence level for the portfolio held and the benchmark are very similar, the ESR for the active portfolio is quite large. This can arise, for instance, through rating upgrades for some issuers held in the benchmark but not in the portfolio, which results in a difference in relative performance. Measuring only the downside risks of the portfolio and benchmark independently does not capture the relative risk of underperformance between the two portfolios.

The relative risk between the benchmark and the portfolio could be a result of intentional deviations taken by the portfolio manager. If this is not the case, then identifying the major sources that contribute to this risk is required to decide on suitable trades that can reduce this risk. This information can be derived from the unexpected loss contribution report shown in Exhibit 9.6. This exhibit identifies the exposure difference between the portfolio and the benchmark to a Ba2-rating grade being responsible for a significant part of the risk. Alternatively, one can also attribute a significant

**EXHIBIT 9.6**    Unexpected Loss Contributions to UL of Active Portfolio

| Across Ratings | | Across Industries | | Across Sectors | |
|---|---|---|---|---|---|
| Rating | %ULC (bp) | Industry | %ULC (bp) | Sector | %ULC (bp) |
| Aaa | 0 | BAC | 3.7 | Industrials | 46.7 |
| Aa1 | 0 | CCL | 7.0 | Utilities | 5.3 |
| Aa2 | 0 | CNC | 3.6 | Financials | 37.6 |
| Aa3 | 0 | COT | 14.2 | | |
| A1 | 5.2 | ENE | 0 | | |
| A2 | 4.6 | TRA | 18.2 | | |
| A3 | 2.2 | UTL | 5.2 | | |
| Baa1 | 17.2 | BNK | 3.7 | | |
| Baa2 | 0 | BRO | 0 | | |
| Baa3 | 0 | FIN | 5.4 | | |
| Ba1 | 0 | INR | 28.5 | | |
| Ba2 | 34.9 | | | | |
| Ba3 | 7.3 | | | | |
| B1 | 18.2 | | | | |
| B2 | 0 | | | | |
| B3 | 0 | | | | |
| Caa–C | 0 | | | | |

part of this risk to the difference in exposure to the insurance and reits (INR) sector.

Exhibit 9.7 examines the various credit risk measures under the assumption that the joint distribution of asset returns of obligors is multivariate $t$ rather than multinormal. Examining Exhibit 9.7, one can see that the relative credit risk has reduced marginally under the multivariate $t$ assumption. This might appear surprising at a first glance. However, note that under the multivariate $t$ distribution there is greater tail dependence between the obligor asset returns. Hence, an extreme movement in asset returns will be more correlated than that modeled by a multinormal distribution. This has the implication that the risk of an underperformance due

**EXHIBIT 9.7**    Credit Risk Measures Under Migration Mode and Multivariate $t$ Distribution for Asset Returns

| Description | Portfolio Held (bp) | Benchmark (bp) | Active Portfolio (bp) |
|---|---|---|---|
| %EL | 27.1 | 34.0 | −7.0 |
| %UL | 123.4 | 105.6 | 86.8 |
| %CrVaR$_{90\%}$ | 79.5 | 96.6 | 33.8 |
| %ESR$_{90\%}$ | 252.6 | 256.2 | 112.5 |

**EXHIBIT 9.8**  Unexpected Loss Contributions to UL of Active Portfolio

| Across Ratings | | Across Industries | | Across Sectors | |
|---|---|---|---|---|---|
| Rating | %ULC (bp) | Industry | %ULC (bp) | Sector | %ULC (bp) |
| Aaa | 0 | BAC | 3.6 | Industrials | 46.3 |
| Aa1 | 0 | CCL | 7.0 | Utilities | 5.0 |
| Aa2 | 0 | CNC | 3.6 | Financials | 35.5 |
| Aa3 | 0 | COT | 13.9 | | |
| A1 | 4.9 | ENE | 0 | | |
| A2 | 4.4 | TRA | 18.3 | | |
| A3 | 2.1 | UTL | 5.0 | | |
| Baa1 | 16.3 | BNK | 3.4 | | |
| Baa2 | 0 | BRO | 0 | | |
| Baa3 | 0 | FIN | 5.0 | | |
| Ba1 | 0 | INR | 27.0 | | |
| Ba2 | 33.5 | | | | |
| Ba3 | 7.3 | | | | |
| B1 | 18.3 | | | | |
| B2 | 0 | | | | |
| B3 | 0 | | | | |
| Caa–C | 0 | | | | |

to exposure differences to various obligors in the portfolio and the benchmark will be less severe than that implied by the multinormal distribution. The unexpected loss contributions to the unexpected loss of the active portfolio from different credit ratings and industry sectors under the multivariate $t$ distribution are shown in Exhibit 9.8.

## Risk Reporting During Economic Contractions

The foregoing credit risk reports can be regarded as standard reports, which are valid during normal market conditions. This is because the recovery rate values and the rating transition matrix used to generate the risk report reflect historical averages over many economic cycles. During period of economic contraction, however, empirical evidence indicates that the recovery values are lower and rating downgrade and default probabilities are usually higher than historical averages. Other stylized facts are an increase in yield spreads between rating categories and a greater asset return correlation between obligors during periods of economic contraction.

To adequately capture the risks under such market conditions, it is important to include risk reports generated by appropriately modifying the input parameters of the credit risk model. Interpreted differently, such

**EXHIBIT 9.9** Modified 1-Year Rating Transition Matrix Under 20 Percent Stress Factor

| | Aaa | Aa1 | Aa2 | Aa3 | A1 | A2 | A3 | Baa1 | Baa2 | Baa3 | Ba1 | Ba2 | Ba3 | B1 | B2 | B3 | Caa–C | Default |
|---|---|---|---|---|---|---|---|---|---|---|---|---|---|---|---|---|---|---|
| Aaa | 86.872 | 7.392 | 3.648 | 0.588 | 0.888 | 0.348 | 0.204 | 0.000 | 0.000 | 0.000 | 0.048 | 0.000 | 0.000 | 0.000 | 0.000 | 0.000 | 0.000 | 0.012 |
| Aa1 | 2.650 | 75.570 | 9.840 | 8.232 | 2.892 | 0.396 | 0.060 | 0.228 | 0.000 | 0.000 | 0.108 | 0.000 | 0.000 | 0.000 | 0.000 | 0.000 | 0.000 | 0.024 |
| Aa2 | 0.740 | 3.050 | 77.838 | 10.584 | 4.956 | 1.704 | 0.732 | 0.204 | 0.000 | 0.000 | 0.000 | 0.000 | 0.060 | 0.096 | 0.000 | 0.000 | 0.000 | 0.036 |
| Aa3 | 0.080 | 0.640 | 3.520 | 78.624 | 11.160 | 3.936 | 1.068 | 0.300 | 0.264 | 0.204 | 0.000 | 0.048 | 0.108 | 0.000 | 0.000 | 0.000 | 0.000 | 0.048 |
| A1 | 0.030 | 0.110 | 0.620 | 5.760 | 78.360 | 9.000 | 3.600 | 0.972 | 0.336 | 0.168 | 0.444 | 0.312 | 0.060 | 0.144 | 0.012 | 0.000 | 0.000 | 0.072 |
| A2 | 0.050 | 0.060 | 0.300 | 0.800 | 5.570 | 78.256 | 8.976 | 3.588 | 0.996 | 0.492 | 0.348 | 0.132 | 0.144 | 0.036 | 0.084 | 0.036 | 0.036 | 0.096 |
| A3 | 0.050 | 0.110 | 0.050 | 0.240 | 1.550 | 8.680 | 72.616 | 8.436 | 4.596 | 1.800 | 0.684 | 0.240 | 0.276 | 0.420 | 0.060 | 0.060 | 0.012 | 0.120 |
| Baa1 | 0.080 | 0.020 | 0.140 | 0.190 | 0.210 | 2.840 | 8.040 | 71.920 | 9.276 | 3.948 | 1.308 | 0.576 | 0.444 | 0.696 | 0.108 | 0.024 | 0.024 | 0.156 |
| Baa2 | 0.070 | 0.110 | 0.130 | 0.180 | 0.180 | 0.920 | 3.870 | 7.270 | 72.966 | 8.880 | 2.124 | 0.660 | 0.828 | 0.612 | 0.564 | 0.324 | 0.036 | 0.276 |
| Baa3 | 0.030 | 0.000 | 0.030 | 0.080 | 0.190 | 0.610 | 0.690 | 3.420 | 9.920 | 68.542 | 8.148 | 3.312 | 2.424 | 1.020 | 0.396 | 0.432 | 0.204 | 0.552 |
| Ba1 | 0.090 | 0.000 | 0.000 | 0.030 | 0.240 | 0.130 | 0.730 | 0.820 | 3.200 | 8.360 | 69.492 | 6.000 | 5.064 | 1.464 | 1.656 | 1.488 | 0.432 | 0.804 |
| Ba2 | 0.000 | 0.000 | 0.000 | 0.030 | 0.040 | 0.160 | 0.140 | 0.390 | 0.770 | 2.530 | 9.180 | 67.068 | 8.184 | 2.208 | 4.884 | 2.484 | 0.696 | 1.236 |
| Ba3 | 0.000 | 0.020 | 0.000 | 0.000 | 0.040 | 0.170 | 0.190 | 0.190 | 0.280 | 0.750 | 2.940 | 5.470 | 68.866 | 6.300 | 6.720 | 4.008 | 1.104 | 2.952 |
| B1 | 0.020 | 0.000 | 0.000 | 0.000 | 0.060 | 0.100 | 0.160 | 0.080 | 0.260 | 0.320 | 0.450 | 2.690 | 6.090 | 67.870 | 6.696 | 8.160 | 2.280 | 4.764 |
| B2 | 0.000 | 0.000 | 0.060 | 0.010 | 0.110 | 0.000 | 0.070 | 0.180 | 0.120 | 0.190 | 0.300 | 1.690 | 3.050 | 5.950 | 58.402 | 14.040 | 4.584 | 11.244 |
| B3 | 0.000 | 0.000 | 0.070 | 0.000 | 0.020 | 0.040 | 0.070 | 0.120 | 0.130 | 0.220 | 0.200 | 0.380 | 1.280 | 4.410 | 3.690 | 63.894 | 9.012 | 16.464 |
| Caa–C | 0.000 | 0.000 | 0.000 | 0.000 | 0.000 | 0.000 | 0.540 | 0.000 | 0.540 | 0.540 | 0.710 | 0.000 | 1.520 | 2.060 | 1.370 | 3.200 | 54.540 | 35.520 |
| Default | 0.000 | 0.000 | 0.000 | 0.000 | 0.000 | 0.000 | 0.000 | 0.000 | 0.000 | 0.000 | 0.000 | 0.000 | 0.000 | 0.000 | 0.000 | 0.000 | 0.000 | 100.00 |

reports can be regarded as stress reports under adverse market conditions. Under such an interpretation, the factor by which certain input variables of the credit risk model are modified to reflect increased risks arising from a weak economy can be referred to as the stress factor. In general, the group responsible for the risk reporting usually decides the appropriate stress factors to be used. For purpose of illustration, I consider the stress factor here to be 20 percent. Note that, in general, the stress factors do not have to be the same for all input variables.

To generate the credit risk report under the 20 percent stress factor, the following input variables to the credit risk model were changed as follows:

- A decrease in the recovery rates by 20 percent from the historical average.
- An increase in the yield spreads between rating categories by 20 percent from the values given in Exhibit 5.8 in Chapter 5.
- An increase in the asset return correlation between obligor pairs by 20 percent.
- An increase in the rating downgrade and default probabilities by 20 percent.

The normalized rating transition matrix under the 20 percent stress factor is shown in Exhibit 9.9. Note that the increase in the downgrade and default probabilities is assumed to occur at the expense of a lower probability of the obligor remaining in the same rating grade at the end of the 1-year horizon.

Exhibit 9.10 shows the credit risk measures generated with the 20 percent stress factor under the migration mode and multivariate *t*-distribution assumption for asset returns. One can infer from this exhibit that there is a significant increase in the credit risk measures for the active portfolio, which suggests that the magnitude of underperformance against the benchmark can be much greater under these market conditions.

**EXHIBIT 9.10** Credit Risk Measures for 20 Percent Stress Factor Under Migration Mode and Multivariate *t* Distribution for Asset Returns

| Description | Portfolio Held (bp) | Benchmark (bp) | Active Portfolio (bp) |
|---|---|---|---|
| %EL | 38.8 | 47.2 | −8.5 |
| %UL | 157.1 | 139.3 | 98.2 |
| %CVaR$_{90\%}$ | 121.6 | 141.4 | 43.4 |
| %ESR$_{90\%}$ | 348.9 | 356.7 | 141.5 |

## PORTFOLIO MARKET RISK REPORT

Although the major preoccupation here has been to measure and report the credit risk of a corporate bond portfolio, presenting the market risk report of the portfolio constitutes an integral part of the risk-reporting requirement for a corporate bond portfolio. Reports for market risk are much more standardized in terms of what the appropriate risk quantities presented should be. Effective duration and effective convexity are almost standard risk quantities that are presented in a market risk report. Tracking error defined in Chapter 4 is also a standard risk measure that is presented. It is useful to remark that duration provides an estimate of the potential loss in market value if the yield curve shifts up by 100 basis points. However, the probability associated with such an event occurring is not known. Quantities such as tracking error, value at risk, and expected shortfall risk, on the other hand, capture both the magnitude of potential underperformance and its associated probability.

The tail risk measures for market risk also can be quantified if one knows the shape of the return distribution arising from market risk. If one follows standard practice, the distribution of returns driven by market risk can be assumed to be normal. This information coupled with the knowledge of the standard deviation of returns of the portfolio or the benchmark allows computation of the value at risk (VaR) and the expected shortfall risk arising from market risk at the desired confidence level. To compute VaR at the 90 percent level of confidence, the standard deviation of the portfolio returns given by equation (4.32) in Chapter 4 has to be scaled by the factor 1.28. To compute ESR at the 90 percent level of confidence, the appropriate scaling factor by which the standard deviation of portfolio returns has to be multiplied can be determined by solving the following integral equation:

$$\lambda = \frac{1}{1 - 0.9} \times \frac{1}{\sqrt{2\pi}} \int_{1.28}^{\infty} x \exp(-0.5x^2)\, dx \qquad (9.6)$$

Computing this integral gives the scaling factor to be equal to 1.76.

The relative tail risk measures can be computed by appropriately scaling the tracking error of the portfolio against the benchmark. For instance, to compute relative ESR at the 90 percent confidence level, one needs to multiply the tracking error by 1.76. Dividing the resulting figure by the market value of the portfolio gives %ESR at the same confidence level. Exhibit 9.11 shows a typical market risk report for the corporate bond portfolio given in Exhibit 9.1 managed against the benchmark portfolio given in Exhibit 6.7 in Chapter 6 with the necessary drill-down capability to analyze the risks and the risk sources.

**EXHIBIT 9.11**  Market Risk Report

| Description | Portfolio | Benchmark |
|---|---|---|
| Effective yield (%) | 5.55 | 5.58 |
| Effective duration | 3.512 | 3.548 |
| Effective convexity | 15.47 | 16.20 |
| %VaR (90% confidence level) (%) | 3.37 | 3.41 |
| %ESR (90% confidence level) (%) | 4.63 | 4.69 |
| Shift sensitivity (USD swap curve) (bp) | 35.19 | 35.56 |
| Twist sensitivity (USD swap curve) (bp) | −2.90 | −2.55 |
| Shift sensitivity (EUR swap curve) (bp) | 0 | 0 |
| Twist sensitivity (EUR swap curve) (bp) | 0 | 0 |
| Exchange rate sensitivity (bp) | 0 | 0 |
| Implied yield volatility sensitivity (bp) | 0 | 0 |
| **Relative risk measures** | | |
| Tracking error (bp) | 4.2 | |
| %VaR (90% confidence level) (bp) | 5.4 | |
| %ESR (90% confidence level) (bp) | 7.4 | |

In Exhibit 9.11, shift sensitivity refers to the risk sensitivity to a −10-basis point parallel shift of the swap curve, twist sensitivity refers to the risk sensitivity to a 10-basis point flattening of the swap curve, exchange rate sensitivity refers to the sensitivity to a 1 percent appreciation of any foreign currencies held in the portfolio relative to the base currency of the portfolio, and implied yield volatility sensitivity refers to the sensitivity to a 1 percent increase in the implied yield volatility. The risk model given in Exhibit 4.4 in Chapter 4 was used to compute tracking error and tail risk measures. It is useful to note that the relative risk measures for market risk are significantly lower than the relative risk measures for credit risk. This provides some justification for the focus by portfolio managers primarily on credit risk when managing a corporate bond portfolio.

## Risk Guidelines

So far in this chapter, I have examined how the market and credit risk of a corporate bond portfolio relative to a benchmark can be presented in a simple and intuitive manner such that the effectiveness of risk communication between the portfolio manager and the client is improved. If the portfolio management mandate explicitly stipulates that portfolio managers are permitted to take risks relative to the benchmark to add value, it is important that the level of relative risk permitted be agreed upon in advance. Such agreements are laid down in the risk guidelines document associated with the portfolio management mandate. Risk guidelines are meant to ensure that the client is aware of potential deviations in return between the portfolio and the benchmark that can occur as a result of deviating from the benchmark-neutral positions.

The risk guidelines document can be quite detailed in terms of the permissible size of each bond that can be held in the portfolio, the maximum nominal amount of a bond that can be purchased relative to its issue size, the permissible leverage, and the unhedged foreign currency exposure that can be held in the portfolio. Because these risk guidelines are imposed on directly observable quantities, monitoring them is rather straightforward. Much more difficult risk guidelines to agree upon and subsequently monitor are those that are imposed on the relative risk between the portfolio and the benchmark. In particular, for corporate bond portfolios there are no standards currently available to guide the choice of the relative risk measures and to impose meaningful limits on them. As a result, identifying an appropriate relative risk measure and imposing limits on permissible exposures becomes a rather lengthy consultation process.

Following the discussion so far in this chapter, it is clear that relative risk exposures for a corporate portfolio against its benchmark need to be defined separately for market risk and credit risk. In this connection, the risk reports presented in this chapter provide useful risk measures for which permissible limits can be enforced when a portfolio management mandate is awarded. For instance, the risk guideline can explicitly state that the percentage expected shortfall risk at 90 percent confidence level for the active portfolio should not exceed 200 basis points. Monitoring such risk limits will be easy if the risk reporting framework presented here is adopted.

## PERFORMANCE ATTRIBUTION

Over any reporting period, investors compare the performance of their portfolio mandates relative to the benchmark. In order to judge the investment performance of the portfolio manager, one tries to identify the good and bad allocation decisions that led to the out- or underperformance against the benchmark. This process, which is usually referred to as performance attribution, is a method for attributing the value added arising from the investment management decisions so that both the investment manager and the client are aware of the sources of this value added. Such a report not only helps to increase the transparency of the investment process from the client's perspective, but also allows for more disciplined investment decisions by portfolio managers. A performance attribution report is most useful from the investment manager's perspective if the investment management process is well integrated into the report so that the value added as a result of the investment decisions is clearly identifiable. This allows the investment manager to communicate the investment management process more effectively to the client and to attribute the value added resulting from the investment decisions.

Standard techniques for performance attribution seek to identify the value added resulting from exposures to specific risk factors that model the inherent risks in a portfolio.[2] Such risk factors are usually chosen to model the investment styles of portfolio managers so that the investment decision process will be captured in the attribution report. For instance, fixed-income portfolio managers implement their view on changes to the level of interest rates by taking an active duration bet against the benchmark. Such active duration bets could result in a risk exposure to the parallel shift of the yield curve. In other instances, portfolio managers may implement views held on the evolution of the shape of the yield curve by overweighting or underweighting certain yield curve sectors relative to the benchmark. Such a market view, if implemented, would result in an active curve twist exposure. In this manner, one can identify a set of aggregate risk exposures relative to the benchmark that result from conscious investment decisions. The purpose of the performance attribution report is to attribute the excess return against the benchmark to each of the aggregate risk factors and by doing this, help improve the transparency of the investment management process.

The foregoing factor exposures are mainly representative of high-grade fixed-income portfolios made up of government bonds or bonds issued by agencies and supranational institutions. This is because the major sources of risk in such portfolios result from exposure to market risk, and the factors just mentioned model market risk. For a portfolio comprising corporate bonds, the dominant risk is credit risk. As a result, investment styles of corporate bond portfolio managers differ from those of a traditional government bond portfolio manager. The value added against the benchmark in corporate bond portfolios results primarily from taking a view on the corporate borrowers creditworthiness and correspondingly underweighting or overweighting the exposures to specific issuer names. In this connection, it is tempting to argue that corporate bond portfolio management has much in common with equity portfolio management. In reality, there are substantial differences between the two when it comes to investment styles. To outperform the benchmark, equity portfolio managers try to pick "winners" and avoid "losers." Corporate bond portfolio managers, on the other hand, focus primarily on avoiding "losers." This is because the upside potential on bonds is usually limited, but the downside risk is substantial.

Notwithstanding the differences, it is helpful to review the performance attribution practices in equity portfolio management. One popular technique in equity portfolio management is to perform style analysis, which requires breaking a broad index down into several mutually exclusive components such as large and small caps and value and growth segments. A style analysis model then aims to quantify the exposures of a portfolio to the various style factors. Excess returns against the benchmark are then attributed to different style factors based on the exposures held to these factors during the performance attribution period.

This style analysis, though not directly applicable to corporate bond portfolios, is an appealing technique for attributing performance. For instance, corporate bond portfolio managers try to add value by identifying promising industry sectors and overweighting those sectors. Furthermore, because the credit rating of the issuers influences yield spreads, the relative exposure to different credit rating categories is also an active investment decision criterion. Taking both these aspects into account, I now indicate how a performance attribution model can be developed for corporate bond portfolios.

## A Simple Attribution Model

In an active portfolio management mandate, portfolio managers pursue different investment strategies that offer the prospect of adding value against the benchmark. Ex post, portfolio managers are interested in knowing how well their investment strategies performed and what trades were most successful in terms of adding value. Moreover, client-reporting requirements may even state that the factors that contributed to under- or outperformance against the benchmark be clearly identified. The identified factors should relate to investment styles pursued so that the investment process is well integrated in the attribution report. In this section, I develop a simple model for attributing the excess returns against the benchmark. The approach is to attribute the excess returns against the benchmark to two major components: (a) the relevant style factors and (b) security selection within the style factors. The details are given in what follows.

The first step in developing an attribution model is to identify the relevant style factors to which the return will be attributed. I mentioned that the issuer credit rating and industry sector are factors that influence the investment decisions. In this case, a combination of these attributes can serve as a suitable style factor for performance attribution. Specifically, consider grouping the various credit ratings into three buckets comprising issuers rated Aa or higher, A-rated issuers, and Baa and lower rated issuers. Furthermore, let the industry sectors be broadly classified into financials, industrials, and utilities. Such a categorization results in nine mutually exclusive factors, each of which is a combination of the credit rating and industry sector. For instance, all A-rated issuers belonging to the financial sector constitute one style factor for the return attribution model. In practice, one could increase the number of industry sectors in the attribution model to include more style factors.

Once the relevant style factors for the performance attribution model have been determined, the attribution process requires identifying benchmark and portfolio exposures to each of these style factors. Knowing the exposure weights to the style factors and the returns associated with each style factor, one can attribute excess returns to these style factors. The excess returns generated by security selection within the style factors are then identified. The mathematical details of the attribution process are as follows.

Without loss of generality, I assume that the number of bonds in the benchmark and the portfolio are identical. Under this assumption, the weights for some or many of the bonds in the portfolio are zero. Bonds with zero weights in the benchmark indicate that they are not part of the benchmark but are held in the portfolio. The return attribution model to be developed here uses the following notations:

$w_{B,i}^k$ = Weight of the $i$th bond in the benchmark that is grouped under the $k$th style factor.

$w_{P,i}^k$ = Weight of the $i$th bond in the portfolio that is grouped under the $k$th style factor.

$N_k$ = Number of bonds that are grouped under the $k$th style factor.

$S$ = Number of style factors modeled.

$w_B^k$ = Sum of the weights of all bonds in the benchmark grouped under the $k$th style factor.

$w_P^k$ = Sum of the weights of all bonds in the portfolio grouped under the $k$th style factor.

$r_i^k$ = Return over the investment period of the $i$th bond grouped under the $k$th style factor (includes price return and accrued interest).

$R_B^k$ = Total return over the investment period from all bonds in the benchmark grouped under the $k$th style factor.

$R_P^k$ = Total return over the investment period from all bonds in the portfolio grouped under the $k$th style factor.

$R_B$ = Return over the investment period of the benchmark.

$R_P$ = Return over the investment period of the portfolio.

It is easy to show that the following relations hold:

$$w_B^k = \sum_{i=1}^{N_k} w_{B,i}^k$$

$$w_P^k = \sum_{i=1}^{N_k} w_{P,i}^k$$

$$R_B^k = \sum_{i=1}^{N_k} w_{B,i}^k \times r_i^k$$

$$R_B = \sum_{k=1}^{S} R_B^k$$

$$\sum_{k=1}^{S} w_B^k = 1$$

The main goal of the attribution model is to allocate the excess return of the portfolio against the benchmark to two components: The excess returns as a result of different exposures held to style factors and the excess returns to the specific choice of the securities within each style factor.

The portfolio return resulting from the exposure to the $k$th style factor is a function of the relative weight of the portfolio to this style factor in relation to the benchmark weights and is given by

$$R_P^k = \frac{w_P^k}{w_B^k} \times R_B^k \tag{9.7}$$

The excess return attributed to the $k$th style factor is then the following:

$$R_{style}^k = R_P^k - R_B^k, \quad k = 1,\dots,S \tag{9.8}$$

The excess return attributed to security selection within the $k$th style factor is given by

$$R_{security}^k = \sum_{i=1}^{N_k} w_{P,i}^k \times r_i^k - R_P^k, \quad k = 1,\dots,S \tag{9.9}$$

Excess return that is not attributed either to the style factor or to security selection forms the residual return. This is given by

$$R_{residual} = R_P - R_B - \sum_{k=1}^{S} R_{style}^k - \sum_{k=1}^{S} R_{security}^k \tag{9.10}$$

**EXHIBIT 9.12** Attribution of Excess Returns Over Investment Period

| Bond Total Return (%) | Benchmark Weight (%) | Portfolio Weight (%) | Style Factor | $R_B^k$ (%) | $R_P^k$ (%) | $R_{style}^k$ (%) | $R_{security}^k$ (%) |
|---|---|---|---|---|---|---|---|
| 1.0 | 10 | 30 | Factor 1 | 0.50 | 0.50 | 0.00 | -0.20 |
| 2.0 | 20 | 0 | Factor 1 | | | | |
| 1.5 | 30 | 0 | Factor 2 | 0.95 | 0.57 | -0.38 | 0.18 |
| 2.5 | 20 | 30 | Factor 2 | | | | |
| 0.5 | 10 | 0 | Factor 3 | 0.17 | 0.34 | 0.17 | 0.14 |
| 1.2 | 10 | 40 | Factor 3 | | | | |

The attribution model developed here is best illustrated with the help of a numerical example. Specifically, consider the benchmark to comprise six bonds with three style factors and the portfolio to be invested in three bonds of the six in the benchmark. The active strategy pursued results in an underperformance of 9 basis points. Exhibit 9.12, which is self-explanatory, attributes the return difference versus the benchmark to various style factors and to security selection within the style factors on the basis of the model developed here.

## QUESTIONS

1. What are the important attributes of a good risk report?
2. What is the standard risk measure used to quantify the relative risk of a portfolio against a benchmark? What are the drawbacks of using such a risk measure to quantify portfolio credit risk relative to its benchmark?
3. How is relative credit risk defined? What are the measures used to quantify relative credit risk?
4. What are the advantages of the relative credit risk measures introduced here compared to other relative risk measures commonly used?
5. How is marginal risk contribution defined? Show that the expected loss contribution of individual bonds in the portfolio add up to the unexpected loss of the portfolio.
6. For the example portfolio considered in this chapter, the relative tail risk measures were lower when the joint distribution of asset returns was modeled to be multivariate $t$ distributed. Justify why this is the case.
7. Under the multivariate $t$-distribution assumption for asset returns, will the absolute credit risk measures of the portfolio be higher or lower than those computed under the multinormal distribution assumption for asset returns? Justify your answer.

8. If you were a portfolio manager, what are the various risk reports you would want to send to your clients?

9. To compute ESR for market risk at the 95 percent level of confidence, what is the appropriate scaling factor to be used in conjunction with the tracking error of the portfolio? Assume excess returns resulting from market risk are normally distributed.

10. What is the difference between performance attribution and risk attribution? What purpose does a performance attribution report serve?

11. What are the important risk factors to which performance is attributed in a high-grade government bond portfolio? Is it appropriate to use the same factors for attributing the performance of corporate bond portfolios? Justify your answer.

12. For a corporate bond portfolio, what are the relevant factors to which one can attribute performance?

## CHAPTER 10

# Portfolio Optimization

**S**o far in this book, I have examined how market and credit risk can be quantified and how the relative risk measures versus a given benchmark can be computed. Depending on the nature of the portfolio management mandate, the relative risks versus the benchmark may either be permitted or need to be eliminated to the extent possible. Eliminating all risks against a given benchmark is almost impossible in most practical situations. Therefore, the task of a portfolio manager will be to ensure that the relative risk is kept to a minimum, or in those cases where it is permitted, to take those risks that offer scope for increasing the expected excess returns versus the benchmark. In addition to this, the portfolio manager will have to rebalance the portfolio once every month or once every quarter to ensure that the risk characteristics are replicated when the benchmark composition changes. Performing these tasks would be simplified if tools for portfolio selection were available to help guide the risk-taking, rebalancing, and portfolio construction processes. In situations where the benchmark comprises several hundred bond issuers, performing a proper credit analysis of all the issuers may itself be a very laborious process. Access to portfolio optimization tools in such cases would be of valuable help to portfolio managers.

In this chapter, I introduce techniques for portfolio optimization that achieve the foregoing objectives. First, I provide some background information on bond portfolio optimization and argue why a quantitative approach to the selection of a corporate bond portfolio can be attractive. This is followed by a brief review of optimization methods and subsequently a discussion on the practical difficulties that can arise when using optimization techniques for portfolio selection. I then present different ways to formulate an optimization problem for portfolio construction and portfolio rebalancing. In the final section, I demonstrate the impact model parameters have on the optimal portfolio composition by taking a market capitalization weighted corporate bond benchmark.

## PORTFOLIO SELECTION TECHNIQUES

When performance of a bond portfolio is measured relative to a benchmark, a major concern of the portfolio manager is which bonds to hold in the portfolio. If the benchmark includes only government bonds or Aaa-rated bonds, the portfolio selection problem becomes rather simple. Because the major risks among high-grade issuers is primarily systematic risk, the bonds in the portfolio need to be selected such that the systematic risk factors are hedged. The systematic risk factors for high-grade bond issuers arise from shape changes to the yield curve, which can be captured using two or three risk factors. Typically, five or six bonds can replicate the systematic risk factors of a benchmark comprising government bonds or Aaa-rated bonds. Choosing the appropriate bonds to replicate the systematic risk factors in such cases is a trivial exercise for a portfolio manager.

Extending the portfolio selection technique to the case where the benchmark is a global government bond benchmark is also quite straightforward. In this case, one can construct a risk model comprising the systematic risk factors for every government bond market and then select a portfolio that minimizes the tracking error between the portfolio and the benchmark. Choosing portfolios to replicate a multicurrency government bond benchmark through tracking error minimization is a standard tool most software vendors for fixed-income analytics provide.

Now consider the problem of selecting a portfolio to replicate a benchmark comprising investment-grade corporate bonds. Traditional approaches to addressing this problem follow a technique popularly known as the cell-indexing strategy. In simple terms, the cell-indexing strategy requires identifying different risk attributes for an investment-grade bond benchmark and then selecting bonds that replicate each of these risk attributes. Specifically, one may identify the risk attributes to broadly include bond maturity, industry sector, and rating category. If, for instance, one divides each of these risk categories into three further subcategories, then any bond in the investment-grade benchmark can be assigned to 1 of 27 possible risk buckets or cells. For purpose of illustration, think of the maturity of bonds belonging to the 1- to 5-year sector, the 5- to 10-year sector, or the greater than 10-year sector. Similarly, one could identify the industry sector the bond belongs to as being the industrial sector, the financial sector, or the utilities sector. The credit rating of the bond can be identified as being Baa, A, or Aa and higher rating.

Once the bonds in the investment-grade benchmark have been assigned to 1 of the 27 cells, portfolio replication becomes simply a task of choosing bonds in the portfolio such that they have the same allocation weights as the benchmark to each cell. The drawback of this traditional approach is that the portfolio constructed using the cell-indexing strategy will replicate only the systematic risk factors, 27 of which have been identified in the example cited here. Issuer-specific risk, which constitutes the dominant part of the risk in a corporate bond portfolio, will not be hedged using the cell-indexing strategy.

Another way of looking at the cell-indexing approach is that it minimizes the tracking error arising from the exposure to the risk factors corresponding to each cell. However, tracking error is not a suitable measure for capturing the issuer-specific risk or, equivalently, the credit risk in a corporate portfolio as argued in Chapter 9. This suggests that one has to formulate the portfolio selection problem to replicate the risk profile of a corporate bond benchmark differently.

## Benefits of a Quantitative Approach

The foregoing portfolio selection techniques can be regarded as quantitative approaches to portfolio construction. One may wonder at this point why there is a need to follow a quantitative approach to select a corporate bond portfolio. In fact, some portfolio managers may be tempted to argue that if adding value relative to a benchmark requires identifying "good credits," human judgment can be superior to a quantitative approach. In reality, however, most experienced portfolio managers know that differentiating good credits from bad credits is far from being a trivial exercise. Moreover, when the number of issuers in the benchmark is large, it is practically impossible to do a thorough credit analysis of all bond issuers. In general, the costs involved in carrying out a credit analysis of a large number of issuers can be prohibitively high. In such cases, use of quantitative tools to identify potential issuers to be included in the bond portfolio can be of much help.

Another advantage of following a quantitative approach to portfolio selection is that the risks at the portfolio level can be analyzed directly rather than at the bond level. This allows one to construct a portfolio that exhibits certain desirable risk–return characteristics, which is then subject to review by the portfolio manager.

Other instances where a quantitative approach to portfolio selection is attractive are when the size of the portfolio is large (typically several billions) or the intention is to simply replicate the risk–return characteristics of the benchmark for an indexed portfolio mandate. For large portfolio sizes, levels of market exposure are too great to hold significant overweight positions in a small number of bonds. Hence, such portfolios tend to be more closely aligned to the benchmark composition.

Constructing a portfolio that matches the benchmark composition closely is, however, not a practical alternative either. Reasons for this are that this approach usually leads to odd lot transactions, which are quite expensive, and that many older bond issues may be illiquid with regard to transactions. These considerations suggest that the replicating portfolio will often include only a subset of the bonds in the benchmark. Identifying such a subset of bonds using quantitative methods is the only viable alternative at least in cases where the portfolio management fees do not justify maintaining a large credit research team.

## OPTIMIZATION METHODS

Most readers are familiar with the theory of portfolio optimization in the context of selecting stock portfolios that exhibit certain desirable risk–return tradeoffs. Portfolio optimization theory deals with the process of identifying the best portfolio composition from a collection of alternatives that meet certain desired risk–return tradeoffs without having to explicitly enumerate and evaluate all possible alternatives. The complexity of the process involved in identifying the optimal candidate portfolio depends on the optimization problem formulation.

In broad terms, an optimization problem can be classified as either a linear or a nonlinear programming problem. A special case of a nonlinear programming problem arises if the objective function is a quadratic in the design variables and all the constraint functions are linear. Such an optimization problem is referred to as a quadratic programming problem. The standard portfolio optimization problem based on the Markowitz theory results in a quadratic programming problem. In general, good problem formulation is the key to finding solutions to an optimization problem that are useful in practice. This skill is usually learned through practice and the knowledge of the strengths, weaknesses, and peculiarities of the solutions obtained using optimization theory.

In this section, I discuss different optimization problem formulations and the associated complexities involved in finding the optimal solution with reference to the bond portfolio selection problem. Before proceeding to do this, it is necessary to introduce some terms commonly used in optimization theory. A feasible solution to an optimization problem is a solution vector that satisfies all the constraint functions. The set of all feasible solutions to an optimization problem is referred to as the feasible region. An optimal solution to a minimization problem requires finding a feasible solution that minimizes the objective function value.

### Linear Programming

As the name suggests, linear programming problems define a particular class of optimization problems in which both the constraint functions and the objective function are linear in the design variables. The design variables in the context of the bond portfolio selection problem are the relative weights of the individual bonds in the portfolio. An interesting characteristic of linear programming problems is that if an optimal solution exists, then at least one of the corner points of the feasible region will qualify to be an optimal solution. This property ensures that we need to examine only a finite set of corner points in the feasible region to find the optimal solution. As a result, algorithms for solving linear programming problems are very efficient even when the number of design variables is several thousand.

The computational efficiency of linear programming problems makes it attractive to formulate the bond portfolio selection problem as a linear programming problem. However, if the objective is to find a tradeoff between the relative risk of the portfolio versus the benchmark and the expected excess return, such a problem formulation is not feasible. This is because the portfolio risk is not linear in the relative weights of the individual bonds in the portfolio, which happen to be the design variables in this case.

## Quadratic Programming

A quadratic programming problem is an optimization problem in which the objective function is quadratic and all the constraint functions are linear. Most standard portfolio selection problems are formulated in this framework. Formulating the portfolio selection problem as a quadratic programming problem is attractive because computationally efficient methods exist to solve the optimization problem when the objective function is convex. In such cases, a global minimum to the optimization problem can be found.

A quadratic programming problem can be stated to have the following general form:

$$\text{Minimize} \quad x^T Q x + 2c^T x, \quad x \in R^n$$

$$\text{subject to} \quad l \le \left\{ \begin{array}{c} x \\ Ax \end{array} \right\} \le u$$

Here, $Q$ is a $n \times n$ matrix and $A$ is a $m \times n$ matrix of linear constraint functions. The complexity of solving quadratic programming problems depends on the nature of the $Q$ matrix. If $Q$ is a positive-semidefinite matrix (all eigenvalues are non-negative), efficient algorithms can be designed to solve the optimization problem.

## Nonlinear Programming

Any optimization problem that cannot be classified into a linear or a quadratic programming problem is classified under the category of a nonlinear programming problem. For instance, if the objective function is linear but some of the constraint functions are nonlinear, then the optimization problem is classified as a nonlinear programming problem. Solving nonlinear programming problems is more difficult and the complexity increases considerably as the number of design variables increases. Although a variety of methods exists to solve nonlinear programming problems, no single method is suitable for all types of problems. Certain methods are more efficient than others in solving particular classes of nonlinear programming problems.

A major challenge in solving nonlinear programming problems is that these problems exhibit local minima, and hence finding the global minimum is difficult. The increase in computational complexity arises primarily from the fact that the global minimum will be in the interior of the feasible region rather than on the boundaries as in the case of linear and quadratic programming problems.

An analogy would help here to explain the differences between the different programming problems. If one relates the optimization problem to the process of identifying where a needle is hidden in a haystack, a linear programming problem would only require looking into the eight corner points of the haystack to find the needle. A quadratic programming problem would require that we explore the entire outer surface of the haystack to find the needle. A nonlinear programming problem, on the other hand, would necessitate examining the entire haystack because the needle could be hidden anywhere inside it.

When formulating the optimization problem to select replicating bond portfolios, one should try to restrict the problem to be either a linear or a quadratic programming problem. This makes it computationally tractable in the face of the large number of design variables that are bound to arise in a practical setting.

## PRACTICAL DIFFICULTIES

In the previous section, I indicated the computational difficulties involved in finding solutions to different types of optimization problems. In most practical situations, however, standard software libraries can be used to find the optimal portfolio composition. The major concern when following a quantitative approach to constructing and rebalancing a corporate bond portfolio to replicate a given benchmark is then to question the implementability of the optimal portfolio composition in a practical setting. In other words, is the optimal portfolio composition meaningful to hold after taking into account the transaction costs involved? If the answer to this question is no, finding an optimal portfolio turns out to be simply an academic exercise.

To provide a concrete example, take the case of a portfolio manager who holds a corporate bond portfolio. Imagine that the portfolio manager has to reinvest cash injections and simultaneously rebalance the portfolio because the benchmark composition has changed at the end of the month. The task of the portfolio manager is to buy and sell some bonds in the portfolio so as to meet the objective of replicating the benchmark risk–return characteristics. Of interest is whether an optimization problem can be formulated to identify the bonds to buy and sell to meet the portfolio manager's objective. Unfortunately, the solutions provided by many standard optimization problem formulations require a significant amount of transactions to be done. In most cases, the portfolio manager will ignore these solutions because the transaction costs involved will render the optimal portfolio composition unattractive to hold. In other instances, the optimal portfolio composition may not be a feasible portfolio to hold because many of the bonds could be illiquid.

At this stage, it is important to recognize that the optimal portfolio composition is a manifestation of the objectives and constraints expressed in formulating the portfolio selection problem. If transaction costs are not modeled in the problem formulation, the optimal portfolio composition could be very different from the portfolio being held. Even assuming that one imposes a constraint on the maximum turnover when portfolio rebalancing is done, the optimal portfolio composition may require buying and selling many bonds whose transaction volumes are small. Such trade recommendations will also be rejected by portfolio managers due to the higher transaction cost involved in trading small lot sizes and the risk of increasing operational errors due to the large number of transactions. Enforcing explicit constraints on the number of transactions is usually difficult, though not impossible.

Finally, it is important to realize that the notion of an optimal portfolio is rather subjective. It is subjective from the point of view that the optimal portfolio composition offers the best tradeoff for the given objective function and set of constraints under certain choices for the input parameters of the model. If one modifies the constraint functions of the optimization problem, one might well end up with a very different optimal portfolio composition. Hence, optimization tools should be used primarily as an aid to portfolio selection and to provide trade suggestions to the portfolio manager. In the rest of the chapter, I discuss different ways in which the optimal bond portfolio selection problem can be formulated in order to meet different objectives and constraints that the portfolio manager may wish to express.

## PORTFOLIO CONSTRUCTION

Assuming that a portfolio management mandate has been awarded, the first step in the portfolio management process is to construct a portfolio that replicates the risk–return characteristics of the benchmark. During the portfolio construction process, one is usually interested in selecting a limited number of bonds that replicate the benchmark characteristics. Standard portfolio construction approaches consider minimizing the tracking error of the portfolio versus the benchmark when selecting a replicating portfolio. With respect to a corporate bond portfolio, the tracking error minimization approach can be regarded as the minimization of the unexpected loss of the active portfolio.

However, adopting this approach will not be very useful in the present case. This is because such a problem formulation will lead to a portfolio whose composition is identical to that of the benchmark. To see why this is the case, recall that there is no notion of risk factors in a credit risk model as is commonly the case with market risk. For credit risk, every obligor in the benchmark qualifies to be a risk factor. Clearly, if the objective function tries to minimize the unexpected loss of the active portfolio whose nominal exposures are given by equation (9.1) in Chapter 9, then one will obtain a portfolio composition identical to the benchmark composition. Under this case, the unexpected loss of the active portfolio will be zero. Hence, formulating the portfolio construction problem as unexpected loss minimization of the active portfolio will not give an implementable portfolio under most circumstances.

To formulate an optimization problem that will lead to an implementable portfolio, I briefly review how an optimal portfolio in the equities market is selected. In the context of an equity portfolio, all risks are classified under market risk, which in turn is expressed through the volatility of equity returns. For a given level of market risk, the portfolio that has the highest expected return is considered to be the most efficient portfolio to hold. Such a portfolio can be selected by formulating a quadratic programming problem. This problem formulation is referred to as the mean-variance optimization problem in finance.

The conceptual framework for selecting an efficient portfolio in the equities market can be easily extended to the case of the corporate bond portfolio selection problem. In making this extension, it is important to realize that corporate bonds have both market and credit risk. Hence, one must consider both sources of risk when identifying corporate bond portfolios that are more efficient than others. One could argue that corporate bond portfolio A is more efficient than portfolio B if both portfolios have the same market risk and expected return but portfolio A has lower credit risk. Stated differently, portfolio A is more efficient than portfolio B if the risk-adjusted return of portfolio A is higher. In the present case, portfolio B corresponds to the benchmark portfolio.

Introducing the notion of efficient portfolio makes it possible to formulate the optimal portfolio selection problem. For instance, the credit risk of a corporate bond portfolio can be considered to be the objective function one wishes to minimize. The set of constraint functions can be formulated on the expected return of the portfolio and the market risk exposures. The solution to this optimization problem then provides the portfolio manager with an indicative bond portfolio that can help in the portfolio construction process. In the next section, I establish the set of constraint functions in connection with the optimization problem for constructing a replicating portfolio.

## Setting Up the Constraints

I argued that in order to select implementable portfolios, one has to formulate the optimization problem such that an efficient portfolio is selected compared to the benchmark. I also mentioned that for such an optimization problem the expected return of the portfolio and market risk exposures serve as constraint functions. To help formulate the constraint functions of the optimization problem, denote the set of market risk factors modeled as $\mathbb{N}_\beta$ and the set of permissible bonds that can be held in the portfolio as $\mathbb{N}_\alpha$.

The first set of constraint functions is on the market risk factor exposures of the portfolio. In Chapter 4, I defined six market risk factors and indicated how the sensitivity to these risk factors at the portfolio level can be determined. To set up the constraint functions for the optimal portfolio selection problem, however, one needs to know the sensitivity to various market risk factors at the individual bond level. The sensitivity in basis points of the $i$th bond to the $k$th market risk factor modeled can be determined from

$$f_{ik} = 10{,}000 \times \frac{P^k_{\text{dirty},i} - P_{\text{dirty},i}}{P_{\text{dirty},i}} \tag{10.1}$$

In equation (10.1), $P_{\text{dirty},i}$ denotes the current dirty price of the bond for \$1 face value and $P^k_{\text{dirty},i}$ is the price after a shock to the $k$th market risk factor. If $\text{NE}_i$ denotes the nominal exposure to the $i$th bond in the portfolio, the market risk sensitivity to the $k$th risk factor is given by

$$\frac{1}{M_P} \sum_{i \in \mathbb{N}_\alpha} \text{NE}_i \times P_{\text{dirty},i} \times f_{ik} \tag{10.2}$$

In equation (10.2), $M_P$ denotes the amount that needs to be invested in the portfolio. If the intention is to have the same market risk sensitivity as the benchmark portfolio to the $k$th risk factor, then this constraint can be expressed as follows:

$$\frac{1}{M_P} \sum_{i \in \mathbb{N}_\alpha} \text{NE}_i \times P_{\text{dirty},i} \times f_{ik} = S^k_B \tag{10.3}$$

In equation (10.3), $S_B^k$ denotes the sensitivity of the benchmark to the $k$th market risk factor, which can be determined using equation (4.30) in Chapter 4. In setting up the constraint functions for the optimization problem, one can decide to enforce constraints on all or only some of the market risk factors.

The other constraint is on the expected return of the bond portfolio. The expected return on a corporate bond portfolio is the effective yield of the portfolio less the percentage expected loss on the portfolio. In practice, it is more convenient to split this constraint into two separate constraints, one on the portfolio effective yield and the other on the percentage expected loss of the portfolio. The effective yield of the portfolio is given by

$$y_P = \frac{1}{M_P} \sum_{i \in N_\alpha} NE_i \times P_{\text{dirty},i} \times y_i \tag{10.4}$$

If $y_B$ denotes the effective yield of the benchmark, the constraint on the portfolio effective yield of the portfolio can be expressed as

$$\frac{1}{M_P} \sum_{i \in N_\alpha} NE_i \times P_{\text{dirty},i} \times y_i \geq y_B \tag{10.5}$$

The percentage expected loss on the portfolio is given by

$$\% EL_P = \frac{1}{M_P} \sum_{i \in N_\alpha} NE_i \times \mu_i \tag{10.6}$$

In equation (10.6), $\mu_i$ corresponds to the expected loss on the $i$th bond held in the portfolio having a nominal exposure of \$1. The percentage expected loss given by equation (10.6) is evaluated either under the default mode or under the migration mode depending on whether the optimization problem is formulated under the default mode or the migration mode, respectively. If the percentage expected loss of the benchmark is given by $\% EL_B$, then the constraint on expected loss can be expressed as

$$\frac{1}{M_P} \sum_{i \in N_\alpha} NE_i \times \mu_i \leq \% EL_B \tag{10.7}$$

The constraint functions (10.5) and (10.7) jointly ensure that the expected return of the portfolio is not lower than that of the benchmark.

A standard requirement for any portfolio selection problem is that the portfolio is fully invested. This requirement can be expressed in terms of the following constraint:

$$\sum_{i \in N_\alpha} NE_i \times P_{\text{dirty},i} = M_P \tag{10.8}$$

Finally, to ensure that the portfolio does not have large exposures to a few bonds, one needs to impose constraints on the maximum nominal exposure to any bond issue. For instance, one can impose this constraint in terms of the maximum permissible nominal exposure of the $i$th bond in the portfolio relative to the issue size $\mathbb{S}_i$ of the $i$th bond. If one chooses the exposure limit to be 5 percent of the respective issue sizes for all bonds in the portfolio, this constraint together with the constraint of no short positions can be expressed as

$$0 \leq \text{NE}_i \leq 0.05\mathbb{S}_i, \qquad i \in \mathbb{N}_\alpha \qquad (10.9)$$

In the next section, I formulate an optimization problem to aid the selection of bonds in a portfolio construction process.

## The Optimization Problem

To complete the formulation of the optimization problem, one needs to define the objective function. I indicated earlier that the objective function is the minimization of the credit risk of the portfolio. A useful measure of credit risk is the unexpected loss of the corporate bond portfolio. If the square of the unexpected loss of the portfolio is used as the objective function, then it is easy to show that the optimization problem is a quadratic programming problem. Given the computational attractiveness of quadratic programming problems, I formulate the portfolio construction problem in this framework. The next step is to establish the objective function of the optimization problem.

For notational simplicity, denote the unexpected loss of the $i$th bond for a nominal exposure $\text{NE}_i$ as

$$\text{UL}_i = \text{NE}_i \times \sigma_i \qquad (10.10)$$

In equation (10.10), $\sigma_i$ denotes the unexpected loss of the $i$th bond held in the portfolio for a nominal exposure of \$1. Again, the unexpected loss of the bond can be computed either under the default mode or under the migration mode. If $\rho_{ik}^\ell$ denotes the loss correlation between the $i$th bond and $k$th bond in the portfolio, the square of the percentage portfolio unexpected loss is given by

$$\% \text{UL}_P^2 = \frac{1}{M_P^2} \sum_{i \in \mathbb{N}_\alpha} \sum_{k \in \mathbb{N}_\alpha} \text{NE}_i \times \text{NE}_k \times \sigma_i \times \sigma_k \times \rho_{ik}^\ell \qquad (10.11)$$

It is important to mention that if the unexpected loss of the $i$th bond and the loss correlation between the $i$th and the $k$th bonds in the portfolio are determined under the migration mode, the portfolio unexpected loss will be captured under the migration mode. The objective function of the optimization problem will be the minimization of equation (10.11).

At this stage, many will have recognized the design variable of the optimization problem to be the nominal exposure amount of the $i$th bond in the portfolio. In general, some notational simplicity can be achieved if the design variables are transformed to be the relative nominal weights of the bonds. The relative nominal weight of the $i$th bond in the portfolio is given by

$$w_i = \frac{\mathrm{NE}_i}{M_P} \tag{10.12}$$

The optimization problem to solve to guide the portfolio construction process is now as follows:

Minimize $\quad \displaystyle\sum_{i \in \mathbb{N}_\alpha} \sum_{k \in \mathbb{N}_\alpha} w_i w_k \, \sigma_i \sigma_k \, \rho_{ik}^{\ell}$

subject to the constraints

$$\sum_{i \in \mathbb{N}_\alpha} w_i f_{ik} \, P_{\mathrm{dirty},i} = S_B^k, \qquad k \in \mathbb{N}_\beta$$

$$\sum_{i \in \mathbb{N}_\alpha} w_i \, y_i \, P_{\mathrm{dirty},i} \geq y_B$$

$$\sum_{i \in \mathbb{N}_\alpha} w_i \, \mu_i \leq \% \mathrm{EL}_B$$

$$\sum_{i \in \mathbb{N}_\alpha} w_i \, P_{\mathrm{dirty},i} = 1$$

$$0 \leq w_i \leq 0.05 \frac{S_i}{M_P}, \qquad i \in \mathbb{N}_\alpha$$

It is again useful to emphasize that this optimization problem is a quadratic programming problem in the design variable $w_i$, which represents the relative nominal weight of the $i$th bond in the portfolio. The risk profile of the optimal portfolio composition resulting from solving this quadratic programming problem is presented in the next section.

### Optimal Portfolio Composition

Again consider the 23-bond portfolio given in Exhibit 6.6 in Chapter 6 to serve as the benchmark portfolio. However, instead of the nominal exposure to each bond being USD 20 million, assume that the nominal exposure is USD 200 million. Such a choice ensures that the benchmark risk profile is unaltered. I chose these nominal exposures so that the benchmark composition is representative of a typical market capitalization-based index. In selecting the optimal portfolio composition, assume that the amount to be invested in the corporate bond portfolio is USD 73 million. The optimal portfolio compositions have been determined both under the migration mode (PMM) and the default mode (PDM) assuming asset returns have a multivariate normal distribution. For computing the loss correlation between obligors, the asset return correlations given in Exhibit 6.7 in Chapter 6 were used. The composition of the optimal portfolios under the migration and default modes is shown in Exhibit 10.1.

In Exhibit 10.1, the optimal portfolio under the default mode was computed using KMV's EDFs for the various issuers. Note that the composition

**EXHIBIT 10.1** Composition of Optimal Bond Portfolios[a]

| S. No. | Issuer | Maturity | Coupon (%) | PMM (mn $) | PDM (mn $) | PSM (mn $) |
|--------|--------|----------|------------|------------|------------|------------|
| 1 | Health Care Reit | 15 Aug 07 | 7.500 | 1.721 | 10.000 | 1.230 |
| 2 | Hilton Hotels | 15 May 08 | 7.625 | 1.374 | 2.367 | 1.300 |
| 3 | Apple Computer | 15 Feb 04 | 6.500 | 1.998 | 1.039 | 1.507 |
| 4 | Delta Air Lines | 15 Dec 09 | 7.900 | 1.179 | 2.949 | 0.962 |
| 5 | Alcoa Inc | 01 Jun 06 | 5.875 | 2.150 | 1.661 | 1.692 |
| 6 | ABN Amro Bank | 31 May 05 | 7.250 | 7.548 | 3.974 | 9.373 |
| 7 | Abbey Natl Plc | 17 Nov 05 | 6.690 | 2.729 | 0.483 | 1.651 |
| 8 | Alliance Capital | 15 Aug 06 | 5.625 | 7.187 | 0.000 | 9.206 |
| 9 | Aegon Nv | 15 Aug 06 | 8.000 | 8.406 | 5.551 | 10.000 |
| 10 | Abbott Labs | 01 Jul 06 | 5.625 | 0.038 | 5.401 | 0.122 |
| 11 | Caterpillar Inc | 01 May 06 | 5.950 | 1.579 | 1.401 | 0.253 |
| 12 | Coca Cola Enter | 15 Aug 06 | 5.375 | 0.957 | 0.206 | 0.000 |
| 13 | Countrywide Home | 01 Aug 06 | 5.500 | 0.983 | 0.000 | 0.000 |
| 14 | Colgate-Palm Co | 29 Apr 05 | 3.980 | 0.000 | 6.540 | 0.000 |
| 15 | Hershey Foods Co | 01 Oct 05 | 6.700 | 2.074 | 10.000 | 2.207 |
| 16 | IBM Corp | 01 Oct 06 | 4.875 | 0.235 | 1.412 | 0.000 |
| 17 | Johnson Controls | 15 Nov 06 | 5.000 | 3.134 | 2.632 | 2.286 |
| 18 | JP Morgan Chase | 01 Jun 05 | 7.000 | 5.280 | 0.490 | 4.984 |
| 19 | Bank One NA ILL | 26 Mar 07 | 5.500 | 9.063 | 4.740 | 9.756 |
| 20 | Oracle Corp | 15 Feb 07 | 6.910 | 7.225 | 1.460 | 8.762 |
| 21 | Pub Svc EL & Gas | 01 Mar 06 | 6.750 | 3.709 | 0.520 | 4.095 |
| 22 | Procter & Gamble | 30 Apr 05 | 4.000 | 0.000 | 6.382 | 0.000 |
| 23 | PNC Bank NA | 01 Aug 06 | 5.750 | 0.997 | 1.289 | 0.000 |

[a]PMM, Portfolio composition under migration mode; PDM, portfolio composition under default mode; PSM, portfolio composition under stress mode.

**EXHIBIT 10.2**  Credit Risk Measures for Portfolio Composition Under Migration Mode (PMM)

| Description | PMM Portfolio (bp) | Benchmark (bp) | Active Portfolio (bp) |
|---|---|---|---|
| %EL | 25.1 | 34.0 | −9.0 |
| %UL | 72.6 | 88.8 | 46.8 |
| %CrVaR$_{90\%}$ | 75.9 | 102.9 | 15.3 |
| %ESR$_{90\%}$ | 174.8 | 240.3 | 38.9 |

of the optimal portfolios under the migration and default modes is very different. This is to be expected because the default probabilities for the issuers are completely different if we adopt the KMV framework to estimate them. To provide a comparison of the various risk measures of the optimal portfolio against the benchmark, Exhibits 10.2 and 10.3 show the credit risk and market risk measures for the PMM portfolio.

**Remarks**  Comparing the credit risk measures given in Exhibit 9.5 in Chapter 9 and Exhibit 10.2, one can see that the optimal portfolio has a significantly improved risk–return characteristic compared to the portfolio composition given in Exhibit 9.1 in Chapter 9. The active portfolio, which serves to capture the relative risks, also has significantly lower risks when the PMM portfolio is used for benchmark replication. For instance, the average underperformance in the worst-case 10 percent scenarios is reduced from 126 basis points to 39 basis points when the PMM portfolio is held. The market risk presented in Exhibit 10.3 shows that both the benchmark and the optimal portfolio have identical market risk exposures.

At this stage, there might be some concern that holding any of the optimal portfolios will require buying more than 90 percent of the bonds in

**EXHIBIT 10.3**  Market Risk Measures for Portfolio Composition Under Migration Mode (PMM)

| Description | Portfolio | Benchmark |
|---|---|---|
| Effective yield (%) | 5.58 | 5.58 |
| Effective duration | 3.549 | 3.548 |
| Effective convexity | 15.98 | 16.20 |
| %VaR (90% confidence level) (%) | 3.41 | 3.41 |
| %ESR (90% confidence level) (%) | 4.69 | 4.69 |
| Shift sensitivity (USD swap curve) (bp) | 35.57 | 35.56 |
| Twist sensitivity (USD swap curve) (bp) | −2.56 | −2.55 |

the benchmark. For a benchmark comprising several hundred bonds, such a strategy will be very expensive from the transaction cost point of view. In practice, however, when the benchmark portfolio consists of several hundred bonds, an optimal replicating portfolio comprising only a fraction of the bonds in the benchmark can be found.

Finally, it is important to observe that the optimal portfolio is not a true replicating portfolio because there is still considerable residual credit risk between the benchmark and the optimal portfolio. However, this was not the intention in the first place, as can be seen from the formulation of the optimal portfolio selection problem.

### Robustness of Portfolio Composition

The optimal portfolio composition under the migration mode in Exhibit 10.1 was determined under normal market conditions. A question of practical interest here is how the composition of the PMM portfolio changes if some input parameters used in the credit model are changed. In other words, one is interested in the robustness of the optimal portfolio composition under different model parameter assumptions. To examine this, the credit risk model parameters were changed to introduce a 20 percent stress factor scenario discussed in Chapter 9. The optimal portfolio composition for this scenario was computed under the migration mode with the multivariate $t$-distribution assumption for asset returns. The composition of the optimal portfolio resulting from this exercise is shown in Exhibit 10.1 under the heading PSM.

Notice that in spite of the large changes to the model input parameters, the portfolio composition reveals similar under- and over-weight positions in the bonds relative to the benchmark composition. Clearly, this suggests that the portfolio composition is less sensitive to parameter uncertainty, provided the modeling framework for credit risk measurement remains the same. Based on this observation, it is fair to say that the optimal portfolio selection approach presented here will help a portfolio manager to identify a list of bonds and the relative nominal amounts to be held in the portfolio construction process.

## PORTFOLIO REBALANCING

The focus so far has been on how to construct a portfolio when a new portfolio mandate is awarded. However, this is something that happens rather infrequently in the portfolio management business. A case of much more practical interest to portfolio managers concerns the rebalancing trades that need to be carried out resulting either from changes to the benchmark composition or from injections and withdrawals from the portfolio that may take place periodically. An important requirement when rebalancing trades are performed is to keep the turnover of the portfolio small to minimize the transactions costs. I define turnover as the percentage of the current market value of the portfolio that needs to be liquidated to rebalance the portfolio (excluding the part required to meet cash withdrawals).

Enforcing turnover constraints in portfolio optimization problems is rather difficult. The approach I take to incorporate this constraint is to solve the portfolio-rebalancing problem in a two-step process. In the first step, one identifies a list of tentative sell transactions from the existing portfolio holdings that meets the turnover constraint while reducing the relative credit risk between the portfolio and the benchmark. In the second step, one determines the actual transactions required to be done taking into consideration the sell recommendations. These transactions are chosen such that the rebalanced portfolio has improved risk-adjusted return relative to the benchmark. Following such a two-step process keeps the complexity of the portfolio-rebalancing problem manageable. The details regarding this optimization approach are discussed in what follows.

## Identifying Sell Transactions

In this section, I discuss the formulation of the optimization problem to identify the tentative list of sell transactions. A key requirement in doing this is to keep the portfolio turnover small. If the portfolio rebalancing trades have to be done primarily to meet cash withdrawals, the objective is limited to identifying only the sell transactions. Hence, the problem of greater practical interest is portfolio rebalancing under the condition that the net injection into the portfolio is either zero or positive. I assume that this is the case in the optimization problem formulation.

Before proceeding to set up the optimization problem, I define the following variables, which will be used in formulating the optimization problem. All exposure amounts given are assumed to be in the base currency of the portfolio.

$NE_{i,P}$ = Nominal exposure of the $i$th bond in the current portfolio.

$NE_{i,B}$ = Nominal exposure of the $i$th bond in the benchmark.

$NE_{i,sell}$ = Nominal amount of the $i$th bond in the portfolio to be sold.

$NE_{i,A}$ = Nominal exposure of the $i$th bond in the active portfolio after the bond sale.

$M_P$ = Market value of the current portfolio excluding new cash injections.

$M_B$ = Market value of the benchmark.

$w_{i,P}$ = Weight of the $i$th bond in the current portfolio, given by $NE_{i,P}/M_P$.

$w_{i,B}$ = Weight of the $i$th bond in the benchmark, given by $NE_{i,B}/M_B$.

$w_i$ = Weight of the $i$th bond in the portfolio to be sold, given by $NE_i/M_P$.

$w_{i,A}$ = Weight of the $i$th bond in the active portfolio after the bond sale, given by $NE_{i,A}/M_P$.

$\sigma_i$ = Unexpected loss of the $i$th bond for \$1 nominal exposure.

$\rho_{ik}^\ell$ = Loss correlation between the $i$th and the $k$th bond.

$N_\alpha$ = Set of permissible bonds in the portfolio.

$\tau$ = Maximum permissible turnover as a percentage of current portfolio size.

I mentioned that the sell transactions will be chosen so as to reduce the relative credit risk between the portfolio and the benchmark. The relative credit risk between the portfolio and the benchmark can be defined in terms of the unexpected loss of the active portfolio. Hence, the objective function of the optimization problem that identifies the sell transactions will be some suitable function of the unexpected loss of the active portfolio. I now formulate such an objective function that will enable us to identify the sell transactions.

Assume that a portion $w_i$ of the $i$th bond holding in the portfolio has been sold. Under this scenario, the weight of the $i$th bond in the active portfolio after the bond sale is given by

$$w_{i,A} = w_{i,P} - w_i - w_{i,B}, \qquad i \in N_\alpha \qquad (10.13)$$

Note that if investments are made in bonds that are not contained in the benchmark, then the benchmark weights for those bonds are zero in equation (10.13). The square of the percentage unexpected loss of the active portfolio after the bond sales is given by

$$\% UL_A^2 = \sum_{i \in N_\alpha} \sum_{k \in N_\alpha} w_{i,A} w_{k,A} \, \sigma_i \sigma_k \, \rho_{ik}^\ell \qquad (10.14)$$

In matrix notation, this equation can be compactly written as

$$\% UL_A^2 = w_A^T \Omega \, w_A \qquad (10.15)$$

Here, $\Omega$ is a matrix with elements $\Omega_{ik} = \sigma_i \sigma_k \rho_{ik}^\ell$ and $w_A$ denotes the vector of bond weights in the active portfolio. To develop the objective function of the optimization problem, one needs to expand the right-hand side of equation (10.15) into its component parts. Making use of equation (10.13) gives the following relation:

$$w_A^T \Omega \, w_A = (w_P - w - w_B)^T \Omega \, (w_P - w - w_B)$$
$$= w^T \Omega w + 2(w_B - w_P)^T \Omega w + w_P^T \Omega w_P + w_B^T \Omega w_B \quad (10.16)$$

Noting that the last two terms in equation (10.16) are constants, one can rewrite equation (10.15) as

$$\% \mathrm{UL}_A^2 = w^T \Omega w + 2c^T w + \text{constant} \quad (10.17)$$

where

$$c^T = (w_B - w_P)^T \Omega \quad (10.18)$$

If the objective is to minimize the unexpected loss of the active portfolio, equation (10.17) can serve as a suitable objective function for the optimization problem.

The constraints for the optimization problem are to limit the turnover to be less than $\tau$ and to exclude the possibility of short positions in any bonds. The optimization problem for identifying the sell transactions during the first stage of the rebalancing process with these constraints imposed is given as follows:

Minimize      $w^T \Omega w + 2c^T w$

subject to the constraints

$$\sum_{i \in \mathbb{N}_\alpha} w_i \leq \tau$$

$$0 \leq w_i \leq w_{i,P}, \quad i \in \mathbb{N}_\alpha$$

The optimization problem formulated here is a quadratic programming problem. Solving this quadratic programming problem provides a list of tentative sell transactions. The nominal amounts associated with these sell transactions are given by

$$\mathrm{NE}_{i,\mathrm{sell}} = w_i \times M_P, \quad i \in \mathbb{N}_\alpha \quad (10.19)$$

In the next section, I discuss the second stage of the optimization process that will help identify the actual transactions to be done to rebalance the portfolio.

## Identifying the Rebalancing Trades

The first stage of the optimization problem made it possible to identify the transactions that will reduce the relative risk between the portfolio and the benchmark. For the second stage of the optimization problem, assume that the portfolio holdings have been modified to take into account the sale recommendations. With this change in place, one identifies the actual rebal-ancing trades to be performed such that the rebalanced portfolio replicates the market risk characteristics of the benchmark and offers an improved risk-adjusted return relative to the benchmark. The following mathematical formulation of the optimization problem assumes that all cash holdings have to be fully invested.

Let $C_I$ denote the cash injection into the portfolio. The new market value of the portfolio after the cash injection is given by

$$M'_P = M_P + C_I \tag{10.20}$$

The new bond holdings in the portfolio assuming the nominal amounts given by equation (10.19) are sold is given by

$$NE'_{i,P} = NE_{i,P} - NE_{i,\text{sell}}, \qquad i \in \mathbb{N}_\alpha \tag{10.21}$$

The relative weight of the $i$th bond in the portfolio after the tentative bond sales is given by

$$x_{i,P} = NE'_{i,P}/M'_P, \qquad i \in \mathbb{N}_\alpha \tag{10.22}$$

If $NE_{i,\text{buy}}$ denotes the nominal amount of the $i$th bond that is bought, the relative weight of this bond in the portfolio is given by

$$x_i = NE_{i,\text{buy}}/M'_P \tag{10.23}$$

After executing these transactions, the relative weight of the $i$th bond in the portfolio is $x_i + x_{i,P}$. The square of the percentage unexpected loss of the portfolio with these bond holdings is given by

$$\%\,UL_P^2 = \sum_{i \in \mathbb{N}_\alpha} \sum_{k \in \mathbb{N}_\alpha} (x_i + x_{i,P})(x_k + x_{k,P})\sigma_i\sigma_k\rho_{ik}^\ell \tag{10.24}$$

In matrix notation, this equation can be compactly written as

$$\%\,UL_P^2 = (x + x_P)^T\Omega(x + x_P)$$
$$= x^T\Omega x + 2x_P^T\Omega x + x_P^T\Omega x_P \tag{10.25}$$

Considering that the relative weight vector $x_P$ is a constant, equation (10.25) can be rewritten as

$$\%\,UL_P^2 = x^T\Omega x + 2b^T x + \text{constant} \tag{10.26}$$

I mentioned that the buy transaction will be driven by the motivation to improve the risk-adjusted return of the portfolio relative to the benchmark.

In this case, equation (10.26) can serve as a suitable objective function to the optimization problem. It is useful to note that the design variables for the optimization problem are the relative weights $x_i$ of the $i$th bond to be bought.

The constraint functions for the optimization problem are very similar to the ones imposed for the portfolio construction process. The only difference is that the design variables here are the relative weights of the incremental buy transactions, whereas earlier they were the relative weights of the bonds in the portfolio. Taking account of this difference in the constraint function formulations, the optimization problem to determine the buy transactions can be stated as follows:

Minimize       $x^T \Omega x + 2b^T x$

subject to the constraints

$$\sum_{i \in N_\alpha} x_i f_{ik} P_{\text{dirty},i} = S_B^k - \sum_{i \in N_\alpha} x_{i,P} f_{ik} P_{\text{dirty},i}, \qquad k \in \mathbb{N}_\beta$$

$$\sum_{i \in N_\alpha} x_i y_i P_{\text{dirty},i} \geq y_B - \sum_{i \in N_\alpha} x_{i,P} y_i P_{\text{dirty},i} - \text{tolerance}$$

$$\sum_{i \in N_\alpha} x_i \mu_i \leq \% \text{EL}_B - \sum_{i \in N_\alpha} x_{i,P} \mu_i$$

$$\sum_{i \in N_\alpha} x_i P_{\text{dirty},i} = 1 - \sum_{i \in N_\alpha} x_{i,P} P_{\text{dirty},i}$$

$$0 \leq x_i \leq 0.05 \frac{S_i}{M_P'} - x_{i,P}, \qquad i \in \mathbb{N}_\alpha$$

Note that the constraint function for the portfolio yield introduces a small tolerance for deviation below the benchmark's yield. Introducing this tolerance provides some flexibility in finding suitable rebalancing trades while meeting the turnover constraint. I chose a 5-basis point tolerance for yield deviation in the numerical examples presented in the next section.

**Remarks**   Practitioners may find the constraint function on the market risk factors $k \in \mathbb{N}_\beta$ rather restrictive. In this case, some of the market risk factors can be relaxed or some tolerances could be set. One could also consider collapsing all the market risk factor constraints into a single constraint on the effective duration of the portfolio. For instance, if $D_B$ denotes the effective duration of the benchmark and $D_i$ the effective duration of the $i$th bond in the portfolio, the market risk constraint can be expressed simply as

$$\sum_{i \in N_\alpha} x_i D_i = D_B - \sum_{i \in N_\alpha} x_{i,P} D_i$$

If corporate bonds denominated in currencies other than the base currency of the portfolio are held, the resulting exchange rate risk can be hedged through currency forwards separately. Note that if only the effective duration of the portfolio is set to be equal to that of the benchmark, there will be a small residual tracking error arising from market risk factors.

## Numerical Results

Assume that the current portfolio holding is the one given in Exhibit 9.1 in Chapter 9 and the benchmark is the 23-bond portfolio with nominal exposures of USD 200 million each. Consider rebalancing this portfolio with a 10 percent turnover constraint. The two-step optimization process described here has been used to identify the rebalancing trades. Exhibit 10.4

**EXHIBIT 10.4**   Composition of Rebalanced Bond Portfolios[a]

| S. No. | Issuer | Maturity | CPH (mn $) | RMM (mn $) | RDM (mn $) | RSM (mn $) |
|---|---|---|---|---|---|---|
| 1 | Health Care Reit | 15 Aug 07 | 10.000 | 4.791 | 10.000 | 5.613 |
| 2 | Hilton Hotels | 15 May 08 | 0.000 | 0.000 | 0.000 | 0.000 |
| 3 | Apple Computer | 15 Feb 04 | 0.000 | 1.497 | 1.018 | 1.655 |
| 4 | Delta Air Lines | 15 Dec 09 | 0.000 | 3.289 | 2.817 | 3.073 |
| 5 | Alcoa Inc | 01 Jun 06 | 10.000 | 10.000 | 10.000 | 10.000 |
| 6 | ABN Amro Bank | 31 May 05 | 0.000 | 0.000 | 1.089 | 0.000 |
| 7 | Abbey Natl Plc | 17 Nov 05 | 10.000 | 10.000 | 10.000 | 10.000 |
| 8 | Alliance Capital | 15 Aug 06 | 0.000 | 0.000 | 0.000 | 0.000 |
| 9 | Aegon Nv | 15 Aug 06 | 0.000 | 0.000 | 1.319 | 0.000 |
| 10 | Abbott Labs | 01 Jul 06 | 0.000 | 0.000 | 0.000 | 0.000 |
| 11 | Caterpillar Inc | 01 May 06 | 0.000 | 0.000 | 0.000 | 0.000 |
| 12 | Coca Cola Enter | 15 Aug 06 | 0.000 | 0.000 | 0.000 | 0.000 |
| 13 | Countrywide Home | 01 Aug 06 | 10.000 | 10.000 | 5.348 | 10.000 |
| 14 | Colgate-Palm Co | 29 Apr 05 | 10.000 | 10.000 | 10.000 | 10.000 |
| 15 | Hershey Foods Co | 01 Oct 05 | 0.000 | 0.000 | 0.000 | 0.000 |
| 16 | IBM Corp | 01 Oct 06 | 0.000 | 0.000 | 0.000 | 0.000 |
| 17 | Johnson Controls | 15 Nov 06 | 0.000 | 0.000 | 0.056 | 0.000 |
| 18 | JP Morgan Chase | 01 Jun 05 | 0.000 | 0.000 | 0.000 | 0.000 |
| 19 | Bank One NA ILL | 26 Mar 07 | 0.000 | 2.925 | 1.297 | 3.021 |
| 20 | Oracle Corp | 15 Feb 07 | 10.000 | 8.854 | 7.606 | 8.700 |
| 21 | Pub Svc EL & Gas | 01 Mar 06 | 10.000 | 9.055 | 9.746 | 8.386 |
| 22 | Procter & Gamble | 30 Apr 05 | 0.000 | 0.000 | 0.000 | 0.000 |
| 23 | PNC Bank NA | 01 Aug 06 | 0.000 | 0.000 | 0.000 | 0.000 |

[a]CPH, Current portfolio holding; RMM, rebalanced portfolio under migration mode; RDM, rebalanced portfolio under default mode; RSM, rebalanced portfolio under stress mode.

**EXHIBIT 10.5**  Credit Risk Measures for Rebalanced Portfolio Under Migration Mode (RMM)

| Description | RMM Portfolio (bp) | Benchmark (bp) | Active Portfolio (bp) |
|---|---|---|---|
| %EL | 33.6 | 34.0 | −0.4 |
| %UL | 101.9 | 88.8 | 63.4 |
| %CrVaR$_{90\%}$ | 105.6 | 102.9 | 26.3 |
| %ESR$_{90\%}$ | 251.0 | 240.3 | 76.3 |

shows the composition of the rebalanced portfolios when different credit risk aggregation methods are used. Also shown in this exhibit is the rebalanced portfolio under a 20 percent stress factor scenario and multivariate $t$ distribution for asset returns.

Note that although the composition of the rebalanced portfolios under the migration mode and the stress mode are very similar, the portfolio composition under the default mode is somewhat different.

Exhibit 10.5 provides a comparison of various credit risk measures of interest for the portfolio and the benchmark. Comparing Exhibit 9.5 in Chapter 9 and Exhibit 10.5 shows that the credit risk measures of the portfolio are more aligned with the benchmark's credit risk measures after the rebalancing. One can also infer this from the relative risk measures captured by the active portfolio. For instance, the ESR at 90 percent level of confidence for the rebalanced portfolio is roughly 50 basis points lower than for the original portfolio composition. The market risk measures given in Exhibit 10.6 indicate that there is very little relative market risk between the portfolio and the benchmark.

**EXHIBIT 10.6**  Market Risk Measures for Rebalanced Portfolio Under Migration Mode

| Description | Portfolio | Benchmark |
|---|---|---|
| Effective yield (%) | 5.55 | 5.58 |
| Effective duration | 3.549 | 3.548 |
| Effective convexity | 16.05 | 16.20 |
| %VaR (90% confidence level) (%) | 3.41 | 3.41 |
| %ESR (90% confidence level) (%) | 4.69 | 4.69 |
| Shift sensitivity (USD swap curve) (bp) | 35.57 | 35.56 |
| Twist sensitivity (USD swap curve) (bp) | −2.56 | −2.55 |

## DEVIL IN THE PARAMETERS: A CASE STUDY

Practitioners view the use of optimization techniques for portfolio selection with skepticism. A major criticism of optimization techniques is that the composition of the optimal portfolio is very sensitive to the choice of the input parameters. Because the errors in the input parameter estimates can be large, the practical value of the optimal portfolio composition is often put to question. Much of this criticism has been directed against mean-variance portfolio optimization for which the estimate of the expected return of assets in the portfolio plays an important role in the composition of the optimal portfolio. It is natural that practitioners will have similar concerns as regards the portfolio composition derived using optimization techniques for replicating a corporate bond benchmark. In particular, practitioners would wish to know how the composition of the optimal portfolio changes for a different parametrization of the credit risk model as applied to a real-world portfolio construction problem.

To address this, I consider the bond portfolio selection problem presented in Ramaswamy (2002) for replicating a single-A rated corporate benchmark in the 1- to 5-year sector of the U.S. dollar market.[1] This benchmark, constructed as of 31 August 2001, contains 655 bonds. Contrasting the optimal portfolio composition presented in that study with the optimal portfolio composition resulting from the use of the modeling parametrization suggested in this book will provide an interesting case study for practitioners. This is because both approaches are similar in terms of formulating the portfolio selection problem. However, the model parameters for computing credit risk used in the study are quite different from the ones used here. The important differences are that the recovery rate and its volatility are estimated for each industry sector and correlation between industry index returns is used to infer the asset return correlation between obligors. Furthermore, for computing portfolio credit risk, loss given default values instead of loss on default and default correlation rather than loss correlation are used.

The question of interest is how the composition of the optimal portfolio will differ from the one reported in Ramaswamy (2002) when the parametrization suggested in this book for modeling credit is used. A more important question, however, is whether it is possible to explain the differences in the portfolio composition on the basis of the model parameters used to quantify credit risk. If it is possible to relate the differences in portfolio composition to particular model parameter choices, then it will be possible to make value judgments as to how one can deviate from the optimal portfolio composition if it is deemed necessary from an implementation perspective. To address the last point, I briefly review the important differences in the choice of the credit risk model parameters.

The most obvious difference in model parameter values is the recovery rate statistic used to quantify credit risk at the obligor level. Whereas the approach taken in this book does not distinguish between recovery rate statistics for senior unsecured bonds at the obligor level, the approach taken in Ramaswamy (2002) makes this distinction explicit, the details of which are shown in Exhibit 10.7. The recovery rate statistics shown in Exhibit 10.7 are based on a study reported by Altman and Kishore, which documents the observed variations in recovery rates across industry sectors using defaulted bond data over the period 1971 to 1995.[2]

The second important difference is the choice of the asset return correlation values between obligor pairs in the Ramaswamy study. Motivated by the approach taken in the CreditMetrics Technical Document, correlations between different industry index returns are used as a proxy for inferring asset return correlation between obligor pairs. Specifically, obligors are mapped to different industry sectors (38 in all) and the equity industry index return correlations are scaled by a factor of 0.4 to proxy asset return correlations between obligors.

To make the comparisons meaningful, I adopt the default mode approach to construct the optimal portfolio. Furthermore, I use the 1-year EDFs provided by KMV Corporation as of end of July 2001 as an estimate of the default probabilities for obligors in the benchmark as in the Ramaswamy study. The composition of the optimal portfolios and the benchmark broken down at the industry sector level are shown in Exhibit 10.8. In this exhibit, the column under Study corresponds to the optimal portfolio composition reported in the Ramaswamy study and the column under Book corresponds to the optimal portfolio composition when the model parameters suggested in this book are used.

Examining Exhibit 10.8 shows some significant differences in exposures to various industry sectors when different model parametrizations are used. For instance, the Book composition has almost benchmark-neutral exposure to banks but has a significant overweight relative to the Study composition. Both portfolios overweight the utilities sector relative to the benchmark, but the Study composition has a significantly greater exposure to utilities. A careful examination of the recovery rate statistics for these two industry sectors reveals that the assumed recovery rate for the banking sector is 29.3 percent and that for the utilities sector is 70.5 percent, both being widely different from the industrywide average recovery rate of 47 percent.[3] This leads to a large overweight of the utilities sector and a significant underweight of the banking sector in the optimal portfolio composition under Study.

Besides the actual recovery rate values, the volatility of the recovery rate values also appears to have a marginal influence on the portfolio composition. For instance, the textiles and apparel sector has very low recovery

**EXHIBIT 10.7** Recovery Rate Statistics for Various Industries

| MSCI Industry[a] | Code | Recovery (%) | LGD (%) | Vol LGD (%) |
|---|---|---|---|---|
| Aerospace and military technology | AERO | 38.4 | 61.6 | 28.0 |
| Construction and housing | CONS | 35.3 | 64.7 | 28.7 |
| Data processing and reproduction | DP | 37.1 | 62.9 | 20.8 |
| Electrical and electronics | EL | 46.1 | 53.9 | 20.1 |
| Electronic components, instruments | ECOM | 46.1 | 53.9 | 20.1 |
| Energy equipment and services | ENEQ | 47.4 | 52.6 | 20.1 |
| Industrial components | INDC | 47.4 | 52.6 | 25.0 |
| Machinery and engineering | MACH | 50.5 | 49.5 | 25.0 |
| Appliances and household durables | APP | 40.1 | 59.9 | 25.0 |
| Automobiles | AUTO | 42.3 | 57.7 | 25.0 |
| Beverages and tobacco | BEV | 45.3 | 54.7 | 21.7 |
| Food and household products | FOOD | 45.3 | 54.7 | 21.7 |
| Health and personal care | HLTH | 26.5 | 73.5 | 22.7 |
| Recreation and others | REC | 40.2 | 59.8 | 25.7 |
| Textiles and apparel | TEX | 31.7 | 68.3 | 15.2 |
| Energy sources | EN | 67.3 | 32.7 | 18.0 |
| Utilities, electrical and gas | UT | 70.5 | 29.5 | 19.5 |
| Banking | BANK | 29.3 | 70.7 | 25.7 |
| Financial services | FIN | 42.1 | 57.9 | 25.7 |
| Insurance | INS | 31.5 | 68.5 | 25.7 |
| Real estate | RE | 34.2 | 65.8 | 28.7 |
| Multi-industry | MULT | 48.7 | 51.3 | 25.0 |
| Gold mines | GOLD | 40.7 | 59.3 | 18.0 |
| Building materials and components | BM | 32.3 | 67.7 | 22.9 |
| Chemicals | CHEM | 58.0 | 42.0 | 27.1 |
| Forest products and paper | FP | 29.8 | 70.2 | 24.4 |
| Metals, nonferrous | MNF | 46.1 | 53.9 | 22.9 |
| Metals, steel | STL | 46.1 | 53.9 | 22.9 |
| Miscellaneous materials and commodities | MMC | 32.2 | 67.8 | 22.9 |
| Broadcasting and publishing | BRD | 39.0 | 61.0 | 20.8 |
| Business and public services | BS | 46.2 | 53.8 | 25.0 |
| Leisure and tourism | LEI | 40.2 | 59.8 | 25.7 |
| Merchandising | MER | 33.2 | 66.8 | 20.5 |
| Telecommunications | TEL | 26.4 | 73.6 | 20.8 |
| Transportation, airlines | AIR | 39.5 | 60.5 | 28.0 |
| Transportation, road and rail | RR | 43.6 | 56.4 | 28.0 |
| Transportation, shipping | SHIP | 38.4 | 61.6 | 28.0 |
| Wholesale and international trade | TRD | 44.0 | 56.0 | 22.1 |

[a]Morgan Stanley Capital International.

**EXHIBIT 10.8**  Sector Concentrations of Benchmark and Optimal Portfolios

| MSCI Industry[a] | Benchmark (%) | Study (%) | Book (%) | MMode (%) |
|---|---|---|---|---|
| Aerospace and military technology | 1.19 | 4.72 | 2.23 | 2.56 |
| Construction and housing | 0.0 | 0.0 | 0.0 | 0.0 |
| Data processing and reproduction | 0.71 | 0.0 | 3.30 | 4.06 |
| Electrical and electronics | 0.27 | 0.0 | 0.44 | 0.88 |
| Electronic components, instruments | 1.53 | 0.0 | 2.94 | 3.71 |
| Energy equipment and services | 1.94 | 4.79 | 3.27 | 6.04 |
| Industrial components | 0.14 | 1.26 | 1.85 | 0.39 |
| Machinery and engineering | 1.51 | 1.80 | 2.37 | 5.38 |
| Appliances and household durables | 0.0 | 0.0 | 0.0 | 0.0 |
| Automobiles | 14.68 | 0.0 | 0.75 | 2.31 |
| Beverages and tobacco | 2.78 | 7.21 | 7.05 | 6.41 |
| Food and household products | 2.23 | 7.56 | 9.66 | 8.83 |
| Health and personal care | 1.67 | 4.16 | 3.73 | 4.62 |
| Recreation and others | 0.52 | 0.0 | 0.0 | 1.45 |
| Textiles and apparel | 0.26 | 2.58 | 1.45 | 0.97 |
| Energy sources | 0.36 | 2.99 | 0.0 | 0.20 |
| Utilities, electrical and gas | 3.62 | 14.17 | 8.34 | 16.01 |
| Banking | 19.73 | 9.64 | 20.03 | 8.09 |
| Financial services | 27.15 | 8.72 | 6.69 | 3.30 |
| Insurance | 3.31 | 7.37 | 4.95 | 3.55 |
| Real estate | 0.0 | 0.0 | 0.0 | 0.0 |
| Multi-industry | 2.09 | 4.88 | 0.90 | 1.26 |
| Gold mines | 0.0 | 0.0 | 0.0 | 0.0 |
| Building materials and components | 0.25 | 2.47 | 2.66 | 1.52 |
| Chemicals | 0.59 | 3.92 | 1.56 | 0.36 |
| Forest products and paper | 0.40 | 1.00 | 0.78 | 0.26 |
| Metals, nonferrous | 0.68 | 5.04 | 1.07 | 1.87 |
| Metals, steel | 0.09 | 0.0 | 0.11 | 0.93 |
| Miscellaneous materials and commodities | 0.0 | 0.0 | 0.0 | 0.0 |
| Broadcasting and publishing | 2.84 | 1.26 | 5.20 | 3.43 |
| Business and public services | 0.0 | 0.0 | 0.0 | 0.0 |
| Leisure and tourism | 0.0 | 0.0 | 0.0 | 0.0 |
| Merchandising | 1.28 | 1.00 | 4.93 | 3.96 |
| Telecommunications | 7.36 | 0.0 | 3.16 | 6.34 |
| Transportation, airlines | 0.14 | 1.12 | 0.0 | 0.11 |
| Transportation, road and rail | 0.51 | 2.35 | 0.01 | 0.96 |
| Transportation, shipping | 0.0 | 0.0 | 0.0 | 0.0 |
| Wholesale and international trade | 0.20 | 0.0 | 0.57 | 0.20 |

[a]Morgan Stanley Capital International.

rate volatility as reported in Exhibit 10.7. Although its recovery value of 31.7 percent is lower than the industrywide average, the volatility of recovery rates is 15.2 percent, which is well below the industrywide average of 25 percent. Because a lower value of recovery rate volatility reduces the unexpected loss at the obligor level, such industry sectors tend to have greater weights in Study. However, the effect of recovery rate volatility on the optimal portfolio composition is not very significant.

The other parameter that can influence the optimal portfolio composition is the asset return correlation between obligors. To test the sensitivity of the portfolio composition to changes in asset return correlation, asset return correlations were increased by 20 percent and the portfolio construction problem re-solved. It was observed, however, that this change had no significant influence on the relative portfolio allocations to different industry sectors. When using an optimization approach to select a corporate bond portfolio, the recovery rates for different industry sectors, if chosen to be different, need to be carefully selected because they have a strong influence on the relative weights among various industry sectors.

To complete the analysis of the effects of alternate model parametrizations on the composition of the optimal portfolio, consider the case of portfolio construction under the migration mode. In this case, the issuer's default probability and rating transiting probabilities are determined by the rating transition matrix, and these in turn are a function of the current credit rating of the issuer. The credit risk model parameters used for portfolio construction under the migration mode are identical to those used for computing the portfolio composition of Book except for the use of the rating migration matrix to define the default and transition probabilities. In particular, the recovery rate statistics were not differentiated among issuers, and the average recovery rate was set to 47 percent and the volatility of the recovery rate was set to 25 percent. The composition of the optimal portfolio under the migration mode is also shown in Exhibit 10.8 under the heading MMode. The important difference between this portfolio composition and the composition of the Book portfolio is that there is a significant overweight assigned to the utilities sector and the allocation to banking sector is small relative to the benchmark weight.

## Risk Reduction

The discussions so far focused on examining the differences in industry sector concentrations of the optimal portfolios. From a portfolio manager's perspective, it is also important to know the level of risk reduction relative to the benchmark and the number of bonds required to replicate the benchmark. Because the parameters used to quantify credit risk are different for each of the optimal portfolios, the most meaningful way to measure the

**EXHIBIT 10.9**   Risk Diversification Ratios

| Optimal Portfolio | EL Ratio | UL Ratio | No. of Bonds |
|---|---|---|---|
| Study | 0.379 | 0.391 | 75 |
| Book | 0.344 | 0.366 | 120 |
| MMode | 0.855 | 0.644 | 142 |

reduction in credit risk for the optimal portfolios is to examine the expected and unexpected loss ratios relative to the benchmark. Specifically, the expected loss ratio is defined as the ratio between the expected loss of the portfolio and the expected loss of the benchmark, where both losses are computed using the same model parametrization. The unexpected loss ratio is similarly defined. Exhibit 10.9 shows the loss ratios for the three optimal portfolios considered here.

It is interesting to note that both Study and Book portfolios achieve similar levels of risk reduction relative to the benchmark. For instance, the optimal portfolio denoted Book has an expected loss ratio of 0.344. This corresponds to a risk reduction of the expected loss by 65.6 percent relative to the benchmark. The risk reduction of the unexpected loss of this portfolio relative to the benchmark is 63.4 percent. In terms of the number of bonds required to construct the optimal portfolio, the Book portfolio requires considerably more, but it is still less than 20 percent of the bonds in the benchmark. An interesting observation is that the risk reduction for the MMode portfolio is substantially less relative to what is achieved when the default mode is used for quantifying credit risk. The reason for this is that when the rating transition matrix is used, the relative differences in default probabilities between single-A rated obligors are significantly lower than in the case when EDF values are used to determine default probabilities. As a result, the possible risk reduction is also correspondingly limited. Note also that the number of bonds required for benchmark replication is considerably more for the MMode portfolio.

## QUESTIONS

1. With reference to a corporate bond portfolio, what are the benefits of taking a quantitative approach to portfolio selection?
2. What is the difference between a quadratic programming problem and a nonlinear programming problem? Why is it computationally more difficult to solve a nonlinear programming problem?
3. A portfolio selection problem is posed as the minimization of the tracking error of the portfolio subject to the constraint that the portfolio

duration and benchmark duration are identical. What type of a programming problem is this?

4. What are the practical difficulties that can arise when a quantitative approach is used to either construct or rebalance corporate bond portfolios?

5. The portfolio construction problem was posed as a quadratic programming problem. Is it possible to formulate the optimal portfolio construction problem as a linear programming problem? Justify your answer.

6. What are the practical difficulties involved in determining rebalancing trades using the portfolio construction problem formulation?

7. Briefly explain the motivation for solving the portfolio-rebalancing problem using a two-step process.

8. Consider the case where the objective function of the portfolio-rebalancing problem is chosen to minimize the turnover of the portfolio. What type of an optimization problem is this?

9. The devil-in-the-parameters case study showed that the composition of the optimal portfolios is influenced by the choice of the credit risk model parameters. Which model parameters require careful estimation?

## CHAPTER 11

# Structured Credit Products

**S**o far in this book, I have analyzed how credit risk in a corporate bond portfolio can be quantified and how the relative risk of the portfolio against a benchmark can be measured and managed. The risk quantification techniques presented in the earlier chapters can be used to analyze the credit risk inherent in structured credit products whose collateral pool comprises corporate bonds. Examples of such structured credit products include Morgan Stanley's Tradable Custodial Receipts (Tracers) and Lehman Brothers Targeted Return Index Securities (Trains). Tracers and Trains provide investors with the opportunity to trade a portfolio of corporate bonds through one trade execution.

Other popular structured credit products that are backed by a collateral pool of securities or bank loans come under the broad category of collateralized debt obligations (CDOs). The cash flows generated through interest income and principal repayments from the collateral pool are allocated to a prioritized collection of CDO securities referred to as tranches. The standard prioritization scheme used is simple subordination: Senior CDO notes are paid before mezzanine and lower subordinated notes, and any residual cash is paid to an equity tranche. A CDO structure can hold in its collateral pool of assets corporate bonds, bank loans, emerging market debt, or asset-backed securities. A CDO structure can also gain exposure to these assets synthetically. The annual CDO issuance has grown from roughly $4 billion prior to 1996 to above $120 billion in 2000.

This chapter provides a brief introduction to the structured credit products CDOs and Tracers. In the first part of this chapter, I focus on CDOs and explain the main features of this product. I then discuss how rating agencies evaluate the credit risk inherent in CDOs and assign ratings to different tranches of the CDO. In the second part of this chapter, I give a brief introduction to tradable corporate bond baskets and explain why this and similar products are attractive from an investor's perspective. I then focus on the structured credit product Tracers and explain the main features of this product. This is followed by an outline of a procedure to evaluate the risks in Tracers using the credit risk quantification approach presented in the earlier chapters of this book. By deriving an implied credit rating of this structured credit product using a tail risk measure, I highlight the differences in credit rating that can result from using the approach presented here as opposed to the rating agency approaches.

## INTRODUCTION TO CDOs

A CDO is a structured credit product that can be broadly categorized into two distinct groups: balance sheet CDOs and arbitrage CDOs. Balance sheet CDOs are packaged by transferring the loans or assets from the balance sheet and hence have an impact on the balance sheet of the originator. Arbitrage CDOs, on the other hand, are packaged by buying bonds or other assets in the market, pooling them together, and then securititizing the assets. The prime objective in balance sheet CDOs is the reduction of regulatory capital, whereas for arbitrage CDOs the objective is to make arbitrage profits. A further subclassification of CDOs is possible depending on whether the collateral can be traded or not. In the former case, the CDO is referred to as a cash flow CDO, and in the latter case, as a market value CDO. Besides these classifications, it is possible to group CDOs into cash and synthetic CDOs. Cash CDOs are those that invest directly in bonds, loans, or other securities that constitute the collateral pool, whereas synthetic CDOs gain exposure to the collateral pool through credit default swaps or total return swaps.

As an asset class, CDOs are grouped under the asset-backed securities market because of the similarities in the fundamental structures that govern both asset classes. For instance, a CDO is a debt obligation issued by a bankruptcy-remote special-purpose vehicle (SPV) secured by some form of receivable. The receivables are the interest and principal payments from the securitized assets held in the bankruptcy-remote SPV. CDO securities typically consist of credit tranches ranging from triple A to single B or unrated, a feature common to asset-backed securities (ABS). Furthermore, the rating of each CDO tranche is determined by credit enhancement, ongoing collateral credit performance, and the interest payment priority from the cash flows generated from the collateral pool. In all these respects, a CDO transaction is fundamentally similar to an ABS transaction.

In this section, I briefly examine the major differences among various types of CDOs and discuss the motivation for CDO issuance. I also indicate what characteristics make CDOs appealing to a wide investor base.

### Balance Sheet versus Arbitrage CDOs

CDOs can be classified as either balance sheet or arbitrage CDOs depending on the motivation behind the securitization and the source of the assets.

Balance sheet CDOs are initiated by holders of securitizable assets, such as commercial banks, that desire to sell part of their risky assets to investors. The main motivation for issuing balance sheet CDOs is to either reduce the regulatory capital requirement or reduce risk concentrations to certain industry sectors arising from the bank lending activities. Balance sheet CDOs can be initiated through a cash sale of the assets into a SPV, which are then securitized into different CDO credit tranches and sold to investors. If the assets that constitute the collateral pool are made up of bank loans, the CDO transaction is referred to as a collateralized loan obligation (CLO). The bank originating the CLO usually retains the first-loss piece, or equivalently, the equity tranche. The sale of the loans into the SPV will free up regulatory capital charge, and the bank originating the CLO can use the regulatory capital freed to fund other business activities.

To illustrate how a CLO transaction helps free up capital for a bank, consider a bank that has a loan book of $1 billion, which consumes 8 percent capital charge, that is, $80 million. By doing a CLO transaction, the bank can sell 98 percent of its loan book to investors and retain an equity piece worth 2 percent of the $1 billion. This equity piece will incur a 100 percent capital charge, which is equal to $20 million. By doing this CLO transaction, the bank has reduced its regulatory capital charge by $60 million and this freed-up capital can be used to fund other prospective or high-margin business activities. CLO transactions originated by a bank to free up regulatory capital are usually large and consist mostly of investment-grade commercial and industrial loans having short maturities. These loans usually represent revolving lines of credit and the members of the pool are anonymous. To help analyze the investment risks, investors are supplied with statistical information on the distribution of the credit quality of the loans and the prepayment risks in the pool.

In an arbitrage CDO, the sponsor raises funds in the capital markets through the issuance of CDO securities to finance the purchase of a portfolio of assets in the open market. Typically, the sponsor will begin to accumulate the assets during a warehousing period prior to the CDO issuance and complete the acquisition of the assets during a 60- to 90-day ramp-up period after the CDO closes. The aim of arbitrage CDOs is to capture the arbitrage opportunity that exists in the credit spread differential between the high-yield securities that constitute the collateral and the low-yield liabilities represented by the rated CDO notes.

Sponsors of arbitrage CDOs include insurance companies, investment banks, and asset managers. The sponsor of the arbitrage CDO often invests in a portion of the equity tranche, which represents a leveraged investment in the underlying collateral. Seen from the asset manager's perspective, arbitrage CDOs create a high-return asset by retaining part of the equity tranche and in addition create stable fee income by increasing assets under management. A typical arbitrage CDO contains 30 to 50 securities, which can include both loans and bonds. When the underlying securities in the collateral pool comprises only bonds, it is customary to refer to the CDO as a collateralized bond obligation (CBO). The credit of the collateral pool in arbitrage CDOs tends to be of lower quality than a balance sheet CDO, and is typically of BB to B rating. Transaction sizes also tend to be smaller, typically $200 million to $1 billion compared to $1 billion to $5 billion for balance sheet CDOs.

## Cash Flow versus Market Value CDOs

Depending on whether the collateral pool can be actively traded or not, CDOs can be further classified into cash flow and market value CDOs. In a cash flow CDO, the collateral is a self-amortizing pool of high-yield bonds or bank loans, which are usually not traded unless certain credit triggers occur. The cash flow structure relies on the collateral's ability to generate sufficient cash to pay principal and interest on the CDO notes. An important objective of a cash flow CDO manager is to choose the assets in the collateral pool that will minimize defaults and maximize the coupon returns. Because the collateral pool is not traded actively, the portfolio value of a cash flow CDO is based on the par amount of the collateral securities.

Unlike the case of cash flow CDOs, the collateral of a market value CDO can be actively traded. As a result, the collateral pool of a market value CDO can be substantially different over time, and in this respect market value CDOs are somewhat more similar to a hedge fund than to a traditional ABS structure. Market value CDOs rely on the portfolio manager's ability to generate total returns and liquidate the collateral in a timely manner if deemed necessary to meet the coupon and principal payments. Because the collateral of market value CDOs is actively traded, market value CDOs are usually marked to market either daily or weekly. The debt rating of different tranches of a market value CDO depend on the price volatility of the assets in the collateral pool in addition to the diversity and the credit quality of the pool.

Because cash flow and market value CDOs have different portfolio objectives, the collateral pool of the two CDO structures is somewhat different. For instance, the collateral of cash flow CDOs consists mainly of rated high-yield assets and loans that are current. For market value CDOs, on the other hand, the collateral pool is much more diverse and may include distressed debt and project finance in addition to high-yield bonds and loans. The intention of holding a more diversified collateral pool in market value CDOs is to increase the potential returns to investors in the equity tranche. On the liability side, cash flow CDOs tend to have longer liabilities than market value CDOs.

## Cash versus Synthetic CDOs

CDOs can be characterized as cash or synthetic depending on whether the CDO invests directly in the assets that constitute the collateral through the cash market or invests indirectly through a credit default swap, total return swap, or credit-linked note. In cash CDOs, the assets held as collateral have to be transferred into a bankruptcy-remote SPV. If the assets in the collateral pool comprise bank loans, moving these loans off balance sheet can be difficult. This is because the bank initiating this transaction may need to obtain permission from the borrower to transfer the ownership of its loans. This process can be time consuming, expensive, and potentially harmful to customer relationships. To avoid these problems, synthetic CDOs are used to transfer the credit risk from the balance sheet of the bank. This is achieved through a credit default swap structure to transfer out the credit risk of an underlying basket of loans to a SPV, which are then sold to investors.

A credit default swap structure is similar to an insurance policy where the buyer purchases protection against default risk on a reference pool of assets that can include bonds, loans, or other receivables. If the reference pools of assets comprise bank loans, the structure is referred to as a synthetic CLO. The protection buyer in a synthetic CDO is usually the bank originating the transaction, and the protection seller is the investor. The protection buyer pays a periodic fee to the protection seller, who in turn pays out to the protection buyer if a defined credit event occurs on the reference pool of assets. Most synthetic CDOs are cash settled, where the protection buyer is paid the difference between par and postdefault market value.

Synthetic CDO structures are now widely used in both arbitrage and balance sheet transactions. Structurally, synthetic CDOs have some advantages over cash CDOs. For instance, in a synthetic CDO there is no interest rate risk because the credit default swap is concerned only with credit events on the reference pool of assets. If the there is no credit event, the investors do not face any loss at liquidation even when the reference assets are worth less due to interest rate changes. Other advantages are that investors in a synthetic CDO are not dependent on the cash flows from an underlying pool of bonds or loans and the maturity of the synthetic CDO is governed solely by the maturity of the underlying credit default swap.

## Investor Motivations

I examined the different types of CDOs in the market and the motivation for CDO issuance. Specifically, balance sheet CDOs are intended to provide regulatory capital relief and reduce risk concentrations to particular industry sectors. Arbitrage CDOs, on the other hand, provide CDO managers a stable source of fee income and a share in the returns generated by the equity tranche ownership. In general, creating a CDO structure involves costs, and these costs are returns forgone by CDO investors. In this connection, one may wonder why investors buy CDOs that cost more than the assets held in the CDOs. Investors buy CDOs for a variety of reasons, some of which are as follows.

A first and important reason is that the CDO structure creates custom exposures that investors desire and cannot achieve in other ways. For instance, investors willing to take exposure to the high-yield market may not be able to invest in this market due to investment constraints. To gain access to this asset class, the only opportunity might be to buy a CDO tranche rated investment grade whose collateral pool contains high-yield bonds. Similarly, gaining access to bank loans may only be possible through CDOs because bank loans are not traded.

Other investor motivations for buying CDOs include the following:

- A diversified portfolio can be purchased through one trade execution, which results in reduced transaction costs.
- CDO debt tranches have higher yields than many corporate bonds or asset-backed securities of similar rating and maturity.
- Arbitrage CDOs allow investors to gain exposure to the non-investment-grade market on a highly diversified basis without committing significant resources.
- Investing in the equity tranche of the CDO offers the opportunity for a leveraged investment in the collateral pool of a diversified portfolio.

## ANATOMY OF A CDO TRANSACTION

In the previous section, I discussed the different types of CDOs that are available and the motivation behind their issuance. I also showed that cash CDOs are structured securities whose cash flows stem from the interest and principal income earned on a portfolio of corporate obligations. These obligations form the CDO collateral, and can comprise banks loans, revolving loans, corporate bonds, emerging market debt, and even asset-backed securities. The cash flow from the collateral pool is distributed to the various tranches following a strict priority rule with the more senior tranches receiving payments before the less senior tranches. In this section, I discuss the structure and mechanics of a CDO transaction from the inception stage.

### Capital Structure

A CDO is created using a standard securitization approach. This involves pooling financial assets and issuing debt and equity obligations backed by

**EXHIBIT 11.1**   CDO Capital Structure

| Assets | Liabilities |
|---|---|
| $100 million: Corporate bonds, emerging market debt, bank loans | $80 million: Class A senior notes<br>$15 million: Class B mezzanine notes<br>$5 million: Equity |

the pool of assets. The entity that issues the obligations and buys the pool of assets is called special-purpose vehicle (SPV). The SPV is set up as a bankruptcy-remote entity, which in legal terms means that the CDO investors are taking the risks of ownership of the assets but not the additional risk of bankruptcy of the CDO's sponsor. This is achieved by creating the SPV as a newly established entity with no operating history to exclude the scope of having prior liabilities. Furthermore, the relevant documents of the SPV and the CDO must limit the SPV's activities to those essential for the transaction and should prohibit the SPV incurring additional debt. The SPV is registered as a charitable trust and is usually established in a tax-free jurisdiction.

The capital structure of a CDO consists of the collateral pool held in the SPV on the asset side and a set of CDO notes having different payment obligations and priorities on the liability side. Exhibit 11.1 shows the typical capital structure of a CDO transaction.

In Exhibit 11.1, the CDO structure issues a senior note, a mezzanine note, and a subordinated note or equity. This liability structure is created out of a collateral pool of assets that include corporate bonds, bank loans, and emerging market debt. The process by which claims on cash flows generated by a collateral portfolio are split into an equity share and several classes of notes or "tranches" having varying payment priorities is referred to as tranching. Tranching transforms a less attractive investment on the collateral side into more attractive investments that appeal to a wider investor community. This is achieved through subordination, which is a form of structural credit enhancement. Subordinated CDO debt tranches protect more senior debt tranches against credit losses, and in return for this, receive a higher coupon for taking on greater credit risk. In Exhibit 11.1, the senior notes have a subordination amount of $20 million.

The rating of each CDO tranche depends on its ability to service debt with the cash flows generated by the assets in the collateral pool. The debt-servicing ability depends on the collateral diversification, subordination, and structural protection present in the CDO structure. The senior CDO notes are typically rated triple A to single A and mezzanine notes are typically rated triple B to single B. The equity tranche is generally unrated, and receives all or most of the residual interest proceeds of the collateral.

**EXHIBIT 11.2** Credit Quality Distribution of CDO Capital Structure

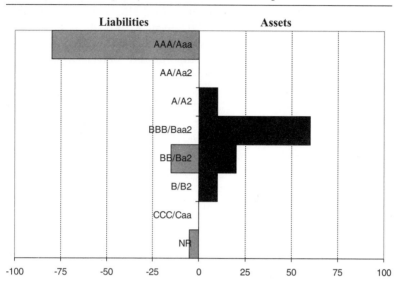

Clearly, as one moves down the CDO's capital structure, the level of risk increases. Exhibit 11.2 shows the distribution of the credit quality of the CDO capital structure from an asset–liability perspective.

Exhibit 11.2 shows that in spite of the fact that the credit quality of the assets in the collateral pool is below AA, the senior CDO note has a triple-A rating. This is possible because of the priority of claims established through subordination. For instance, a default of a single bond in the collateral portfolio reduces the return on the asset side of the CDO structure. However, on the liability side, the single bond default is almost entirely absorbed by the equity tranche. Any loss that cannot be absorbed by the equity tranche is passed on to the mezzanine tranche. Such a subordination of claims ensures that the promised cash flows to the senior notes will only be affected if several bonds in the collateral pool default during the life of the CDO.

## How the Transaction Evolves

Once the decision is made to issue a CDO, the asset types and specific credits to be included in the collateral have to be identified by the asset manager. In most cases, the asset manager starts buying the assets prior to the closing date of the deal with the intention of transferring the assets into the SPV on the closing date. This period, also referred to as the warehousing period, requires a bridge facility to finance the purchase of the assets. The warehousing period can last typically several weeks.

On the closing date of the CDO transaction, the SPV issues multiple debt tranches and an equity tranche to investors. The asset manager then enters into an investment management agreement with the SPV to manage the collateral assets. Subsequently, the assets bought during the warehousing period are transferred to the SPV and the asset manager continues acquiring the collateral assets using the proceeds from the sale of debt and equity tranches. The period during which the assets are acquired is referred to as the ramp-up period, and this can last 3 to 6 months. The ramp-up period is usually followed by a reinvestment period, which could last 3 to 6 years. During the reinvestment period, the cash flows from principal repayments arising from early amortization are reinvested.

Finally, the reinvestment period is followed by an amortization period during which all cash received from repayment of principal is used to redeem the liabilities. Most CDOs follow a sequential schedule for principal repayments. Under this schedule, the principal of the senior notes is repaid fully before the repayment of principal is made to less senior tranches in the capital structure. Some CDOs also repay principal on a "pro rata" basis, where principal is repaid pro rata according to the size of each tranche.

## Parties to a CDO

The major parties involved in a CDO transaction include the asset manager, trustee or custodian, hedge counterparty, and, in some cases, a bond insurer. This list of parties to a CDO is not exhaustive. Typically, it also involves additional parties like the rating agencies that assign ratings to the CDO notes issued and lawyers, structuring experts, and underwriters at the time the transaction is initiated. Exhibit 11.3 shows the typical contractual relationship among various parties involved in a CDO transaction. I now briefly discuss the role of each party in a CDO transaction.

**Asset Manager**    The asset manager plays an important role in the structuring of a CDO transaction. Typically, an asset manager's responsibility includes selecting assets that form the collateral, determining the timing of sale and purchase of subsequent investments, and assessing the quality and adequacy of the collateral in meeting the liabilities. Because the asset manager has considerable flexibility and discretion in trading, his or her skills tend to have an impact on an arbitrage CDO's performance. The role of an asset manager for balance sheet CDOs is rather limited because the assets chosen in the collateral pool are the ones the bank wants to sell for regulatory capital relief or to reduce risk concentrations.

**Trustee**    The trustee or custodian in a CDO transaction has a fiduciary responsibility and is responsible for safe custody of the SPV's assets and for ensuring

**EXHIBIT 11.3** Typical CDO Contractual Relationship

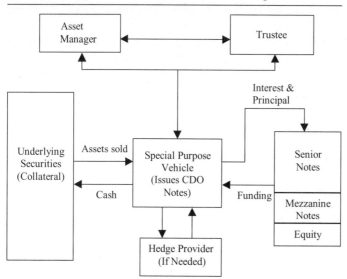

compliance with the CDO's requirements. This may require ensuring that the various collateral tests are met before executing a trade recommended by the asset manager. The compliance testing for CDOs is usually more complex than for typical ABS transactions, which is further complicated when active trading is done in market value CDOs. The trustee issues a monthly report detailing the status of the CDO and cash distributions made by the CDO.

**Hedge Counterparty**   If the collateral assets are primarily fixed-coupon-paying assets and the CDO notes pay floating rates, hedge counterparties will be needed to swap the proceeds so that the cash flows of the assets and liabilities are matched. In different circumstances, hedge counterparties may also provide currency swaps, timing hedges, or total return swaps.

**Bond Insurer**   In some circumstances, if external credit enhancements are required to prop up the rating of a CDO tranche, bond insurers may be involved. The bond insurer guarantees the payment of principal and interest on one or more of the CDO notes issued. Bond insurance results in a reduction in the senior tranche yield.

## Structural Protections

The credit quality of the different debt tranches of the CDO depends on the ability of the CDO to withstand the default losses and still be able to pay the promised cash flows. Clearly, the credit quality of the debt tranches depends on the credit quality of the collateral assets and the structural protections present in the CDO as a function of the seniority of the tranche. In this section, I focus on structural protections, which can be broadly classified into three categories: subordination, collateral quality tests, and collateral coverage tests.

**Subordination**   I mentioned that the CDO capital structure imposes some form of internal credit enhancement through subordination. In practice, one can distinguish between two types of subordination: priority in bankruptcy and priority in cash flow timing. Priority of claims in the event of bankruptcy are always strict, which signifies that proceeds from the liquidation of the collateral assets are first paid to meet the obligations of the senior debt holder. Any proceeds that remain after meeting this claim are distributed to the debt tranche that is second most senior. This procedure is used until all the proceeds are distributed to the various investor groups following this strict priority rule.

In order to maintain tranche priority in cash flows, CDOs may use the sequential or pro rata principal paydown mechanism discussed earlier. The sequential paydown structure has the effect of amortizing the senior CDO tranches first because principal payments are made before the mezzanine or lower tranches are amortized. A variant of this is to use a fast-pay/slow-pay structure in which a greater proportion of principal payments goes to the senior tranche.

**Collateral Quality Tests**   The collateral quality tests for cash flow CDOs include a list of criteria that the collateral portfolio must meet on an ongoing basis. Each of the collateral quality tests is designed by rating agencies to ensure that the collateral assets in the SPV are managed under the guidelines mandated by the transaction's rating. To some extent, these quality tests depend on the type of assets that comprise the collateral portfolio. The commonly used collateral quality tests are as follows:

- *Minimum average rating test.* This test specifies that the minimum weighted average rating of the collateral portfolio must meet a specified level, which is usually B to B+ in cash flow CDOs.
- *Minimum recovery test.* This test specifies that the collateral portfolio meet a minimum weighted average recovery rate.
- *Industry concentration limit.* This limit is specified to ensure that there is sufficient diversification in the collateral portfolio. A typical maximum industry concentration limit is 8 percent, which is determined by the ratio of the total outstanding par amount of collateral securities in

a given industry divided by the total outstanding par amount of the collateral.

■ *Weighted average maturity test.* This test is designed to ensure that there is a predictable amortization profile for the rated securities after the reinvestment period.

**Collateral Coverage Tests**   Collateral coverage tests are designed to protect the rated notes of cash flow CDOs and serve as early warning signals that interest or principal proceeds may be inadequate to meet the payment obligations. When the coverage tests are not met, cash flows are diverted from lower rated notes and equity to pay down the more senior CDO tranches, triggering an early amortization schedule of the senior CDO tranches. There are two types of coverage tests commonly used: interest coverage tests and overcollateralization tests.

The interest coverage (IC) test is designed to ensure that coupon payments received from the collateral assets are adequate to pay fees and interest due on the rated CDO notes. IC tests are usually not employed in market value CDOs.[1]

The overcollateralization (OC) test is designed to ensure that the CDO transaction maintains a preset minimum overcollateralization ratio for each rated tranche. The overcollateralization ratio for any tranche is the ratio of the par amount of the tranche to the par amount of the performing assets in the collateral portfolio plus the expected recovery rate on any defaulted securities. OC tests are employed in market value CDOs as well, with the tests being performed on the basis of the market value of the securities instead of par values.

To illustrate the procedure involved in computing IC and OC tests, consider a collateral portfolio with a par value of $100 million and a weighted average coupon of 8 percent per annum. Let the annual fees, which include trustee fees, hedging premiums, and asset management fees, be $0.5 million. Assume that there are three debt tranches paying semiannual coupons, the details of which are shown in Exhibit 11.4.

**EXHIBIT 11.4**   Liability Structure of a CDO[a]

| Tranche | Par Value (mn $) | Annual Coupon | Min IC Ratio (%) | Min OC Ratio (%) |
|---|---|---|---|---|
| Class A | $P_A = 75$ | $C_A = 5\%$ | 150 | 125 |
| Class B | $P_B = 10$ | $C_B = 6\%$ | 130 | 115 |
| Class C | $P_C = 10$ | $C_C = 8\%$ | 110 | 100 |
| Equity | $P_E = 5$ | — | — | — |

[a]IC, Interest coverage test; OC, Overcollateralization test.

**IC Tests:**

$$IC_{\text{class A}} = \frac{P_{\text{pool}} \times \text{WAC} - \text{Fees}}{P_A \times C_A} = 200\%$$

$$IC_{\text{class B}} = \frac{P_{\text{pool}} \times \text{WAC} - \text{Fees}}{P_A \times C_A + P_B \times C_B} = 172\%$$

$$IC_{\text{class C}} = \frac{P_{\text{pool}} \times \text{WAC} - \text{Fees}}{P_A + C_A + P_B \times C_B + P_C \times C_C} = 146\%$$

**OC Tests:**

$$OC_{\text{class A}} = \frac{P_{\text{pool}}}{P_A} = 133\%$$

$$OC_{\text{class B}} = \frac{P_{\text{pool}}}{P_A + P_B} = 118\%$$

$$OC_{\text{class C}} = \frac{P_{\text{pool}}}{P_A + P_B + P_C} = 105\%$$

In these equations, $P_{\text{pool}}$ denotes the par amount of the collateral pool and WAC the weighted average coupon of the collateral pool. Note that all the coverage tests are passed for the this example.

## MAJOR SOURCES OF RISK IN CDOs

As is the case with any complex financial product, investment in CDOs involve risks arising from a variety of sources. The effective management of these risks by the asset manager has a significant influence on the performance of the CDO tranches. Among the different sources of risk, the dominant risk in a CDO transaction arises from credit risk. In general, credit risk manifests itself in different forms as a result of various structural protection mechanisms built into the CDO structure. In this section, I discuss the different types of risks that are commonly associated with CDO transactions.

### Interest Rate Risk

Interest rate risk in a CDO can arise from a variety of sources, and to some extent will also depend on the complexity of the structure. An important source of interest rate risk is the mismatch between coupon receipts and coupon payments. For instance, the assets in the collateral pool might pay fixed-rate coupons, whereas the CDO might pay floating-rate coupons on the liabilities. This source of interest rate risk can be usually hedged through an interest rate swap. Other interest rate risk sources result from the differences in the periodicity of coupon receipts and coupon payments and the differences in coupon payment dates between assets and liabilities.

Changes to interest rates can also result in significant risks to the CDO. For instance, if the collateral portfolio includes a greater proportion of callable bonds, falling interest rates can lead to large principal prepayments, and these have to be reinvested in a lower yielding asset. Hedging interest rate risk fully is usually difficult in CDO transactions due to the active management of the collateral assets and embedded optionalities that may be present in them.

## Liquidity Risk

The collateral pool of CDOs includes high-yield and emerging market bonds. Because bonds belonging to these asset classes have limited liquidity, CDOs that invest in these asset classes are exposed to liquidity risk. The implication is that the asset manager may not be able to liquidate the assets when needed. In particular, if some of the illiquid assets mature after the legal maturity of the CDO, liquidity risk may have a negative impact on the return of the equity investor.[2] From an investor's perspective, the limited scope for secondary market trading of CDOs leads to liquidity risk.

## Ramp-Up Risk

Arbitrage CDO transactions involve an initial period, known as a ramp-up period, during which a significant portfolio of the collateral assets is acquired. This ramp-up period can last from 3 to 6 months after the CDO notes are issued to investors. The extent of ramp-up risk in a CDO transaction depends on the relative proportion of assets acquired during the ramp-up period and how long it lasts. The major risks that arise during the ramp-up period include the following:

- Negative carry between the earnings on cash deposits and the liabilities due on CDO notes.
- Origination risk due to unavailability of bonds the asset manager intended to buy.
- Adverse credit spread or price movements, which increase the cost of buying the collateral assets.

## Reinvestment Risk

The CDO assets are allowed to be traded during the reinvestment period, which can last 3 to 6 years, provided the collateral coverage and quality tests are met. Reinvestment of collateral cash flows provides the flexibility to maintain collateral quality and portfolio diversification as rating changes, defaults, and early amortizations reconfigure the collateral pool's risk–return profile. Replacing the bonds in the collateral pool gives rise to reinvestment risk. For instance, if a bond matures and the interest rates have declined since the issuance of the CDO notes, the proceeds have to be invested in a lower yielding asset, causing the excess spread to be lower.[3] In other instances, the asset manager may have to invest the proceeds in short-term instruments until suitable investment opportunities are identified. During this period, the CDO will be exposed to negative carry due to investments in a low-yielding asset. Negative carry usually affects the return on the CDO's equity tranche.

## Prepayment Risk

Prepayment risk arises from early amortization triggers resulting from collateral coverage tests not being met. This risk is enhanced in transactions that have tighter collateral coverage ratios. Prepayment risk is mostly borne by the senior note holders in a CDO transaction because the payment waterfall in arbitrage CDOs is mostly sequential. However, when a collateral coverage test is not passed, it will not automatically result in a prepayment. This is because senior notes are repaid from principal payments. If there is no principal payment during a period, prepayment to senior debt holders will be deferred until principal payments on the collateral assets are due.

## Asset Manager Risk

The performance of the various tranches of an arbitrage CDO are strongly influenced by the trading practices and expertise of the asset manager. Specifically, the asset manager's decisions regarding choice of portfolio composition and timing of sale and purchase of assets have an important influence on the CDO's performance. Moreover, the asset manager's decision regarding how to balance the interests of equity stake holders and debt holders in the CDO may also be crucial to the CDO performance. For instance, part of the excess spread could be paid to equity holders early in the life of the CDO provided no collateral quality and coverage tests are violated. This leakage of collateral value, however, may not be in the interests of the debt holders. In other cases, the asset manager may purchase assets trading at a discount to par in order to boost the return to equity stakeholders because it increases the par value of the collateral assets. Such an investment, from the debt holders' perspective, will be seen as a credit deterioration of the collateral pool because they do not participate in the equity's upside potential.

## RATING A CDO TRANSACTION

The ratings assigned to the different tranches of a CDO transaction are linked to the ability of the structure to make timely payments of interest and principal on the outstanding liabilities. This requires modeling the risks associated with future cash flows by taking into account the subordination structure, default rates, recovery amounts, and default correlation between the issuers in the collateral pool of the CDO. If one introduces an additional level of complexity where the composition of the collateral assets change over time, modeling the cash flow risks over the life of a CDO transaction becomes almost intractable. This is particularly true for market value CDOs, which tend to be actively traded. Even in the case of cash flow CDOs, asset managers are given limited freedom to trade the collateral assets. This may be driven by the motivation to reduce further losses on "credit-impaired" assets or to take profit from "credit-improved" assets. Such trades result in a change in the cash flow characteristics of the underlying collateral pool, and, as a consequence, the cash flow risk profile of the new collateral pool can be quite different.

Different trading practices followed by asset managers can also introduce additional risks to a CDO transaction. For instance, some asset managers may pursue "par building" trades to enhance the return for equity tranche holders.[4] This refers to the practice of purchasing deeply discounted bonds and selling par or premium bonds because the collateral coverage tests for cash flow CDOs are based on the par value of the bond rather than market values. Another related asset manager risk arises from how the asset manager employs the excess spread present in the collateral portfolio. If the excess spread is employed to buy additional collateral, this can enhance the credit protection available to senior note holders.

The discussion suggests that rating any tranche of a CDO transaction is a rather complex process. It is complex because the asset pool changes during the life of the transaction resulting from a number of factors: prepayments, collateral triggers, reinvestment of cash flows and excess spread, and trading actions resulting from qualitative decisions taken by asset managers. Modeling the risks associated with the cash flows of a collateral pool that changes over time is usually intractable. Therefore, modeling the cash flow risks of the CDO structure can only be done with respect to the current composition of the collateral pool.

The general approach taken by rating agencies for assigning a credit rating to a particular CDO tranche is a function of the expected loss associated with the tranche after taking into account the cash flow priorities. Many alternative methods can be used for estimating the expected loss, ranging from Monte Carlo simulation techniques to simple credit-event-driven scenario analysis.[5] The technique used to compute the expected loss of a given tranche differs among the different rating agencies. In this section, I briefly describe the different approaches used by rating agencies to rate a CDO tranche.

## Moody's Method

Moody's rating methodology for cash flow CDOs compares the credit risk inherent in the collateral portfolio with the credit protection offered by the structure to different tranches. The CDO's credit protection is quantified in terms of the maximum collateral loss the structure is able to withstand without affecting the cash flows of the rated notes. In determining an appropriate rating for the various CDO tranches, Moody's evaluates the collateral portfolio's credit risk and the credit protections present in the CDO structure. Because the rating of the CDO tranche is based on the expected loss concept, the first step in the ratings process is to model the credit risk of the collateral portfolio. Rather than modeling correlated credit events, Moody's approach transforms the actual pool of collateral assets into a pool of uncorrelated assets through a concept known as the diversity score. Stated simply, the diversity score represents the equivalent number of uncorrelated assets in a comparison portfolio that exhibits a similar degree of default risk as the original portfolio with correlated assets. Moody's make the further assumption that the probability of default of each obligor in the comparison portfolio is identical using a weighted average rating factor. The estimate of the expected loss of the collateral portfolio is then derived based on the assumption that the loss distribution of a portfolio of uncorrelated assets follows a binomial distribution. I briefly describe here Moody's methodology, referred to as a binominal expansion technique (BET), for determining the credit rating of a cash flow CDO tranche.

**Binomial Expansion Technique**   As mentioned earlier, Moody's approach consists in transforming a collateral pool of correlated assets into a pool of uncorrelated assets through the diversity score concept. The diversity score of a pool of correlated assets is computed by examining the degree of diversification to various industries present in the asset pool. Moody's define a list of 33 industry categories, and the default risk between two obligors belonging to different industry groups is assumed to be uncorrelated. The diversity score for a two-obligor portfolio where both obligors belong to the same industry is defined to be equal to 1.5. Exhibit 11.5 shows how Moody's assigns the diversity score as an increasing number of assets in the collateral portfolio belong to the same industry group.

The collateral portfolio's diversity score is computed by summing the diversity scores of all industries represented in the portfolio. For purposes

**EXHIBIT 11.5**   Moody's Diversity Score

| Number of Firms in Same Industry | Diversity Score |
| --- | --- |
| 1 | 1.00 |
| 2 | 1.50 |
| 3 | 2.00 |
| 4 | 2.33 |
| 5 | 2.67 |
| 6 | 3.00 |
| 7 | 3.25 |
| 8 | 3.50 |
| 9 | 3.75 |
| 10 | 4.00 |

*Source:* Adapted from Table 4 in Alan Backman and Gerard O'Connor, "Rating Cash Flow Transactions Backed by Corporate Debt 1995 Update," *Moody's Investors Service,* April 1995, p. 11. © Moody's Investors Service, Inc., and/or its affiliates. Reprinted with permission. All rights reserved.

of illustration, if the collateral portfolio comprises 30 bonds belonging to 30 different industries, the diversity score is 30. On the other hand, if there are only 10 industries represented in the portfolio with groups of three bonds belonging to a particular industry category, then the diversity score of this portfolio is only 20. Notice that a higher diversity score corresponds to a greater diversification in the collateral portfolio. The foregoing diversity score calculation makes the assumption that the par amounts for the bonds in the portfolio are equal. Moody's adjusts the diversity score if the par amounts of the bonds in the collateral portfolio are not equal.

Apart from computing the diversity score for the portfolio, the default probabilities of the individual assets in the portfolio have to be specified in order to estimate the expected loss of the comparison portfolio. Again, Moody's makes the simplifying assumption that the default probabilities of every asset in the comparison portfolio are equal to some average probability of default. The average probability of default is inferred by first computing a weighted average rating factor (WARF) for the collateral portfolio. This requires transforming the letter rating of the bond obligor into an equivalent numeric rating factor. The numeric rating factors used by Moody's are given in Exhibit 11.6. If $A_i$ denotes the par amount of the $i$th bond in the collateral portfolio and $RF_i$ its corresponding rating factor, then

**EXHIBIT 11.6**   Moodys's Rating Factors

| Credit Rating | Rating Factor |
| --- | --- |
| Aaa | 1 |
| Aa1 | 10 |
| Aa2 | 20 |
| Aa3 | 40 |
| A1 | 70 |
| A2 | 120 |
| A3 | 180 |
| Baa1 | 260 |
| Baa2 | 360 |
| Baa3 | 610 |
| Ba1 | 940 |
| Ba2 | 1,350 |
| Ba3 | 1,780 |
| B1 | 2,220 |
| B2 | 2,720 |
| B3 | 3,490 |
| Caa | 6,500 |
| Ca–C | 10,000 |

*Source:* Adapted from Table 8 in Alan Backman and Gerard O'Connor, "Rating Cash Flow Transactions Backed by Corporate Debt 1995 Update," *Moody's Investors Service,* April 1995, p. 18. © Moody's Investors Service, Inc., and/or its affiliates. Reprinted with permission. All rights reserved.

the WARF of an $n$-bond collateral portfolio is given by

$$\text{WARF} = \frac{\sum_{i=1}^{n} A_i \times \text{RF}_i}{\sum_{i=1}^{n} A_i} \tag{11.1}$$

Given the WARF for the collateral portfolio, one can assign an average probability of default $p$ over the life of the CDO that reflects the historical cumulative probability of default for the rating. For instance, if the WARF for the collateral portfolio is equal to 280, then $p$ can be set equal to the cumulative probability of default of a Baa2-rated issuer over the life of the CDO.

Given a diversity score $D$ and a cumulative probability of default $p$ for the comparison portfolio, the probability of $k$ defaults during the life of the

CDO is given by the following binomial distribution:

$$P_k = \frac{D!}{(D-k)!} p^k (1-p)^{D-k} \qquad (11.2)$$

To compute the expected loss of a particular CDO tranche, we need to compute the tranche loss $L_k$ when $k$ defaults occur in the comparison portfolio. Computing $L_k$ for any tranche requires taking into account the waterfall structure, the credit protections available in the CDO structure, and the assumed recovery rates for the assets in the collateral portfolio. Given $P_k$ and $L_k$, the expected loss for the tranche can be computed as follows:

$$\text{expected loss} = \sum_{k=1}^{D} P_k L_k \qquad (11.3)$$

Once the expected loss for a given CDO tranche is computed, the implied cumulative default probability of the tranche can be computed, given a certain recovery rate assumption, as follows:

cumulative default probability = expected loss/(1 − recovery rate)   (11.4)

Given an estimate of the cumulative probability of default, the implied credit rating of the CDO tranche can be estimated using Moody's idealized cumulative probability of defaults estimated for different ratings as a function of the maturity of the security.[6] In practice, the cumulative default probabilities are multiplied by a stress factor before the actual mapping to a credit rating is done.

In assigning a credit rating to a specific CDO tranche, Moody's does not rely exclusively on a quantitative valuation framework. Instead, the quantitative factors are evaluated in conjunction with qualitative factors such as asset manager risk and the legal and structural risks inherent in the CDO transaction before rating a CDO tranche.

**Rating Market Value CDOs**   In a market value CDO, the asset manager has much more freedom in trading the collateral assets. To take this into consideration, the collateral coverage tests are performed using the market value of the collateral portfolio rather than the par value as in the case of cash flow CDOs. The market value of the collateral portfolio is influenced by a variety of factors, including changes in credit rating of the collateral assets, changes in interest rates, changes in investor preferences that result in changes to credit spreads, and, finally, the actual defaults that can occur to the collateral assets. Because an important additional source of risk in a market value CDO is the price volatility of the collateral portfolio if market values are used for collateral coverage tests, Moody's takes into account the price volatility in the rating process through a set of advance rates.

Advance rates can be described as the adjustments that need to be made to the value of each asset so as to provide a cushion against market risk. Specifically, the overcollateralization test described earlier is carried out on the market value of the collateral assets discounted by an appropriate advance rate. Thus, advance rates can be seen as representing "haircuts" that provide credit enhancement for the rated CDO note. Advance rates vary by asset type: Assets with greater price volatility require lower advance rates. The degree of diversification present in the collateral portfolio also affects advance rates; a portfolio with greater diversification has higher advance rates.

Moody's approach to choosing the advance rates is based primarily on historical simulations. However, in cases where historical data are limited, the volatility of asset returns and correlation between assets are usually adjusted upward. Once an appropriate advance rate is calculated and the collateral asset values are properly discounted to account for the collateral portfolio's volatility, the method used for inferring the credit rating of the CDO tranche is very similar to the case of the cash flow CDO.

## Standard & Poor's Method

The approach taken by Standard & Poor's to rate the different CDO tranches gives greater emphasis to modeling the correlation between asset returns of various obligors in the collateral portfolio. In this respect, the rating approach of Standard & Poor's is fundamentally different from Moody's approach. Standard & Poor's rating process involves three main steps. First, the default rate distribution of the collateral portfolio over the life of the CDO is generated. Second, a set of scenario default rates (SDRs) for different tranches based on the default rate distribution of the collateral portfolio is derived. Finally, the cash flow analysis of the CDO transaction is carried out in conjunction with the calculated SDRs to determine the appropriate ratings for the various tranches. I briefly describe this three-step process in rating a CDO tranche.

**Default Rate Distribution**    Considering that the CDO rating is ultimately linked to the probability of joint defaults of the collateral portfolio, an estimate of the default rate distribution is an important input variable. To generate the default rate distribution of the collateral portfolio, Standard & Poor's uses a proprietary model called the CDO Evaluator.[7] This proprietary model uses the Monte Carlo simulation technique to generate the probability distribution of default rates as a percentage of the total principal balance for the collateral portfolio. The default rate simulation takes into consideration the credit rating, the size and the maturity of each asset, and the asset return correlation between the assets in the collateral portfolio. Standard & Poor's makes the following assumptions for simulating the default rate distribution of the collateral portfolio:

- The asset return correlation between corporate obligors is taken to be .3 if the obligors belong to the same industry sector. The asset return correlation between corporate obligors that do not belong to the same industry sector is considered to be zero (there are 39 industry sectors in Standard & Poor's industry classification).
- The default rates of the assets are differentiated by asset type, maturity, and credit rating of the obligor. For example, the asset default rate for a triple-A-rated corporate bond maturing in 4 years is set to be 0.19 percent, whereas for a triple-B-rated corporate bond with the same maturity this is set to be 21.45 percent. The choice of these default rates is based on Standard & Poor's default study of corporate obligors.

**Scenario Default Rates**   Once the default rate distribution of the collateral portfolio over the life of the CDO transaction has been simulated, Standard & Poor's computes an indicative tranche size for a given target credit rating. This is done by deriving the scenario default rate that is applicable to the target credit rating of the tranche. The SDR represents the default rate that the CDO tranche with a given credit rating should be able to withstand under various cash flow scenarios modeled by Standard & Poor's rating criteria. The determination of the SDR is done through a two-step process. In the first step, a trial SDR is derived from the default rate distribution. This is done by first identifying the default rate for a corporate bond having the same tranche credit rating and weighted average maturity of the collateral portfolio. Subsequently, the portfolio default rate that will not be exceeded by more than this identified default rate for the corporate bond is chosen to be the trial SDR. This process is best explained using Exhibit 11.7, which shows the typical shape of the simulated portfolio default rates for a transaction having weighted average maturity of 10 years.

From Exhibit 11.7, one can infer that there is a 1 percent chance that the default rate on the collateral portfolio will exceed 30 percent during the life of the CDO transaction. Because the default rate of 1 percent over a 10-year period is the historical cumulative probability of default of a triple-A-rated corporate bond, the trial SDR is equal to 30 percent for the CDO tranche with triple-A rating. This simple example provides the motivation for introducing the SDRs for various tranches: It makes it possible to determine the respective tranche sizes and their corresponding credit ratings. In this example, an SDR of 30 percent corresponds to an initial estimate of

**EXHIBIT 11.7**   Probability Distribution of Portfolio Default Rates

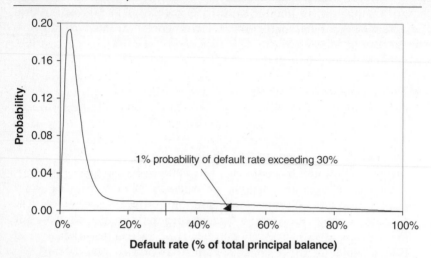

the triple-A tranche size to be 70 percent of the par value of the collateral assets.

The initial estimate of the SDR is refined in the second step by multiplying it by an adjustment factor. Standard & Poor's does not provide details of how these adjustment factors are computed. For a triple-A-rated tranche, the adjustment factor is 1.20, and this leads to the final SDR of 36 percent.[8] Based on this SDR, the indicative tranche size for a triple-A rating should not exceed 64 percent (100 percent minus 36 percent) for this collateral portfolio.

**Cash Flow Analysis**   Once the SDR for a target tranche credit rating has been derived, a cash flow analysis is carried out taking into account all the structural elements of the transaction. The purpose of this exercise is to verify that each CDO tranche can continue to pay principal and interest notwithstanding defaults up to the SDR on the collateral portfolio. During the cash flow analysis, recoveries on the defaulted debt and timing of defaults are taken into account. The final size of the CDO tranches are selected through an iterative procedure where the tranche size is increased as long as its losses are lower than the SDR for the tranche.

## Method of Fitch Ratings

The rating methodology of Fitch for cash flow CDOs shares many similarities with Moody's approach. For instance, the CDO tranche's expected loss is used to derive the credit rating for the tranche, a practice also followed by Moody's. However, an important difference between Moody's approach and the Fitch approach is that Fitch does not use the diversity score concept and the binomial expansion technique to derive the cumulative probability of default. Instead, Fitch simulates the cash flows specific to the transaction and takes into account the timing of defaults, interest rate risks, and assumptions on recovery rates and default probabilities. These simulations are also used to determine the appropriate level of credit enhancements required to support the CDO tranche rating.

In rating different tranches of the CDO, Fitch's method focuses on the following issues:

■ When evaluating asset managers, Fitch looks for strong credit under-writing skills and demonstrated ability to manage portfolios through credit cycles. Superior portfolio management skills are evaluated by examining the stability of risk-adjusted ratios generated over time on managed portfolios against an index by the asset manager. Evaluation of asset manager skills during the rating process reflects the opinion of Fitch that asset manager skills play an important role in the overall performance of the CDO transaction.

■ Collateral quality tests are based on the weighted average rating factor for the collateral portfolio using Fitch rating factors, which are different from Moody's rating factors.[9] In recognition of the fact that weighted average ratings can change over time resulting from credit migration, Fitch permits asset managers to freely trade the collateral even for cash flow CDOs. However, Fitch requires that the weighted average rating and weighted average coupon values specified in the CDO guideline documentation are not violated when collateral is traded.

■ Concerning collateral diversification, Fitch takes the view that enforcing explicit requirements on industry diversification may be counterproductive. This is because such a requirement may force asset managers to take exposures to certain industry sectors that they do not feel comfortable with. Moreover, the strong positive asset return correlation between obligors belonging to different industry sectors limits the potential diversification benefits. As a result of these observations, Fitch requires only a minimum of 10 industry exposures. Among these 10 industry exposures, exposures to 3 industry sectors are allowed to exceed the 10 percent exposure limit provided the total exposure to the 3 industries does not exceed 35 percent.

■ Structural protections are enforced through overcollateralization and interest coverage tests. For nondefaulted assets, these tests are based on the par value of the assets. Defaulted assets, on the other hand, are valued at the lower of the recovery assumption for the asset class and the market value of the asset. Interest coverage tests are performed as frequently as coupon payments are made and whenever the collateral assets are traded.

## TRADABLE CORPORATE BOND BASKETS

A major concern of many investors in corporate bonds is the lack of liquidity in the corporate bond market compared to the government bond market. Institutional fixed-income investors, in particular, would like to have the option to execute large buy or sell orders for corporate bonds without incurring significant transaction costs. Unfortunately, the average issue size for many corporate bonds is in the range $300 to $500 million and hence deal sizes for many corporate bonds are typically in the region of $10 million. As a consequence, institutional investors wishing to take on or shed sizable diversified corporate credit exposures are exposed to significant liquidity risk. To address this concern, major investment banks have issued securities that are backed by a portfolio of corporate bonds that can be traded using one deal execution. Examples of such tradable corporate bond baskets include Morgan Stanley's Tradable Custodial Receipts (Tracers) and Lehman Brothers Targeted Return Index Securities (Trains).[10] Tracers and Trains are designed to balance the liquidity concerns with the need to represent the broad investment-grade bond market. The average lot sizes for these products are around $100 million, which is quite attractive from the perspective of large institutional investors. An important difference between tradable bond baskets and CDOs backed by a portfolio of corporate bonds is that tradable bond baskets are not tranched.

Other examples of tradable corporate bond baskets include the iShares GS $ InvesTop exchange-traded fund (ETF) launched by Barclays Global Investors, which is indexed to a portfolio consisting of 100 investment-grade corporate bonds denominated in U.S. dollars. Because it is exchange traded, it allows investors to take short positions and execute limit orders. Furthermore, transaction costs are lower compared to taking a similar diversified exposure through mutual funds. As a result of this flexibility, the major investors in this fund include hedge funds and retail investors. However, the investment guidelines of many institutional investors do not permit them to buy this fund because ETFs trade as a stock. As of April 2003, the outstanding amount of the iShares corporate bond fund was close to $2 billion.

In the following sections, I focus primarily on Tracers issued in the cash market backed by a portfolio of investment-grade corporate bonds. I provide a brief description of the characteristics of Tracers and explain how investors can assess the relative value of this structured product compared to buying a single corporate bond with similar credit rating and market risk characteristics. In connection with this, I discuss a technique for inferring the implied credit rating of Tracers and similar structured credit products.

## Main Features of Tracers

Tracers are custody receipts that represent an ownership interest on a pro rata basis in an equal par-weighted portfolio of investment-grade corporate bonds. Tracers typically contain 30 to 35 investment-grade corporate bonds with an outstanding issue size of $1 billion or more and have a diversified exposure to different industry sectors. Investors holding Tracers have the option of either selling the custody receipts or redeeming for the appropriate pro rata share of the underlying securities on a weekly basis. Depending on investor demand for Tracers, Morgan Stanley has the option of creating additional Tracer receipts on a weekly basis, which is done by depositing additional securities with Bank of New York, the custodian. Tracers have a sinking fund structure and mature when the bond with the longest maturity in the portfolio expires.

Tracers are issued by maturity (5, 10, and 30 years) and they roll-down the yield curve. Tracers are quoted and traded on a spread basis to the U.S. Treasury yield curve, and the transaction costs are in the range of 3 to 5 basis points in yield. Morgan Stanley charges 4 basis points in administrative fee for managing the bond portfolio, which is subtracted from the coupons on the bonds as they are received.[11] The custodian pays the coupon and principal received from the underlying bonds to the investors 1 day after they are received.[12] Only qualified institutional investors can buy Tracers, because they are considered private securities due to the trust structure.

The portfolio composition of Tracers is designed to be static to improve transparency. However, the underlying portfolio composition can change as a result of the following credit events and corporate actions:

- If any bond held in the portfolio is downgraded below investment grade either by Moody's or Fitch, the administrative agent auctions the bond and distributes the proceeds to investors.
- If the bond obligor defaults, the bond is auctioned and the proceeds are distributed to the investors.
- In the event a corporate action arises for one of the bonds held in the portfolio, the administrative agent auctions the bond if there is a lack of unanimity of opinion among the investors.

In each of these circumstances, the investor has the right to opt out of the auction and take physical delivery of the impacted security.

## Portfolio Composition and Risk Characteristics

Because any given Tracers series is primarily a portfolio of corporate bonds, analyzing the risks of this structured credit portfolio can be performed using the methodology presented in the earlier chapters to quantify credit risk. This is particularly important for investors who may wish to analyze the relative value of buying, say, the 10-year Tracer versus buying a comparable-maturity corporate bond that carries a similar risk profile. To address this question, I consider the series 2001-1 Tracer, whose portfolio composition is given in Exhibit 11.8. The series 2001-1 Tracer matures on 15 September 2011 and had an average coupon of 7.252 percent as of 2 April 2003.

**EXHIBIT 11.8** Composition of 2001-1 Series Tracer as of 2 April 2003

| S. No. | Ticker | Issuer Rating | Maturity | Coupon (%) | Nominal (mn $) | Clean Price | Yield (%) | Modified Duration |
|---|---|---|---|---|---|---|---|---|
| 1 | AA | A2 | 01 Jun 11 | 6.500 | 54.50 | 111.52 | 4.778 | 6.290 |
| 2 | AOL | Baa1 | 15 Apr 11 | 6.750 | 54.50 | 106.05 | 5.797 | 6.029 |
| 3 | AWE | Baa2 | 01 Mar 11 | 7.875 | 54.50 | 111.89 | 5.966 | 5.938 |
| 4 | BAC | Aa3 | 15 Jan 11 | 7.400 | 54.50 | 118.28 | 4.580 | 5.996 |
| 5 | BRITEL | Baa1 | 15 Dec 10 | 8.375 | 54.50 | 121.83 | 4.931 | 5.765 |
| 6 | C | Aa2 | 01 Oct 10 | 7.250 | 54.50 | 117.10 | 4.533 | 5.914 |
| 7 | COP | A3 | 25 May 10 | 8.750 | 54.50 | 124.95 | 4.610 | 5.401 |
| 8 | DCX | A3 | 18 Jan 11 | 7.750 | 54.50 | 113.09 | 5.648 | 5.866 |
| 9 | DD | Aa3 | 15 Oct 09 | 6.875 | 54.50 | 117.04 | 3.895 | 5.227 |
| 10 | DT | Baa3 | 15 Jun 10 | 8.000 | 54.50 | 117.70 | 5.037 | 5.502 |
| 11 | F | A3 | 01 Feb 11 | 7.375 | 54.50 | 92.04 | 8.800 | 5.670 |
| 12 | FON | Baa3 | 30 Jan 11 | 7.625 | 54.50 | 104.45 | 6.878 | 5.805 |
| 13 | FRTEL | Baa3 | 01 Mar 11 | 7.750 | 54.50 | 119.61 | 4.747 | 6.062 |
| 14 | GE | Aaa | 19 Jan 10 | 7.375 | 54.50 | 117.03 | 4.442 | 5.392 |
| 15 | GM | A2 | 15 Sep 11 | 6.875 | 54.50 | 97.91 | 7.209 | 6.276 |
| 16 | GS | Aa3 | 15 Jan 11 | 6.875 | 54.50 | 112.88 | 4.866 | 6.040 |
| 17 | HSBC | A2 | 15 May 11 | 6.750 | 54.50 | 110.48 | 5.153 | 6.172 |
| 18 | IADB | Aaa | 15 Jan 10 | 7.375 | 54.50 | 122.60 | 3.590 | 5.438 |
| 19 | JPM | A2 | 01 Feb 11 | 6.750 | 54.50 | 110.88 | 5.049 | 6.085 |
| 20 | K | Baa2 | 01 Apr 11 | 6.600 | 54.50 | 113.34 | 4.588 | 6.308 |
| 21 | MER | Aa3 | 17 Feb 09 | 6.000 | 54.50 | 110.04 | 4.060 | 4.947 |
| 22 | NI | Baa3 | 15 Nov 10 | 7.875 | 54.50 | 114.28 | 5.549 | 5.689 |
| 23 | ONE | A1 | 01 Aug 10 | 7.875 | 54.50 | 120.86 | 4.500 | 5.682 |
| 24 | Q | A1 | 22 Jan 11 | 6.125 | 54.50 | 112.87 | 4.174 | 6.224 |
| 25 | S | Baa1 | 01 Feb 11 | 7.000 | 54.50 | 103.24 | 6.464 | 5.928 |
| 26 | SBC | A1 | 15 Mar 11 | 6.250 | 54.50 | 110.87 | 4.601 | 6.314 |
| 27 | ULVR | A1 | 01 Nov 10 | 7.125 | 54.50 | 117.91 | 4.327 | 5.852 |
| 28 | USB | Aa3 | 01 Aug 11 | 6.375 | 54.50 | 112.64 | 4.534 | 6.496 |
| 29 | VIA | A3 | 15 May 11 | 6.625 | 54.50 | 113.16 | 4.658 | 6.239 |
| 30 | VZ | A2 | 01 Dec 10 | 7.250 | 54.50 | 116.04 | 4.728 | 5.883 |
| 31 | WB | Aa3 | 18 Aug 10 | 7.800 | 54.50 | 121.16 | 4.407 | 5.744 |
| 32 | WMT | Aa2 | 10 Aug 09 | 6.875 | 54.50 | 117.01 | 3.832 | 5.206 |

Because Tracers can be seen simply as a portfolio of corporate bonds, we can try to quantify the risk of holding this corporate bond portfolio over a 1-year horizon using the technique presented in Chapter 6. To simplify matters, I assume the asset return correlation between every obligor pair to be 30 percent when computing various portfolio credit risk quantities of interest under the migration mode. In performing the simulations, the joint distribution of asset returns was assumed to be multinormal with mean recovery rate of 47 percent across all bonds. To examine the impact on portfolio credit risk due to an increase in asset return correlation between obligors, a second simulation run was performed with an asset return correlation of 45 percent across obligor pairs. The weighted average rating factor for this portfolio based on current market values was also computed using Moody's rating factors given in Exhibit 11.6. The aggregate portfolio risk characteristics of the series 2001-1 Tracer are shown in Exhibit 11.9.

Moody's rated the series 2001-1 Tracer Baa1 as of April 2003. Given this information, an investor might be confronted with the following question: Is the investment risk in Tracers the same as the risk of holding a Baa1-rated corporate bond? I address this important question in the next section.

## Implied Credit Rating

Driven by the desire to reduce downside risk, investors hold a portfolio rather than a single security. Holding a diversified portfolio protects investors from large losses that may otherwise occur when only a single financial security is held. Given this observation, it is more likely that an investor would prefer to buy a Tracer with a Baa1 rating than a Baa1-rated bond having a similar duration risk and yield. This brings up the following

**EXHIBIT 11.9** Risk Characteristics of a Tracer Portfolio

| Description | Asset Return Correlation 30 Percent | Asset Return Correlation 45 Percent |
|---|---|---|
| Average yield (%) | 4.97 | 4.97 |
| Modified duration | 5.85 | 5.85 |
| Moody's WARF | 181 | 181 |
| Expected loss (bp) | 32.1 | 32.1 |
| Unexpected loss (bp) | 90.3 | 113.0 |
| CrVaR at 90 percent confidence (bp) | 111.6 | 113.3 |
| ESR at 90 percent confidence (bp) | 229.4 | 272.1 |

question: How do rating agencies rate a portfolio of corporate bonds? Some insight into how rating agencies assess the risk of a portfolio of corporate bonds can be obtained on the basis of the rating agencies methodology for CDOs presented earlier. Both Moody's and Fitch, for instance, use the expected loss of the portfolio as an input parameter to determine an appropriate credit rating.

This approach can be extended to Tracers; the implied credit rating for the underlying portfolio of bonds in a Tracer can be derived using the following simple rule:

- First, compute the expected loss of the corporate bond portfolio.
- In the next step, compute the set of expected losses for a bond having the same duration and yield as the portfolio, but with different credit ratings.
- Finally, identify the credit rating under which the expected loss for the bond is approximately equal to the corporate bond portfolio's expected loss.

At first glance, this procedure may appear rather naive for computing a corporate bond portfolio's credit rating. Even for a casual observer it will be evident that no risk measure is being used to derive the implied credit rating of the portfolio. To investigate whether this simple procedure will lead to a Baa1 rating for the series 2001-1 Tracer as assigned by Moody's, consider a bond with the following characteristics as of trade date 2 April 2003: a 7.252 percent annual coupon, maturing on 20 September 2010, and trading at a clean price of $114.10. Such a bond will have an identical yield, modified duration, and convexity as the bond portfolio that constitutes the series 2001-1 Tracer. The expected and unexpected losses of this bond under the migration mode assuming different credit ratings for the bond are given in Exhibit 11.10. In deriving the expected and unexpected loss, a recovery rate of 47 percent was assumed.

Comparing Exhibits 11.9 and 11.10, one see infer that on the basis of the expected loss information, the series 2001-1 Tracer will be assigned a Baa1 rating. As mentioned earlier, this also happens to be the rating assigned by Moody's to this structured portfolio. Note that we were able to

**EXHIBIT 11.10**  Credit Risk Measures for a Bond with Same Duration as a Tracer

| Description | A1 Rated | A2 Rated | A3 Rated | Baa1 Rated |
|---|---|---|---|---|
| Expected loss (bp) | 22.5 | 24.4 | 38.7 | 32.9 |
| Unexpected loss (bp) | 196.4 | 224.3 | 267.0 | 301.9 |
| ESR at 90 percent confidence (bp) | 272.6 | 308.0 | 463.7 | 508.1 |

arrive at Moody's credit rating for this portfolio without having to model the obligor asset return correlations. A similar conclusion holds for the implied credit rating of the portfolio if the WARF score is examined. For example, WARF for the portfolio is 181, and this is higher than the threshold value of 180 for an A3-rated bond. This also leads to the conclusion that the bond portfolio has a Baa1 rating.

Unfortunately, both WARF as well as the implied credit rating of the portfolio established on the basis of expected loss information lead to improper interpretation of the actual risk associated with the underlying portfolio. The credit risk facing an investor holding a single bond rated Baa1 is fundamentally different from the credit risk faced by an investor holding a Baa1-rated series 2001-1 Tracer even if they both have identical market risks. This is evident from examining the unexpected loss of the replicating bond shown in Exhibit 11.10 under different credit ratings. In fact, the unexpected loss of the Tracer assuming 45 percent asset return correlation between obligor pairs is only half of that of an A2-rated bond.

Having established that the true risks are not reflected in the credit rating assigned by rating agencies in the portfolio context, one can explore alternative methods of arriving at an implied credit rating for a portfolio that better reflect the risks. In arriving at this implied credit rating, assume that the investor is interested in comparing the potential downside risks between the series 2001-1 Tracer and a bond having the same market risk profile. One measure that can be used to quantify this downside risk is the expected shortfall risk introduced in Chapter 7.[13] The ESRs at 90 percent level of confidence for the replicating bond are shown in Exhibit 11.10 assuming different credit ratings for the bond. Under the assumption that the bond has an A1 rating, the ESR at 90 percent level of confidence is equal to 272.6 basis points. This value is close to ESR at 90 percent confidence level for the series 2001-1 Tracer when the asset return correlation between obligors is assumed to be 45 percent.

Clearly, an investor worried about the downside risk will consider buying the series 2001-1 Tracer as being equivalent to buying a bond rated A1 with the same market risk characteristics. Because the numerical results suggest that the 1-year expected loss of an A1-rated bond is 10 basis points lower than that for the Tracer, the investor would break even if the yield of the series 2001-1 Tracer is 10 basis points more than an A1-rated bond of comparable maturity. Finally, it is important to note that the use of a downside risk measure as opposed to expected loss to infer the credit rating of a portfolio leads to a three-notch rating difference for the example considered here. Such a large difference in the implied credit rating of a structured credit product suggests that further research is needed to resolve these differences and to find the best approach to be used for rating structured credit products.

## QUESTIONS

1. What are the similarities and differences between CDOs and asset-backed securities?
2. What factors make a CDO attractive from an investor's perspective?
3. What is subordination and how does it provide credit enhancement to senior CDO tranches?
4. Explain what "par-building" trades mean and how this practice can lead to worsening of collateral quality.
5. What is diversity score and what purpose does it serve?
6. What are the advantages and disadvantages of using market value tests for cash flow CDOs?
7. You are asked to provide a list of relative merits between buying an A1-rated cash flow CBO and an A1-rated Tracer, both maturing in 3 years, to your management. What are the important points you will list?

# Solutions to End-of-Chapter Questions

## CHAPTER 2

1. This experiment leads to a random variable that has a binomial distribution. The random variable $X$ of a binomial distribution counts the number of successes in $n$ trials. If $p$ is the probability of an event occurring in a given trial, the probability of this event occurring $r$ times in $n$ trials is given by

$$P(X = r) = \frac{n!}{r!(n-r)!} \times p^r (1-p)^{n-r}$$

The probability that the face 6 will show up at least two times is 1 minus the probability that the face 6 shows up once in 10 trials. These are given, respectively, by

$$P(X \geq 2) = 1 - P(X = 1) = 1 - \tfrac{101}{91} \times \left(\tfrac{1}{6}\right)^1 \times \left(\tfrac{5}{6}\right)^9 = 0.6770$$

and

$$P(X = 2) = \frac{10!}{2! \times 8!} \times \left(\tfrac{1}{6}\right)^2 \times \left(\tfrac{5}{6}\right)^8 = 0.2907$$

2. The mean and variance of the random variable are given, respectively, by

$$\mu = \sum_{i=1}^{n} x_i\, p(x_i) = \sum_{i=1}^{6} i \times \tfrac{1}{6} = 3.5$$

and

$$\sigma^2 = \sum_{i=1}^{6} (x_i - \mu)^2\, p(x_i) = \sum_{i=1}^{6} (i - 3.5)^2 \times \tfrac{1}{6} = 2.917$$

3. The 10th percentile of the distribution corresponds to the 0.1 quantile. If $x_p$ is the 0.1 quantile of a normal distribution, $x_p$ solves the following equation:

$$\frac{1}{\sqrt{2\pi}\sigma} \int_{-\infty}^{x_p} \exp\left(-\frac{(x-\mu)^2}{2\sigma^2}\right) dx = 0.1$$

For $\mu = 0.5$ and $\sigma = 1.2$, this gives $x_p = -1.0378$

4. For a beta distribution, the mean and variance are given, respectively, by

$$\mu = \frac{\alpha}{\alpha + \beta} \quad \text{and} \quad \sigma^2 = \frac{\alpha\beta}{(\alpha + \beta)^2(\alpha + \beta + 1)}$$

For $\alpha = 1.4$ and $\beta = 1.58$, we have $\mu = 0.47$ and $\sigma = 0.25$.

If $f(x)$ denotes the density function of a beta distribution, the probability that the recovery rate lies between 20 and 80 percent of par value during simulations is given by

$$\int_{0.2}^{0.8} f(x)dx = \int_{-\infty}^{0.8} f(x)dx - \int_{-\infty}^{0.2} f(x)dx = 0.7095$$

5. The mean and volatility of the recovery rate process are given, respectively, by

$$\mu = \frac{a+b}{2} = \frac{0.2 + 0.8}{2} = 0.5$$

and

$$\sigma = \frac{b-a}{\sqrt{12}} = \frac{0.8 - 0.2}{\sqrt{12}} = 0.173$$

6. Take, for example, $3 \times 3$ matrices and show this is true. The general case follows easily. Let the matrices $A$ and $B$ be given by

$$A = \begin{bmatrix} a_{11} & a_{12} & a_{13} \\ a_{21} & a_{22} & a_{23} \\ a_{31} & a_{32} & a_{33} \end{bmatrix} \quad \text{and} \quad B = \begin{bmatrix} b_{11} & b_{12} & b_{13} \\ b_{21} & b_{22} & b_{23} \\ b_{31} & b_{32} & b_{33} \end{bmatrix}$$

If $C$ denotes the product $A \times B$, then the first row of this matrix is given by

$$c_{11} = a_{11}b_{11} + a_{12}b_{21} + a_{13}b_{31}$$

$$c_{12} = a_{11}b_{12} + a_{12}b_{22} + a_{13}b_{32}$$

$$c_{13} = a_{11}b_{13} + a_{12}b_{23} + a_{13}b_{33}$$

For any Markov matrix, the sum of the row elements must add to one. To see if this is true, check the following identity:

$$c_{11} + c_{12} + c_{13} = a_{11}(b_{11} + b_{12} + b_{13}) + a_{12}(b_{21} + b_{22} + b_{23})$$
$$+ a_{13}(b_{31} + b_{32} + b_{33}) = a_{11} + a_{12} + a_{13} = 1$$

This follows from the fact that $A$ and $B$ are Markov matrices. Similarly, one can show that the other rows of the matrix $C$ also add up to one, and hence, the result.

7. Applying a result from linear algebra, one can represent any matrix $A$ in terms of its eigenvector decomposition given by

$$A = S\Lambda S^{-1}$$

where $S$ is the matrix formed using eigenvectors of $A$ and $\Lambda$ is a diagonal matrix containing eigenvalues of $A$. Using this relation, one has

$$A^2 = S\Lambda S^{-1}S\Lambda S^{-1} = S\Lambda^2 S^{-1}$$

Note that the eigenvalues of the matrix $A^2$ are the diagonal elements of the matrix $\Lambda^2$. The last exercise showed that if $A$ is Markov, then $A^2$ is also Markov. Denote the Markov matrix $A^2 = P$ and let the eigenvalues of $P$ be given by the diagonal matrix $\Lambda_P = \Lambda^2$. It follows then that

$$P^{1/2} = S\Lambda S^{-1} = S\Lambda_P^{1/2}S^{-1} = A$$

Because $A$ is by construction a Markov matrix, so is $P^{1/2}$, using the eigenvalue decomposition. In the general case, it follows that for any integer value $n$, the decomposition

$$P^{1/n} = S\Lambda_P^{1/n}S^{-1}$$

is a Markov matrix.

8.
$$P^{1/12} = \begin{bmatrix} 0.9555 & 0.0380 & 0.0065 \\ 0.0127 & 0.9681 & 0.0192 \\ 0 & 0 & 1 \end{bmatrix}$$

$$P^{1/2} = \begin{bmatrix} 0.7670 & 0.1879 & 0.0451 \\ 0.0626 & 0.8296 & 0.1078 \\ 0 & 0 & 1 \end{bmatrix}$$

9. The eigenvalues are $\lambda_1 = 5.8284$, $\lambda_2 = 2.0$, and $\lambda_3 = 0.1716$. The eigenvectors are

$$\vec{x}_1 = \begin{bmatrix} -0.3827 \\ -0.9239 \\ 0 \end{bmatrix}, \quad \vec{x}_2 = \begin{bmatrix} 0 \\ 0 \\ 1 \end{bmatrix}, \quad \vec{x}_3 = \begin{bmatrix} -0.9239 \\ -0.3827 \\ 0 \end{bmatrix}$$

The Cholesky decomposition is $A = LL^T$, where

$$L = \begin{bmatrix} 1 & 0 & 0 \\ -2 & 1 & 0 \\ 0 & 0 & 1.4142 \end{bmatrix}$$

10. The first two principal components explain a variance of

$$\frac{\lambda_1 + \lambda_2}{\lambda_1 + \lambda_2 + \lambda_3} = \frac{7.8284}{8} = 97.85 \text{ percent}$$

11. The normalized direction vectors are $\ell_1 = [0.7071 \ 0 \ 0.7071]^T$ and $\ell_2 = [1 \ 0 \ 0]^T$. Thus $\sigma_1^2 = \ell_1^T A \ell_1 = 1.5$, $\sigma_2^2 = \ell_2^T A \ell_2 = 1.0$, $\rho = 0.5773$
    The variance explained by these factors is

$$\frac{\sigma_1^2 + \sigma_2^2(1 - \rho)}{\lambda_1 + \lambda_2 + \lambda_3} = 24.03 \text{ percent}$$

## CHAPTER 3

1. Different forms of bond collateralization used for securitization include the following:
   a. Mortgage bonds backed by real estate or other physical property.

    b. Collateral trust bonds secured by financial assets such as stocks, bonds, and other securities, which are deposited with a trustee.

    c. Equipment trust certificates, which are secured by ownership of specific equipment, usually capital in nature, with the title to this equipment held by a trustee.

    d. Asset-backed securities, which are secured by home-equity loans, credit card receivables, and auto loans.

2. Major investment risks that face corporate bond investors can be classified under the following categories:

    a. Credit risk, which arises from either the bond obligor becoming bankrupt or the obligor being downgraded to lower credit quality.

    b. Market risk, which results from an increase in the general level of interest rates.

    c. Liquidity risk, which arises from the lack of marketability of a bond.

    d. Economic risk, which arises from a general slowdown of the global economy, which in turn leads to lower corporate profits and therefore lower debt-repaying capacity of many corporate borrowers.

3. Corporate bond trading is done through a broker/dealer market. Bonds not sold back to investors and held in inventory for longer time periods incur capital charges. Bond dealers also face the risk of the bond obligor being downgraded, which results in a lower trade price for the bond. Higher bid–ask spreads charged to compensate for these risks force investors to trade corporate bonds infrequently. This is turn reduces turnover in corporates, and, as a consequence, increases the risk of holding bonds in inventory by dealers longer than they would normally wish. The sum total of these effects contributes to higher trading costs for corporate bonds.

4. Trading cost per year is given by $2.5 \times 5 \times 1.25 = 15.625$ basis points.

5. During periods of economic crisis, corporate bonds offer economic enterprises an alternative funding source when banks cut down on lending. This diversity of funding sources provides insurance against a financial problem turning into economywide distress. Furthermore, because funding in the capital markets competes with bank lending, borrowing costs for corporates are lower during normal times. Corporate bonds also provide investors with alternative investment opportunities. Finally, well-developed corporate bond markets bring market discipline and reduce the scope for misdirected credit allocations.

6. Carrying out a historical performance analysis of various asset classes can help identify relationships between them that are otherwise not evident. Experience suggests that historical performance analysis is very useful for predicting future volatility of returns of the asset class and reasonably useful for predicting the correlation between the returns of different asset classes. Furthermore, to evaluate the potential

risks associated with investment decisions, an analysis of historical performance is required.

7. Holding larger than necessary level of foreign currency reserves incurs costs in real resources. Reserve managers are faced with the challenge of reducing these costs by increasing return on reserves. However, given the public scrutiny of the investment returns, losses arising from investment decisions need to be kept to a minimum. This requires investments in high-grade, low-volatility assets, which, however, deliver low returns. The major challenge faced by reserve managers is to meet the objective of generating higher returns without taking much credit or interest rate risk.

8. Given the yield pickup over comparable-maturity U.S. Treasury securities, corporate bonds offer the opportunity to generate higher returns than investments in Treasury securities. Furthermore, investment in corporate bonds lowers the volatility of returns relative to an investment in Treasuries with similar duration. Finally, the correlation of corporate bond returns with Treasury and other high-grade credits being less than one will lead to some diversification benefit. This will have the effect of reducing the volatility of returns on the overall reserves if there is increased exposure to corporates in the reserves portfolio.

9. Under the new accounting rules, the pension fund assets have to be marked to market and the present value of pension liabilities has to be computed by discounting future liabilities by the long-term yield of corporate bonds. During periods of economic recession, these rules will have the effect of increasing the present value of liabilities due to a fall in long-term yields while at the same time producing lower valuations for the assets due to the falling equities market. The impact of these two will be quite serious for those pension funds that have greater exposure to equities, because the coverage ratio (pension assets divided by pension liabilities) will fall. In a defined benefit scheme, this will force corporations to increase pension contributions to keep the coverage ratio above the mandatory minimum level. To minimize this risk, pension sponsors may have a tendency to include a greater proportion of corporate bonds to serve as a better hedging instrument under the new accounting rules.

10. In a defined benefit pension scheme, the pension sponsor has to make additional pension contributions if pension assets do not generate sufficient returns to cover actuarial liabilities. This risk is referred to as surplus risk, which is the risk that the assets will fall short of liabilities. To reduce surplus risk, plan sponsors have to ensure that the sensitivity to modeled risk factors across assets and liabilities are broadly matched. For example, liabilities are higher if the long-term yields on corporate bonds decline. To ensure that pension assets are also higher under this scenario, greater exposure to corporate bonds is required in the pension assets. The amount of surplus risk, in practice, has to be balanced

against the expected return on the pension assets, which has to be in line with the expected growth rate of real earnings. This is required to ensure that the pension contribution rate for the plan sponsor is not too high.

# CHAPTER 4

1. The yield to maturity is 4.674 percent, the modified duration is 3.748, the convexity is 16.85, and the approximate price change is $-\$0.955$.
2. The yield to maturity is 4.412 percent, the modified duration is 5.623, and the convexity is 44.10. The bond manager's view is that the yields will decrease and the yield curve will flatten.
3. The motivation for doing principal component analysis of the yield curve is to understand the correlation structure between yields across different maturities. Because yields across maturities are correlated, principal component analysis helps to reduce the number of independent factors required to explain the yield curve dynamics.
4. Let $\vec{\ell}_s$ denote the normalized shift vector and $\Sigma$ the covariance matrix of yield changes. The second factor $\vec{\ell}_t$ can be determined by solving the following optimization problem: Maximize $\vec{\ell}_t^T \Sigma \vec{\ell}_t$ subject to the constraints $\vec{\ell}_s^T \Sigma \vec{\ell}_t = 0$ and $\vec{\ell}_t^T \vec{\ell}_t = 1$.
5. The tracking error of a portfolio is the annualized standard deviation of the weekly or daily return differences between the portfolio and the benchmark. This definition leads to an ex post measure of tracking error. A monthly tracking error of 25 basis points corresponds to $25\sqrt{12} = 86.6$ basis points annualized tracking error.
6. The market value of the portfolio is $M_p = \$3,646,265$; the market value after the yield curve shift is $M_p^s = \$3,666,849$; and the market value after the yield curve twist is $M_p^t = \$3.650,741$. Then,

$$\text{shift sensitivity} = \frac{M_p^s - M_p}{M_p} = 56.45 \text{ basis points}$$

$$\text{twist sensitivity} = \frac{M_p^t - M_p}{M_p} = 12.27 \text{ basis points}$$

# CHAPTER 5

1. Given $A_0 = \$12$, $F = \$10$, $\mu = 5$ percent, and $\sigma_A = 10$ percent, use the equation

$$D = \frac{\ln(A_0/F) + (\mu - 0.5\sigma_A^2)T}{\sigma_A \sqrt{T}}$$

Substituting the foregoing values gives $D = 2.273$. The 1-year default probability is given by $PD = N(-D)$, or

$$PD = \frac{1}{\sqrt{2\pi}} \int_{-\infty}^{-D} \exp(-0.5x^2)\,dx = 0.0115$$

2. Many of the assumptions made under Merton's approach to determine the default probability of a firm are violated in practice. These include the following: (a) firms seldom issue zero-coupon debt and there are usually multiple liabilities, (b) firms in distress may be able to draw on lines of credit that will result in a change in the liabilities, and (c) asset returns of firms may deviate from a normal distribution. As a result, applying Merton's method in practice to determine the default probability of a firm is usually difficult.

   The KMV approach resolves these difficulties as follows: (a) The default point that triggers bankruptcy is assumed to be the sum of the short-term and one half of the long-term liabilities and (b) the distance to default variable is mapped to a historical default statistics database to estimate the probability of default.

3. The structural approach leads to default probability estimates that are more responsive to current economic environment. The empirical approach, on the other hand, leads to default probability estimates that reflect long-term averages. Although increased responsiveness to changes in economic conditions on the firm's default probability has many advantages, this feature may be undesirable if the estimates are used for the purpose of economic capital allocation. Another potential drawback of the structural approach followed by KMV is that default probability predictions for regulated banks tend to be higher than what historical data would suggest. This is primarily because the historical default database contains mainly corporates and not banks.

4. Recovery rates on defaulted bonds are estimated based on the trading price of the bond in the secondary market approximately 1 month after the default event. The factors that influence recovery rates include the seniority of the bond issue, the industrial sector to which the bond issuer belongs, the state of the economy, and the credit rating of the issuer 1 year prior to default.

5. Rating outlooks are forward-looking assessment of the creditworthiness of issuers over the medium term published by rating agencies. Rating outlooks assess the potential direction of an issuer's rating change over the next 6 months to 2 years. Changes in rating outlooks influence bond prices, and sometimes significant price changes may occur after such changes in outlook are published. Price changes occur because a

change in rating outlook is considered by market participants as a signaling event used by rating agencies before eventually upgrading or downgrading an issuer's credit rating.

6. Here, $P_{\text{dirty}} = \$103.50$, PD = 0.002, RR = 0.47, $\sigma_{\text{RR}} = 0.25$, NE = \$10 million, and LD = 1.035 − 0.47 = 0.565. Thus EL = NE × PD × LD = \$11,300

$$UL = NE \times \sqrt{PD \times \sigma_{\text{RR}}^2 + LD^2 \times PD(1 - PD)} = \$276,075$$

7. Empirical evidence indicates that recovery rates are negatively correlated with default rates. Reduced-form models do not take this relationship into account. Reduced-form models assume that recovery rate and default rate processes are independent.

8. Yields on corporate bonds vary significantly across issuers. These yield differences for a given maturity can be significant even among issuers having identical credit rating and belonging to the same industrial sector. As a result, yield curves that are constructed for a specified credit rating introduce large pricing errors if bonds are priced off these yield curves. Because bonds have to be repriced under rating change scenarios, computing meaningful price changes under rating changes across all bonds would be practically impossible.

   Although pricing bonds off generic yield curves runs into difficulties, generic yield curves for different credit ratings can still be constructed and used in a meaningful way if these yield curves are used primarily to compute yield spreads across different maturities and credit ratings. This gives a richer description of yield spreads, which are differentiated by maturity and credit rating. Moreover, this also reflects the current yield spreads when estimating credit risk under the migration mode rather than the static values used for illustration purposes in this book. Yield spreads derived using such curves could be used in conjunction with the duration and the convexity of the bond to compute the price changes.

9.
$$EL = NE \times \sum_{k=1}^{18} p_{ik} \times \Delta P_{ik}$$

$$= 10{,}000{,}000 \times 0.001892 = \$18{,}920$$

$$UL = NE \times \sqrt{PD \times \sigma_{\text{RR}}^2 + \sum_{k=1}^{18} p_{ik} \times \Delta P_{ik}^2 - \left(\sum_{k=1}^{18} p_{ik} \times \Delta P_{ik}\right)^2}$$

$$= 10{,}000{,}000 \times \sqrt{0.002 \times 0.25^2 + 3.768 \times 10^{-4} - 0.001892^2}$$

$$= \$223{,}208.5$$

## CHAPTER 6

1. Aggregation of portfolio credit risk requires estimating the standard deviation of loss (unexpected loss) of the securities held in the portfolio and the correlation between security losses. Aggregation of market risk requires estimating the standard deviation of returns of the securities held in the portfolio and the correlation between security returns. In this respect, aggregation of credit risk and market risk are quite similar in principle. The major difference, however, is that the distribution of security losses resulting from credit events is highly skewed, whereas the distribution of security returns driven by market-related events is approximately normal. The knowledge of the standard deviation of a normally distributed random variable is sufficient to derive tail risk statistics. Deriving tail risk measures for credit risk requires performing a Monte Carlo simulation. The other difference between market and credit risk pertains to the ease with which data required to compute these measures can be obtained. For market risk, one only needs daily or weekly time series of security returns, which is observed in the market. Variables that are required to aggregate credit risk are usually not observed and therefore require making assumptions.

2. As the term suggests, asset return correlation between two obligors is the correlation between asset returns of the obligors. Default correlation is the correlation between the default indicators for the two obligors, typically over a 1-year time horizon. Loss correlation is the correlation between the credit losses of the two obligors, where the credit losses are usually measured over a 1-year time horizon. Default correlation is typically an order of magnitude less than asset correlation. Loss correlation magnitude depends on whether the credit risk is to be aggregated under the default mode or the migration mode. Under the migration mode, the credit loss resulting from rating changes is also included and hence will be higher than under the default mode.

3. The assessment of the risk of financial securities is based on models that capture the price dynamics of these securities. Model risk refers to the risk that such models may not describe the price dynamics of the financial securities accurately. This could arise, for instance, when simplifying assumptions are made to keep the model complexity manageable. The model risk associated with quantification of credit risk is quite high. This is mainly due to the many simplifying assumptions that have to be made to keep the model tractable. Furthermore, many variables that are used for modeling credit risk are not directly observable. This tends to increase model risk further by introducing an additional layer of uncertainty.

4. Under the assumption that recovery rates are positively correlated, the expected value of the joint losses is higher. This results in higher loss correlation between the two obligors. One can verify this from the following relation for the joint expected value of two random variables:

$$E(XY) = E(X)E(Y) + \rho_{XY}\sigma_X\sigma_Y$$

Clearly, $E(XY)$ is higher if the random variables are positively correlated.

5. The joint default probability in this case is $5.7033 \times 10^{-6}$. The expected loss of the portfolio is $1,009.6. The unexpected loss using the default correlation is $26,135.5. The unexpected loss using the loss correlation is $6,123.8.

6. The leverage ratio of a firm is defined as the ratio between the face value of outstanding debt and the asset value of the firm. If $w_i$ denotes the leverage ratio of the $i$th firm, the asset return of the $i$th firm can be approximated as follows:

$$r_A^i = (1 - w_i) \times r_S^i + w_i \times r_F^i$$

Here, $r_S^i$ is the equity return of the firm and $r_F^i$ is the return on a risk-free bond issued by the firm. This equation allows one to approximate the asset return covariance between two firms $i$ and $k$ using the equity return covariance between these firms as follows:

$$\text{cov}(r_A^i, r_A^k) = (1 - w_i) \times (1 - w_k) \times \text{cov}(r_S^i, r_S^k) + w_i \times w_k \times \text{cov}(r_F^i, r_F^k)$$

If the leverage ratio is high, the last term in the above equation will dominate. Because the correlation between two risk-free bonds will be much higher than the equity return correlation between two firms, the asset return correlation between two firms with high leverage ratio will be much higher than the equity return correlation between the firms.

7. Because asset returns are not observable, computing the asset return correlation between obligors requires inferring this value using indirect approaches. Factor models render the task of estimating the asset return correlation between obligors easy by identifying common factors to which the business risks of two companies are exposed. Moreover, if a company's business changes as a result of mergers and acquisitions, the future prospects of the company change. This leads to a change in the asset return correlation against other companies. Factor models capture these changes by recognizing the changes in the sensitivities to common factors for the company.

8. The $z$-threshold values will be different if the true mean and standard deviation of asset returns are used in the calculations. One can show using change of variables that if $z_i$ is the $z$-threshold under the true mean and standard deviation of the asset returns, then the new threshold will be given by

$$w_i = \frac{(z_i - \mu)}{\sigma}$$

9. The loss correlation is 0.03598, $EL_P = \$4,740$, and $UL_P = \$31,210$.

## CHAPTER 7

1. The convergence of a Monte Carlo simulation can be speeded up by using quasi-random sequences or by performing importance sampling. Quasi-random sequences are sequences of $n$-tuples that fill $n$-dimensional space more uniformly than uncorrelated points generated by pseudo-random sequences. Hence, fewer simulations are required to get the same convergence efficiency with quasi-random sequences than with pseudo-random sequences. Importance sampling helps to speed up the simulations by generating random numbers around the region of interest. This is useful when one is interested in computing tail risk measures.

2. The loss distribution resulting from credit risk is a skewed distribution with a long, fat tail. Given the first two moments of this distribution, it is not possible to gain much insight into the credit losses around the tail of the distribution. For a fat-tailed distribution, a measure of the tail risk is critical for examining the scope for large losses to occur. The only way to measure this risk is by performing a Monte Carlo simulation to generate the credit loss distribution.

3. The main computational steps involved in simulating the credit loss distribution are the following:
   a. Simulate correlated random numbers that model the joint distribution of asset returns of the obligors in the portfolio
   b. Infer the implied credit rating of each obligor based on simulated asset returns
   c. Compute the potential loss in value based on the implied credit rating, and in those cases where the asset return value signals an obligor default, compute a random loss on default value by sampling from a beta distribution function.

   Repeating the above simulation runs many number of times allows one to compute the distribution of credit losses.

4. The expected and unexpected losses are the same in both cases. This is because the expected and the unexpected loss of the portfolio are dependent only on the mean and the standard deviation of the recovery rates. Evidence for this follows from the analytical expressions derived for expected and unexpected loss where the knowledge of the recovery rate distribution was not required to derive these expressions.

5. The only modification required in the Monte Carlo simulations is to draw correlated recovery rate vectors during the simulation runs. This, of course, requires making an assumption on the appropriate joint distribution for the recovery rate variables.

6. For a normal distribution, knowledge of the mean and the standard deviation of the distribution allows one to completely characterize the shape of the distribution. Hence, any tail statistic of interest can be derived knowing the mean and the standard deviation of the distribution. This suggests that if the distribution of credit losses happened to be normally distributed, performing a Monte Carlo simulation for computing tail risk measures will be not necessary if the expected and the unexpected loss of the distribution are given.

7. Yes, one should be willing to play the game. Because the expected payoff is equal to the initial investment to play the game, this is a fair game.

8. Because the expected payoff is still equal to the initial investment, it is still a fair game. However, because there are eight balls with zero payoff, there is 8 percent chance of loosing $5 and 13 percent chance that the loss will be $4 or more. This increases the downside risk considerably. If, as an investor, one focuses on the downside risk, one should not be willing to play this game.

9. The various statistical parameters of interest for Question 7 are mean = $5, $\sigma$ = $1.378, VaR(90%) = $2, and ESR(90%) = $3. The statistical parameters of interest for Question 8 are mean = $5, $\sigma$ = $1.851, VaR(90%) = $3.333, and ESR(90%) = $4.667.

## CHAPTER 8

1. Financial time series data exhibit a property known as tail dependence. Under tail dependence, there is greater degree of co-movement of returns across firms during periods of large market moves compared to those observed during normal market conditions. Because multivariate normal distributions do not exhibit tail dependence, modeling the joint distribution of asset returns as multivariate normal will fail to model herding and contagion behavior in financial markets, which represent large correlated market moves.

2. The multivariate $t$ distribution exhibits tail dependence and hence will be able to capture correlated extreme market moves. Moreover, Student's $t$ distribution inherits the correlation matrix of normal distributions. Hence, the correlation matrix for multivariate $t$ distribution is easy to calibrate. Finally, it is quite easy to generate sequences of multivariate $t$-distributed random variables, which makes the task of performing numerical simulations to evaluate credit risk fairly simple.

3. As the number of degrees of freedom in the multivariate $t$ distribution is reduced, the degree of tail dependence increases. This has the implication that the portfolio credit loss distribution will have fat tails and hence tail risk measures will increase significantly.

4. (a) $-2.576$; (b) $-3.355$.

5. (a) \$26,803; (b) \$26,680.

6. The following are the steps involved in generating an $n$-dimensional sequence of multivariate $t$-distributed random variables with $v$ degrees of freedom:

   ***Step 1.*** Compute the Cholesky factor $L$ of the matrix $C$, where $C$ is the $n \times n$ asset return correlation matrix.

   ***Step 2.*** Simulate $n$ independent standard normal random variates $z_1$, $z_2, \ldots, z_n$ and set $\vec{u} = L\vec{z}$.

   ***Step 3.*** Simulate a random variate $\omega$ from a chi-square distribution with $v$ degrees of freedom that is independent of the normal random variates and set $s = \sqrt{v}/\sqrt{\omega}$.

   ***Step 4.*** Set $\vec{x} = s \cdot \vec{u}$, which represents the desired $n$-dimensional $t$ variate with $v$ degrees of freedom and correlation matrix $C$.

   Repeating steps 2 to 4 allows one to generate the sequence of multivariate $t$-distributed random variables.

## CHAPTER 9

1. The important attributes of a good risk report are the following:
   - Provides insight into the main sources of relative risk between the portfolio and its benchmark.
   - Is simple and intuitive so that it improves the effectiveness of risk communication.
   - Makes it possible to quantify the magnitude of potential underperformance of the portfolio against its benchmark and the probability of this occurring.
   - Provides different levels of granularity to meet reporting requirements of different interest groups.

2. The standard risk measure used to quantify relative credit risk is tracking error. A forward-looking or ex ante tracking error is usually estimated

based on a risk model. Such a risk model, however, is merely a representation of market-driven volatility and correlation observed among the modeled risk factors and estimated using daily or weekly time series data. Because credit risk is the risk of a rare event occurring, a risk model based on a few years of historical data will not adequately capture the risk.

3. The relative credit risk of a portfolio against a benchmark is defined as the risk of a new portfolio constructed such that it has net long and short exposures to the bonds contained in the benchmark and the portfolio. These net long and short positions can be seen as resulting from taking the difference between the relative weights of the bonds in the portfolio and the relative weights of the bonds in the benchmark. Relative credit risk can be quantified using the following measures: expected loss, unexpected loss, credit value at risk, and expected shortfall risk.

4. The main advantage of the relative credit risk measures introduced here over traditional measures is that it allows one to compute both the magnitude and the probability of underperformance of the portfolio against its benchmark. Under a lack of knowledge of the shape of the credit loss distribution, a standard relative risk measure such as tracking error will fail to provide any confidence estimates to the estimated credit loss.

5. The marginal risk contribution of a bond is defined as the rate of change in risk for a small percentage change in the bond holdings. The unexpected loss contribution of the $i$th bond in the portfolio is given by

$$\sum_{i=1}^{n} \mathrm{ULC}_i = \frac{\sum_{i=1}^{n} \mathrm{UL}_i \times \sum_{k=1}^{n} \mathrm{UL}_k \times \rho_{ik}^{\ell}}{\mathrm{UL}_P}$$

$$= \frac{\sum_{i=1}^{n} \sum_{k=1}^{n} \mathrm{UL}_i \mathrm{UL}_k \, \rho_{ik}^{\ell}}{\mathrm{UL}_P} = \frac{\mathrm{UL}_P^2}{\mathrm{UL}_P} = \mathrm{UL}_P$$

6. The relative credit risk between the portfolio and the benchmark arises because of net long and short positions in the individual bonds. Under the multivariate $t$ distribution, there is greater correlation among asset returns when large market movements occur. This effect tends to mitigate the relative risk exposure arising from net long and short positions because asset returns tend to move more in tandem during extreme market conditions. This explains why the relative tail risk

measures are lower under the multivariate $t$-distribution assumption for asset returns.

7. Obligor asset returns tend to be more correlated during periods of large market moves when their joint distribution is modeled as a multivariate $t$ distribution than when they are modeled to have a multivariate normal distribution. Hence, the credit risk measures of the portfolio are higher under the multivariate $t$-distribution assumption than under the multivariate normal distribution assumption for obligor asset returns.

8. As a portfolio manager, I would like to send the following risk reports to the clients:

   - A market risk exposure report that presents measures such as yield, duration, and convexity for the portfolio and the benchmark and the tracking error arising from exposure to market risk factors.
   - A credit risk exposure report that quantifies risk measures such as unexpected loss and expected shortfall risk for both the portfolio and the benchmark, and the relative credit risk quantified using these measures.
   - A marginal credit risk exposure report highlighting the sources that contribute to the relative credit risk between the portfolio and the benchmark.
   - A credit risk report that is applicable during economic contractions, where the recovery rates are lower and asset return correlations are higher than under the normal economic environment.

9. At the 95 percent level of confidence, the scaling factor $\alpha$ for computing VaR is determined by solving the following integral expression:

$$0.05 = \frac{1}{\sqrt{2\pi}} \int_{\alpha}^{\infty} \exp(-0.5x^2)\, dx$$

This gives $\alpha = 1.645$. The appropriate scaling factor for computing ESR at the 95 percent level of confidence is given by

$$\lambda = \frac{1}{1 - 0.95} \frac{1}{\sqrt{2\pi}} \int_{1.645}^{\infty} x \exp(-0.5x^2)\, dx = 2.06$$

10. In the portfolio management context, performance attribution refers to the process of attributing the excess returns of the portfolio against the

benchmark to various sources that contributed to this excess return. Risk attribution, on the other hand, refers to the process of attributing the relative risk (measured in terms of tracking error or relative VaR) to various risk factor sources. The performance attribution report helps the portfolio manager to communicate the investment management process more effectively to the client and to attribute the value added against the benchmark to the investment decisions. Such a report not only helps to increase the transparency of the investment process, but also allows for more disciplined investment decisions by the portfolio manager.

11. In a high-grade government bond portfolio, performance is usually attributed to the yield curve risk factors such as duration and curve risk. The main risk drivers in a corporate bond portfolio, however, are changes in the perceived credit quality of the obligors. Because yield curve risk factors do not model obligor creditworthiness, a performance attribution report designed for high-grade government bond portfolios will be inappropriate for a corporate bond portfolio.

12. Relevant factors to which performance can be attributed for a corporate bond portfolio include industry sector and obligor credit ratings. These factors primarily capture the excess returns resulting from credit selection. For market risk factors, one could attribute the excess returns resulting from yield curve exposures versus the benchmark. However, in a corporate bond portfolio context, the excess returns from yield curve exposures are usually small and hence could be integrated into the factors used for explaining credit selection.

## CHAPTER 10

1. The benefits of taking a quantitative approach to portfolio selection are the following:
   - It allows risk analysis to be performed at the portfolio level rather than at the bond level.
   - The operational costs are lower because this approach does not require maintaining a large pool of credit analysts.
   - As the number of bond issuers in the benchmark increases, it becomes practically impossible to perform a thorough credit analysis of all issuers, and hence taking a quantitative approach provides a reasonable alternative for bond selection.

2. In a quadratic programming problem, the objective function is quadratic and the constraint functions are linear. In a nonlinear programming problem, the objective function and the constraint functions can

be any nonlinear function in the design variables. The optimal solution to a nonlinear programming problem usually occurs at the interior point of the hypercube formed by the constraint functions. Searching for a solution inside the hypercube is a time-consuming exercise.

3. Because tracking error is a quadratic function in the portfolio weights and the constraint functions are linear in the portfolio weights, this is a quadratic programming problem.

4. The practical difficulties that can arise when a quantitative approach is used for portfolio construction or rebalancing are the following:
   - Many bonds in the optimal portfolio composition may be illiquid and hence difficult to transact.
   - In a portfolio-rebalancing context, the required number of transactions and/or turnover may be too large, and therefore, not implementable.

5. The answer is no, because the credit risk of the portfolio cannot be modeled as a linear function.

6. An important requirement when portfolio rebalancing is performed is to keep the turnover small. Because the optimal portfolio construction problem formulation does not take into consideration the existing bond holdings, the portfolio turnover will be large if the portfolio construction problem is used to rebalance an existing corporate bond portfolio.

7. When portfolios are rebalanced, turnover of the portfolio has to be kept to a minimum in order to reduce transaction costs. Imposing turnover constraints in a corporate bond portfolio optimization problem is difficult. To overcome this difficulty, one can pose the rebalancing problem such that a set of potential sell transactions is first identified from the existing portfolio that does not exceed a specified maximum turnover. During the second step, the actual rebalancing trades can be identified taking into account the sell recommendations. Breaking the rebalancing problem into two steps keeps the complexity of the optimization problem simple while simultaneously imposing the turnover constraint.

8. If the objective function of the portfolio-rebalancing problem is chosen to minimize the portfolio turnover, then the optimization problem is a nonlinear programming problem. This is because one of the constraint functions in the optimization problem is the reduction of the active portfolio's unexpected loss. Because such a constraint function is quadratic in the design variables, the optimization problem is a nonlinear programming problem.

9. The recovery rate for the obligor is the one that has to be carefully selected because the composition of the optimal portfolio is most sensitive to this parameter.

## CHAPTER 11

1. The major similarities between ABSs and CDOs are the following:
   - Both are backed by a collateral pool of assets held in a bankruptcy-remote special-purpose vehicle.
   - The rating of each tranche of an ABS or a CDO is a function of the credit enhancement, interest and principal payment priorities, and ongoing collateral credit performance.

   The major differences are the following:
   - Unlike in the case of ABSs, CDOs do not have a service provider.
   - The collateral assets of a CDO can be traded, whereas for ABS this is not the case.

2. The factors that make a CDO attractive from an investor's perspective are the following:
   - A diversified portfolio can be purchased through one trade execution, resulting in reduced transaction costs.
   - CDO debt tranches have higher yields than many corporate bonds or asset-backed securities of similar rating and maturity.
   - Arbitrage CDOs provide an opportunity to gain exposure to the non-investment-grade market on a highly diversified basis without committing significant resources.

3. Subordination is a form of internal credit enhancement that is used to protect senior tranches against credit losses. This is achieved by giving priority to senior tranches in the event of bankruptcy and in cash flow timing. Priority in the event of bankruptcy is always strict. Priority in cash flows is achieved either through a sequential paydown structure for the different tranches or through a pro rata principal paydown mechanism.

4. Par-building trades are those in which collateral asset managers sell bonds that are close to par value and buy bonds that sell at deep discounts. Because for cash flow CDOs collateral coverage tests are based on the par value of the collateral pool, this practice leads to a declining credit quality for the collateral pool, but ensures that the coverage tests are passed. Par-building trades tend to favor equity investors at the expense of senior tranche holders.

5. The diversity score of a portfolio represents the equivalent number of uncorrelated assets in a comparison portfolio that exhibits a similar degree of default risk as the original portfolio containing correlated assets. The diversity score makes it possible to estimate the loss distribution of a portfolio of correlated assets using a binomial distribution rather than through simulation.

6. The main advantage of using market value tests for cash flow CDOs is that they prevent par-building practices, which tend to favor equity tranche holders at the expense of debt tranche holders. However, the

use of market value tests may force an asset manager to trade more frequently due to changes in the market value of the collateral arising from interest rate changes or rating changes.

7. The relative merits between buying a CBO and a Tracer of similar maturity are as follows:

   ■ Evaluating the market and credit risks of a Tracer is simpler than for a CBO.

   ■ Computing a fair market price for a Tracer is easy and there is greater pricing transparency.

   ■ For a CBO, it is possible to choose among different tranche ratings, but this option does not exist for a Tracer.

   ■ CBOs are exposed to asset manager risk, but Tracers do not have this.

   ■ There is considerable market liquidity for Tracers, but CBOs are quite illiquid.

# Notes

## CHAPTER 3

1. Euro-denominated corporate bonds are quoted as a spread over the euro swap curve. The practice of quoting U.S. dollar-denominated corporate bonds as a spread versus U.S. Treasuries is on the decline and some market players are willing to quote corporate bonds as a spread over the U.S. dollar swap curve.
2. The modified duration concept is discussed in Chapter 4.
3. Portfolio turnover is defined as one half of the market value of the buy and sell transactions divided by the market value of the portfolio. A simpler definition, assuming no injections or withdrawals from the portfolio, is the sum of all buy transactions divided by the size of the portfolio.
4. Alan Greenspan, "Lessons from the Global Crises," Remarks before the World Bank Group and the International Monetary Fund, Annual Meetings Program of Seminars, Washington, DC, September 27, 1999.
5. Nils H. Hakansson, "The Role of a Corporate Bond Market in an Economy—and in Avoiding Crisis" (Working Paper RPF–287), Institute of Business and Economic Research, University of California, Berkeley, 1999.
6. The Lehman Brothers multiverse index is representative of the investible universe of fixed-income securities in all currencies including high-yield bonds.
7. William F. Sharpe, "Asset Allocation," in John L. Maginn and Donald L. Tuttle (eds.), *Managing Investment Portfolios: A Dynamic Process*, New York: Warren, Gorham & Lamont, 1990.
8. *72nd Annual Report*, Bank for International Settlements, July 2002, p. 82.
9. The duration of reserve portfolios of most central banks is typically between 6 months and 21 months.
10. This statement is true under the assumption that the central bank is able to replicate the returns of a broad corporate benchmark. How this can be done using a subset of bonds contained in the benchmark is dealt with in Chapter 10.
11. These changes are reflected in the accounting rule International Accounting Standard 19 and, in the United Kingdom, in Financial Reporting Standard 17.

## CHAPTER 5

1. Peter J. Crosbie and Jeffrey R. Bohn, "Modeling Default Risk," KMV Corporation, January 2002.
2. Jay A. Siegel, Robert Young, and Edward Young, "Analysis of Rating Linkages Between Manufacturers and Their Finance Subsidiaries," *Moody's Investors Service,* November 2001.
3. David T. Hamilton, Richard Cantor, and Sharon Ou, "Default and Recovery Rates of Corporate Issuers," *Moody's Investors Service,* February 2002, p. 16.
4. See, for example, Karen VandeCastle and David Keisman, "Recovering Your Money: Insights Into Losses from Defaults," Standard & Poors Corporation, 1999; Karen VandeCastle, "Suddenly Structure Mattered: Insights into Recoveries of Defaulted Debt," Standard & Poors Corporation, May 2000; David T. Hamilton, Richard Cantor, and Sharon Ou, "Default and Recovery Rates of Corporate Issuers," *Moody's Investors Service,* February 2002.
5. Edward I. Altman, Andrea Resti, and Andrea Sironi, "The Link Between Default and Recovery Rates: Effects on the Procyclicality of Regulatory Capital" (Working Paper No. 113), Bank for International Settlements, July 2002.
6. Edwin J. Elton, Martin J. Gruber, Deepak Agrawal, and Christopher Mann, "Factors Affecting the Valuation of Corporate Bonds" (Working Paper), Stern Business School, New York University, 2002.

## CHAPTER 6

1. Sanjiv R. Das, Laurence Freed, Gary Geng, and Nikunj Kapadia, "Correlated Default Risk" (Working Paper 01/02-22-WP), Santa Clara University, Santa Clara, CA, January 2002.
2. Bin Zeng and Jing Zhang, "Measuring Credit Correlations: Equity Correlations are not Enough!" KMV Corporation, January 2002.
3. See Chapter 8 in Greg M. Gupton, Christopher C. Finger, and Mickey Bhatia, *CreditMetrics* (Technical Document), New York: RiskMetrics Group, April 1997.
4. Stephen Kealhofer and Jeffrey R. Bohn, "Portfolio Management of Default Risk," KMV Corporation, May 2001.

## CHAPTER 7

1. For a discussion of finance applications of Monte Carlo techniques, see Bruno Dupire (ed.), *Monte Carlo: Methodologies and Applications for Pricing and Risk Management,* London: Risk Books, 1998.

2. For details, see William H. Press, Saul A. Teukolsky, William T. Vetterling, and Brian P. Flannery, *Numerical Recipes in C: The Art of Scientific Computing*, Cambridge: Cambridge University Press, 1993, pp. 287–289.
3. If the estimated covariance matrix $C$ happens to be singular, one can add a small diagonal perturbation matrix to $C$ as explained in Chapter 2 to make it positive definite.
4. For a discussion of importance sampling, see Paul Glasserman, Philip Heidelberger, and Perwez Shahabuddin, "Variance Reduction Techniques for Estimating Value-at-Risk," *Management Science*, Vol. 46, No. 10, October 2000, pp. 1349–1369.
5. For a discussion of the relative merits of value at risk and expected shortfall, see Yasuhiro Yamai and Toshinao Yoshiba, "On the Validity of Value-at-Risk: Comparative Analyses with Expected Shortfall" (IMES Discussion Paper No. 2001-E-4), Bank of Japan, 2001.

## CHAPTER 8

1. For an empirical study of fitting alternate joint distribution functions to model correlated defaults, see Sanjiv R. Das and Gary Geng, "Modeling the Processes of Correlated Default" (Working Paper), Santa Clara University, Santa Clara, CA, May 2002.
2. Rüdiger Frey, Alexander J. McNeil, and Mark A. Nyfeler, "Modeling Dependent Defaults: Asset Correlations Are Not Enough!" (*RiskLab Research Paper*), retrieved from www.risklab.ch March 2001.
3. Charles W. Dunnett and Milton Sobel, "A Bivariate Generalization of Student's *t*-Distribution with Tables for Certain Special Cases," *Biometrika*, Vol. 41, 1954, pp. 153–169.

## CHAPTER 9

1. For an exposition of risk modeling for fixed-income portfolios, see Lev Dynkin and Jay Hyman, "Multi-Factor Fixed-Income Risk Models and Their Applications," pp. 665–696 in Frank J. Fabozzi and Harry M. Markowitz (eds.), *The Theory and Practice of Investment Management*, New York: Wiley, 2002.
2. See, for example, Srichander Ramaswamy, "Fixed Income Portfolio Management: Risk Modeling, Portfolio Construction and Performance Attribution," *Journal of Performance Measurement*, Vol. 5, Summer 2001, pp. 58–70; Lev Dynkin, Jay Hyman, and Vadim Konstantinovsky, "A Return Attribution Model for Fixed Income Securities," Chapter 21 in Frank J. Fabozzi (ed.), *Handbook of Portfolio Management*, New York: Wiley, 1998.

## CHAPTER 10

1. Srichander Ramaswamy, "Managing Credit Risk in a Corporate Bond Portfolio," *Journal of Portfolio Management*, Vol. 28, Spring 2002, pp. 67–72.
2. Edward I. Altman and Vellore M. Kishore, "Almost Everything You Wanted to Know about Recoveries on Defaulted Bonds," *Financial Analysts Journal*, November/December 1996, pp. 57–64.
3. In a practical setting, one could use Moody's methodology for predicting recovery rates on defaulted bonds. See Greg M. Gupton and Roger M. Stein, "LossCalc™: Moody's Model for Predicting Loss Given Default (LGD)," *Moody's Investors Service*, February 2002.

## CHAPTER 11

1. Market value transactions use instead a minimum net worth test. This test requires that the excess market value of the collateral after taking into account all debt due never falls below a certain percentage of the equity face value. This test is performed for each debt tranche, with a typical percentage for senior debt at 60 percent of equity.
2. Collateral quality guidelines will indicate whether this is permitted or not.
3. Excess spread refers to the difference between the interest rate earned on the collateral assets and the interest rate paid to the CDO debt holders. Excess spread provides an additional layer of loss protection to senior debt holders.
4. For a discussion on par-building trading practices, see David Tesher, "CDO Spotlight: Par-Building Trades Merit Scrutiny," Standard & Poor's Corporation, July 2002.
5. In Chapter 6, I showed that the expected loss of a portfolio comprising defaultable securities is not dependent on the correlation between obligor defaults in the portfolio. On the basis of this information, one may suspect that the notion of diversification in the underlying collateral portfolio is irrelevant for purposes of estimating expected loss. In fact, by taking a bond portfolio for which Moody's assigns a rating, I show in the last section of this chapter that Moody's credit rating can be inferred without modeling the asset return correlation between the obligors in the portfolio.
6. For a discussion on CDO valuation methodology and deriving implied credit ratings, see Sivan Mahadevan and David Schwartz, "CDO Insights: A Framework for Secondary Market CDO Valuation," Morgan Stanley Fixed Income Research, October 2001.

7. For details, see Sten Bergman, "CDO Evaluator Applies Correlation and Monte Carlo Simulation to Determine Portfolio Quality," Standard & Poor's Corporation, November 2001.

8. The adjustment factor used here is reported in a study by Domenico Picone, "Collateralised Debt Obligations," retrieved from www.default risk.com/pdf—files/Collateralised—Debt—Obligations.pdf September 2002.

9. Fitch rating factors are given in "Rating Criteria for Cash Flow Collateralized Debt Obligations," (Loan Products Special Report), p. 6, Fitch Ratings, November 2000.

10. Exposure to a broad basket of corporate bonds can also be acquired by trading synthetic Tracers issued by Morgan Stanley. Recently issued synthetic Tracers use a pool of 100 equally weighted credit default swaps to represent the exposure to the U.S. investment-grade corporate bond market.

11. For exchange-traded bond funds, the administrative fee is around 15 basis points.

12. This tends to make the accrued interest calculations for Tracers different from those for conventional bonds, and sometimes these are a challenge to back-office accounting.

13. The use of a tail risk measure to derive an implied credit rating for the portfolio shares many common principles with the way economic risk capital is allocated in banks to target desired solvency standards.

# Index